Changing Human
Service Organizations

Changing Human Service Organizations

POLITICS AND PRACTICE

George Brager
Stephen Holloway

THE FREE PRESS
NEW YORK

The Free Press
A Division of Simon & Schuster
1230 Avenue of the Americas
New York, NY 10020

Manufactured in the United States of America
10 9 8 7 6 5 4 3 2 1

Library of Congress Cataloging-In-Publication Data

Brager, George A.
        Changing human service organizations.
        Includes index.
        1. Social service.   2. Organizational change.
3. Organizational behavior.   I. Holloway, Stephen,
joint author.   II. Title.
HV40.B815   361   77-87572
ISBN 978-0-7432-3785-7

For information regarding special discounts for bulk purchases, please contact Simon &
Schuster Special Sales at 1-800-456-6798 or business@simonandschuster.com

To

Robert and Amy Brager
whose youth and enthusiasm for ideas
kept their father growing and on his toes

and to
Janet Holloway

Contents

Preface

THE LITERATURE on organizational problem solving and change has two major emphases. The first is on how top-level managers can induce lower-ranking members to comply with administratively inspired innovation. The second, stemming from the organizational-development field, highlights the process by which third-party consultants can assist top management in creating a more open organizational system. Both emphases imply a view of change as a process initiated at the top of an organizational hierarchy and then disseminated downward; and both pay scant attention to the special case of the human service organization.

Our interest is in change initiated by those with limited formal responsibility for organizational problem solving. This approach inverts the usual lens by focusing on the ways in which organizational actors with less formal power can influence those with more formal power. Middle-level supervisors and line workers are most affected by this concern, but even many administrators are responsible to superordinates and may be "bosses" in relative terms only. The traditional emphasis on "top down" change provides only a partial understanding of the process, thus distorting significant realities of organizational behavior.

Our frame of reference is the human service organization. Increasingly, human service professionals of all ranks have come to recognize that organizational policies and programs affect the services they are able to provide their clients. The vast majority of human services are delivered through formal organizations, and, typically, the professional holds a position of limited influence in such organizations. It is not uncommon for such a worker to find himself embroiled in organizational problems that compromise the quality of service available to clients and yet to lack the authority necessary to change the situation for the better.

In part, the same may be said for staff of other types of organizations. That is, they have an interest in changing one or another aspect of the organization's functioning so as to advance its mission but lack the requisite resources and skills to do so. Thus, although our arguments are elaborated in a human services context, the generalizations that emerge are also applicable to other low-power participants—be they social workers, psychologists, mental health workers, department heads, teachers, school principals and nurses, on the one hand, or accountants, production workers, and editors of publishing houses, on the other. Similarly, the organizations that receive major attention are the not-for-profit public or private bureaucracies such as hospitals, departments of public welfare, public schools, or family service agencies that have collectively come to be referred to as human service organizations. While they differ in important ways from the bureaucracies of the profit-making sector, many of the theoretical and practice principles relating to organizational problem solving and change hold for both.

The book diverges from the current organizational literature in one other important respect—its practice emphasis. Its focus in major part is the development of practice technology for use by staff "on the line" as they attempt to modify agency policy and program. The organizational literature has contributed significant knowledge to our understanding of organizational structure and process and contains elements of practice-relevant theory. For example, it allows us to predict roughly that different structures prompt different behaviors (e.g., an authoritative structure leads to more effective coordination but discourages creativity, whereas the reverse is true of participatory decision-making structures, which make coordination more difficult and creativity more likely). It is one thing, however, to assess the consequences of varying structures and another to identify the interventions required to move from one structure to the other; for example, the acts necessary to transform an authoritative into a participatory structure or the reverse. Organizational theorists have shown little interest in practice process and method, and even the administrative literature that devotes attention to practice theory tends to ignore the steps necessary to move from one condition to another. This book attempts in part to redress this imbalance. It offers a model for integrating the range of theoretical issues that are relevant to change while focusing primary attention on the practice activities necessary for effective intervention within organizations.

Change is a process that cannot be divorced either from the context in which it is occurring or from the specifics of what is being changed. At the same time, there are important principles about human behavior and organizational functioning that should inform the way one plans a particular change effort. Attempting to compensate for this inherent contradiction, we begin the book with a discussion of the genesis of organizational problems that we believe are endemic to *all* organizations and the ways in which these problems affect low-power personnel, moving them either to accommodate to agency mandates or to intervene in order to bring about change. Outlining a scheme for conceptualizing how the change process occurs, we proceed to consider the range of variables stemming from the organization's environment, internal organizational arrangements, and the perceptions of its participants that predispose an organization to change. This largely theoretical discussion is meant to sensitize the reader to identify the range of change possibilities that exist in particular settings— and thus the feasibility of his or her change ideas. It constitutes Part I of the book. The remainder of the volume, devoted to practice technology, details the several stages of a change process and examines the practice issues and methods relevant to each stage.

The case materials used throughout the book represent composite experiences in a range of organizations. They are drawn from our own social work practice and the practice of our colleagues and students. Except in readily apparent instances, the names of agencies and workers have been altered to preserve confidentiality. Although the examples are "true to life," details have been altered, and few of the examples can be considered representative of specific organizations or individuals. The changes depicted are essentially modest ones, purposely so in a book that presents theory and practice technique related to change from within an organization by persons with limited formal power.

Finally, we wish to underscore a dilemma inherent in practice of this kind. We have elaborated a technology that we believe practitioners will find effective in instituting modest change. Yet we cannot be certain that individuals will not seek to apply the principles to areas of self-interest that may or may not impede the organization's humanist mission or run counter to the interests of the recipients of service. The technology can be well or poorly applied, but there is no way to refine the effort so that it furthers only "constructive" change. The risk is worth taking, we believe, in light of the major deficits in service provision, the professional responsibility of human service workers, and the contributions they can—and must —make to provide more effective help to the clients or their organizations. Improved services and client benefit are at the core of the practice we espouse.

Acknowledgments

THE NAMES OF THE AUTHORS of this book are listed alphabetically; we contributed equally to the final product.

We begin by acknowledging our debt and gratitude to Alex Gitterman, Carol Meyer, and Irving Miller of the Columbia University School of Social Work. Their review and criticism of early drafts of chapters contributed significantly to the quality of the final product. Lenore Brager also read the book in its earlier versions. She offered substantive help to both of us, and her nurturing was a source of inestimable support to her husband as well. Gladys Topkis, our editor, challenged us, taught us, and enhanced the clarity of our writing. Audrey Terry was quick, thorough, and patient in typing numerous drafts of chapters and ultimately the final manuscript.

It is often difficult to separate one's own ideas from those of others with whom one has shared professional interests, and we wish to acknowledge their contribution. For Brager, there are his colleagues who met biweekly to develop a course on organizational change, which is required of all students at the Columbia University School of Social Work: Rosalyn Chernesky, Carel Germain, Mary Goldson, and Agnes Louard, in addition to the aforementioned Gitterman, Meyer, and Miller. For Holloway, there are Harvey Hornstein and Morton Deutsch of Teacher's College and Robert Lefferts of the SUNY–Stony Brook School of Social Welfare.

Finally, we are indebted to our students at Columbia and Stony Brook. Many of the examples in this book are drawn from their experience. We warned them, as we taught organizational practice at the two schools, that we were prepared to appropriate some of their ideas for use in the book. We have.

George Brager
Stephen Holloway

1. Organizational Problems and Change from Below

THIS BOOK IS CONCERNED with the process of planned change within human service organizations. Its focus is on innovation initiated by staff at the lower and middle levels of the hierarchy of the organizations they wish to alter. Our "view from the bottom" does not stem from a romanticization of the lower-ranking practitioner, nor do we endorse the neo-populist notion that locates social concern and integrity invariably and exclusively in the lower reaches of the organization's order. Rather, our attention to practitioner-initiated change stems from two factors. Our primary interest is in the provision of human services that are responsive to the needs and rights of the consumers of those services. It is an organizational truism that the closer organizational decision making is to the source of information, the more likely it is that the decision will accurately take account of the information. Since the organizational staff members who interact with clients are line workers, one means of increasing the organization's responsiveness to client needs is to increase the impact of line staff on agency programs and policies.

Secondly, our interest in worker-initiated change derives from the limitations of practitioner influence. Although low- and middle-level staff at times contribute to agency decision making, in general they are relatively powerless. This fact, too obvious to need documentation, makes increasing their impact on service provision a relevant professional concern. This is even more the case when one considers the paucity of both theoretical and practice attention to the matter. With relatively few exceptions, the existing literature is focused on change initiated at the top of the organizational hierarchy and disseminated downward.[1] It treats change

---

[1] Recent exceptions include Rino J. Patti and Herman Resnick, "Changing the Agency from Within," in Beulah R. Compton and Burt Galaway, eds., *Social Work Processes* (Homewood, Ill.: Dorsey, 1975), pp. 499–51; Rino J. Patti, "Organizational Resistance and Change," *Social Service Review* 48, no. 3 (September 1974), pp. 367–83; and Harold Weissman, *Overcoming Mismanagement in the Human Services* (San Francisco: Jossey-Bass, 1973).

1

from the perspective of the upper-level manager and holds only tangential relevance for the lower-power person who is interested in "bottom up" change activity.

The exploration of change theory and practice presented in the subsequent chapters of this book must be preceded by an overall perspective on the problems that face human service organizations, since the worker's perspective provides the platform on which reasoned practice is built. We believe that problems, dysfunctions, and compromise are inevitable in any human service agency, and that they issue largely from the impact of contradictions in the larger society, as well as from the structure or form of complex organizations themselves.

Before we turn to a consideration of these sources of difficulty in the human services field, which lead the practitioner to identify a need for change, let us specify what we mean by the "human services." The term "human service organization" is used here to refer to the vast array of formal organizations that have as their stated purpose enhancement of the social, emotional, physical, and/or intellectual well-being of some component of the population. Examples are mental-health clinics and hospitals, schools, settlement houses, correctional institutions, and welfare agencies. These institutions function with either a public or a private-voluntary charter and increasingly are supported directly or indirectly by public monies. People are either served voluntarily, as is the case with a hospital or mental-health clinic, or through some form of coercion, as is the case with correctional institutions or public schools. The broad goal of human service organizations is the alteration of some aspect of the individuals served. Such alterations, be they in behavior, perspective, social status, or in the individual's share of life-sustaining resources, are defined by the organization to serve the interest of both the client and the larger society. As Hasenfeld and English suggest, these organizations differ from other bureaucracies in two basic ways. First, their "raw material" input is human beings and their output is persons processed or changed in some predetermined fashion. Second, they function with a social mandate to "serve"—that is, to support and enhance the general well-being and functioning of people.[2]

The expansion of these organizations marks a shift in the functions of socialization, support, and control from the family and immediate community to the state. It also reflects the emergence of a range of social technologies that are so costly to develop that they can be implemented only on a large scale.[3] As a consequence, today we have an elaborate network of service institutions designed to meet needs that historically were addressed by family and community, if, indeed, they were defined as needs at all.

[2] Yeheskel Hasenfeld and Richard English, eds., *Human Service Organizations* (Ann Arbor: University of Michigan Press, 1974), pp. 1–2.

[3] *Ibid.*, p. 1.

Conflicting Ideologies: Contradictions for Human Service Agencies

Social institutions are the products of the values and beliefs of the society within which they are located. Whether an organization is a school, a private corporation, or a city council, it reflects and operationalizes the ideologies of its environment. Because ideologies vary among the members of complex societies, may be ambivalently held, and are advanced with differing intensity by different groups, organizations are subject to tension generated by contradictory belief and value systems. In no other sector of the society is this more the case than in the human services.

The human services field is beset by a number of conflicting ideologies. This fact establishes a problematic context to which each human service organization must, in some fashion, accommodate. We specify these contradictions in order to identify some of the antecedents of the intraorganizational problems that inhibit effective service and lead practitioners to think about change. Although an elaborate list might be developed, for the present purpose we restrict ourselves to three major categories. These include the ambivalent sentiments of American society concerning the recognition of and institutional response to human need, the equivocal mandate under which the service organization functions, and the inconsistent belief systems found within the social work profession, a primary professional reference group for the human service field.

SOCIETAL AMBIVALENCE

Considered as a collectivity, Americans are systematically ambivalent on the subject of the efficacy of institutional human services for their fellows. On the one hand, we are concerned that we and our neighbors receive adequate health care, police protection, schooling, and unemployment compensation when necessary. Furthermore, the traditions of New Deal social programs as well as strong themes of liberal and progressive thought mediate toward the allocation of resources for human services programs. While the popularity of such legislation fluctuates with the political and economic climate, viewed from decade to decade, spending figures indicate that Americans have consistently supported expansion in allocations for service programs during this century.[4]

On the other hand, Americans who struggle to support their families balk at having to foot the bill for "welfare freeloaders" and resent the "loafers" living on food stamps, free health care, and so on. While the AFDC mother or recipient of other public services will attest to the fact that dependence on public services for one's sustenance is a grim experience at best, the middle-class taxpayer views the situation quite differently.

---

[4] Paul A. Brinker and Joseph J. Klos, *Poverty, Manpower and Social Security* (Austin: Lone Star Publishers, 1976), p. 35.

bound by agency prescriptions. This adds to the anomolous context of the human service field. Consider, for example, the following statements by three respected social work educators on the appropriate response of a worker who perceives himself as caught in a conflict between the interests of his clients and those of his sponsoring agency. Helen Harris Perlman: "In order to represent the agency, the worker must be psychologically identified with it, at one with its purposes and policies." [9] William Schwartz: "The worker is not exclusively identified with either the client or the agency, but with the process through which they reach out to one another." [10] Charles Grosser: "The worker is often a partisan in a social conflict. His expertise is available exclusively to serve his clients' interests." [11]

A similar contradiction is buried in the ongoing debate between the "individual services" and the "large systems" wings of the profession. At one extreme, the argument is that the need for services dealing with poverty, emotional distress, and the like is rooted in a flawed social order and must be attacked by broad-scale efforts rather than through the provision of services for the "victims" of societal dysfunction. At the other extreme is the argument that the human damage manifest in the range of problems of people seeking help is so compelling that it must receive primary attention. Arguments also range along a continuum between these two extremes, and there are accommodations that can be made between the opposing views.[12] Nevertheless, in actual practice the contradictory positions tend to crystallize around the issue of the primary role of the social worker. Whether the attention of the worker ought to be significantly devoted to social policy and action or whether the worker's sole function is to provide clinical and other services has been the subject of virulent debate. What is perhaps as telling as the argument itself, however, is its moral overlay. Partisans of each viewpoint have at least implicitly criticized the "social irresponsibility" reflected in the emphasis of those holding the opposing view. In short, the social work profession offers conflicting explanations about the origins of social problems, contradictory directives about the methods with which social workers should address these problems, and opposing definitions of the social worker's role when client and organizational needs conflict.

Situated within this tumult of conflicting professional and societal im-

[9] Helen Harris Perlman, *Social Casework* (Chicago: University of Chicago Press, 1958), p. 50.

[10] William Schwartz, "Private Troubles and Public Issues: One Job or Two?" *Social Welfare Forum* (New York: Columbia University Press, 1969).

[11] Charles Grosser, "Community Development Programs Serving the Urban Poor," in Ralph Kramer and Harry Specht, eds., *Readings in Community Organization Practice* (Englewood Cliffs, N.J.: Prentice-Hall, 1969), p. 297.

[12] Alex Gitterman and Carel Germain outline a model of practice that integrates these opposing views in "Social Work Practice: A Life Model," *Social Service Review* 50, no. 4 (December 1976), pp. 601–10.

peratives, the human service organization that has endured for any length of time has developed a variety of means of accommodating to them. For illustrative purposes, we cite three among the many that could be identified. One of the more common strategies is the development of an ambiguous statement of mission which obfuscates contradictions. Goals that are general or unclear hide the agency's *real* priority or mask the fact that the agency is facing in two mutually exclusive directions at once.

Another accommodation is to operate in a "crisis" or present mode of orientation which precludes the development of perspective about the organization's functioning. A closely related accommodation is to ignore societal imperatives, rationalizing them as service issues, so that the agency avoids coming to terms with social forces that are difficult or impossible to overcome in the short term. For example, the human services field has dealt with the paucity of resources available for services at least in part by focusing on information and referral systems (which can be proffered at small cost) rather than more comprehensive services (which are expensive). Or agencies invest considerable energy in attempting internal and external coordination of programs, implicitly assuming that what is currently offered constitutes a coherent system of services. By doing so, they avoid the need to face the glaring gaps and inconsistencies in present offerings.

A third means of responding to conflicting imperatives is for the organization to develop mechanisms that isolate it from inconsistent elements. One tactic is to maintain as much distance from funding sources as it can manage without jeopardizing its financial support, through either infrequent interaction or ambiguous communication. Another and perhaps more typical method of avoidance is for the organization to isolate itself from organized client groups.

These and other accommodations are inevitable if the organization is to reduce the conflict experienced between itself and its outer world, as well as the internal conflict generated by organizational actors who represent diverse external ideologies and interests within the agency. Indeed, accommodation is inevitable if the organization is to enhance its position or maintain itself. Just as inevitably, however, the organization pays a price for using them. Ambiguous mission statements, present-oriented management, isolation mechanisms, and the like lead not only to ineffective and inefficient services but to nonresponsiveness and inconsistency in the organization's relations with its clients.

Organizations as Tension-Producing Instrumentalities

Given the range of conflicting ideologies that characterizes human services, it is clear that any given human service organization will be rife with problematic situations. This is exacerbated by the fact that the form of the human service organization—bureaucracy—embodies contradictions that make it intrinsically problem generating as well. Three basic structural elements of complex organizations—hierarchy of authority, specialization of task and function, and rules and regulations—may be noted to make the point.

HIERARCHY OF AUTHORITY

Although all collectivities have some system of authority relations among participants, bureaucracies range more toward the formal end of a formal-informal continuum than do other systems, such as social networks, for example. This is not to overlook the importance of informal patterns of decision making within organizations. Rather, it suggests the central importance of an explicitly defined and stable system of authority relations as intrinsic to bureaucratic structure.

Authority is necessary to unify and coordinate diverse and conflicting organizational participants and units. It enhances consistency and speed in decision making. It also allocates responsibility and fixes accountability, theoretically at least, in those with most experience and expertise. It is, in short, a requirement of the orderly and efficient functioning of complex systems.

But hierarchy of authority brings conflict in its wake. Persons located at different places in a chain of command are privy to different information and develop different, potentially contradictory perspectives about organizational issues. Their concerns and stake in particular organizational events are therefore different and potentially conflicting as well. Inevitably, then, the "world view" and interests of participants vary with their location on the organizational ladder.[13]

Hierarchy is also organizationally dysfunctional. In fixing responsibility (and the rewards that accompany responsibility), hierarchical arrangements reduce the commitment of those who have less obligation for shaping the decisions reached by the organization as well as their incentives for creativity in problem solving. They also channel communication in a vertical direction, resulting in significant message distortion.

The organizational literature offers prescriptions for minimizing the disadvantages of hierarchy (e.g., participant decision making, expressive supervision, and the like). Although these techniques can reduce problems, they cannot eliminate them, and they often create their own tensions in turn. The difficulties inherent in nonhierachical patterns become clear when one considers the opposite end of the authority continuum—i.e., arrange-

---

[13] Participant interests and the impact of organizational structure on these interests are considered in detail in Chapter 4.

ments in which there is rotating leadership and collective decision making. Apart from the excessive time demands of such a pattern and the uncertainty of direction that leadership turnover and lack of continuity entail, proponents of collective decision making who have observed it in practice have noted other deficiencies. Vacuums in leadership are necessarily filled, so that whatever the pattern, leadership will in fact exist. In avoiding the appearance of unequal influence however, the arrangement encourages leadership that is neither responsible nor accountable.[14] The point, in brief, is that hierarchical arrangements, whether rigid or flexible, are necessary and will by their very nature generate problems.

SPECIALIZATION OF TASK AND FUNCTION

The division of tasks and functions into smaller and simpler tasks is a traditional method of organizing work in industrialized societies to increase productivity and efficiency. The specialization characteristics of human service organizations transcends efficiency goals, however. As knowledge expands, in-depth expertise in ever-growing content areas is impossible to attain. This in part explains the development of different, though related, professional fields (e.g., sociology, psychology, political science, history, philosophy) and the growth of specializations within professions (e.g., surgery, pediatrics, gynecology, to name but three of the numerous medical specialties). Furthermore, human problems have been found to be intractable to single-pronged interventions. People's needs are interdependent, as are the conditions that give rise to them. A comprehensive approach, blanketing diverse professions, subspecialities, and areas of expertise, is necessary for effective performance.

But if the specialization of task and function is a necessary feature of complex human service organizations, it engenders its own set of problems. Organizations are composed of a set of interdependent parts, each of which contributes to and receives something from the whole.[15] Since the behavior of any part of the system has consequences for the other parts, a high degree of interdependence, combined with a high degree of specialization, generates contradictory pressures.

Specialization carries the same dynamics as noted in regard to authority relations. That is, staff who perform different tasks and carry different functions are exposed to different information, develop different perspectives, and have different stakes in the system. Thus, doctors, nurses, social workers, case aides, occupational therapists, and attendants view the

[14] Norman Fruchter and Robert Kramer, "An Approach to Community Organizing Projects," *Studies on the Left* 6, no. 2 (March-April 1966), pp. 31–61.

[15] For further discussion of the systems approach to the study of organizations, see David Silverman, *The Theory of Organizations* (New York: Basic Books, 1971), pp. 26–43.

hospital through varying and contradictory lenses. Conflicts among and between these role partners are to be expected.

Conflict may stem from other aspects of role differentiation as well. Role definitions typically overlap, and it may be difficult to locate where one specialized task ends and another appropriately begins. For example, guidance counselors, social workers, and school psychologists are all charged with enhancing the educational, social, and emotional functioning of children in the schools. Their tasks overlap, creating the conditions for a clash of position. Clashes are also likely to occur when specialized tasks and functions are imprecisely defined or role expectations are unclear.

As with authority arrangements, there are techniques to ameliorate the problems inherent in specialization. Once that is said, however, the problems remain.

RULES AND REGULATIONS

All organizations have rules, sometimes informal rules, more often written ones. The accumulation of rules is developmental; that is, the longer an organization's life cycle, the more codified its procedures and regulations become. Rules and regulations also multiply when an organization is located in a hostile environment,[16] and because of the conflicting ideologies noted earlier, human service agencies are particularly vulnerable to environmental challenge. Rules serve a number of critical functions for organizations—among them, to coordinate diverse tasks without time-wasting interaction, to standardize staff actions so as to assure consistency, to reduce the inefficiency required to make decisions anew in instances of recurring events, and to insure behavior in conformance with the organization's mission.

But rules impact differently on different actors. Because rules are control devices, they generate tension among participants, especially professionals who perceive self- or peer direction rather than the organization as the legitimate authority. They are, furthermore, the source of innumerable contradictions. To cite a few: rules devised for particular circumstances are invoked in apparently similar but actually disparate situations; rules that have historical validity persist after they have become outdated; rules that cannot accommodate complexity or unique events are applied mechanistically to just such circumstances; and one set of rules works at cross-purposes to another set.

Organizations can limit the number of rules and regulations they prescribe. They can define the use of rules for largely routine and standard

---

[16] For example, Rose found that voluntary associations in hostile environments were more likely to elaborate rules and develop formal structures than those in benign environments. Arnold M. Rose, "Voluntary Associations Under Conditions of Competition and Conflict," *Social Forces* 24 (December 1955), pp. 160–61

events. They can insure goal-oriented behavior by selecting ideologically sympathetic staff or training them to internalize the agency's values. Although these methods minimize the tension-producing elements of rule systems, contradictions persist.

To summarize our argument, the characteristics of human service agencies as instrumentalities (i.e., their hierarchical arrangements, specialization of task and function, and rules and regulations) are necessary for the effective organization of services and simultaneously generate contradictions and conflicts for organizational actors. These factors, along with the accommodation stemming from the public's ambivalence concerning the provision of services and people's rights to receive needed services, and the translation of this ambivalence into inconsistent organizational mandates, constitute an ideological and institutional context that inevitably generates problems for human service organizations.

Organizational Problems: The Impetus for Change

From the perspective of the individual organizational actor, a "problem" is an unimplemented or frustrated system of strongly held beliefs and values.[17] Thus, the Roman Catholic belief system asserts that abortion is wrong; hence, the legalization of abortion in this country is a problem for adherents of that ideology. In contrast, the legalization of abortion is not a problem for supporters of other sentiment systems, such as non-Catholic social libertarians or feminists. In the context of the human service organization, any aspect of the organization's functioning that frustrates or fails to implement a set of sentiments that is held strongly by organization members will constitute a "problem" for them. Given the range of conflicting ideologies that characterizes the field of human services and the contradictions embedded in its bureaucratic form of organization, it is clear that any given human service organization will be rife with situations that are perceived as problems by some and not by others.

IDENTIFYING PROBLEM AREAS

If "problems" are relative to the beliefs and values of those who perceive them, something should be said about the "problems" with which the authors of this book are concerned. As noted earlier, our primary interest is in the responsiveness of human service agencies to the needs and rights of their actual or potential consumers. Organizational barriers to client responsiveness, then, constitute the problem arena. But how do these barriers come to be identified in practice?

---

[17] The point applies whether the sentiments are intrinsic to their holder or are used to rationalize the holder's self-interest, as we suggest is the case in Chapter 4.

The means are twofold. The first is through the worker's interaction with the users of the service. Clients come with some adversity, and the activities and procedures of the organization are or are not available to help them cope with or overcome the trouble. Sometimes the organization, while providing help in one area, creates difficulty in another. Thus, hospitals cure illnesses, but their interventions also may induce in patients a loss of self-esteem or a sense of helplessness. In these instances, feelings are shared with the worker or cues emitted that express client worries and complaints. Organizational problems are thus identified, directly or implicitly, by the consumers of the service. The point may seem obvious, but such is hardly the case in practice. Individually oriented workers all too frequently attend to a client's "private troubles" without also recognizing the public (or organizational) issues involved.[18]

Typical is the case of a social worker in a psychiatric hospital whose client was adjudged by the hospital incompetent to handle his finances. The worker sensitively engaged Mr. X on the issue, ultimately concluded that he *was* able to manage his money, and intervened successfully to get the decision reversed. But in defining the problem solely in terms of Mr. X, he did not explore the process by which such a mistake could have been made, whether similar errors had occurred in regard to other clients, and what protections there were for clients like Mr. X apart from the fortuitous intercession of a sympathetic worker. A problem had surfaced through interaction with a client, but its definition as a "private trouble" prevented the pursuit of its solution as a "public issue."

A second means by which organizational problems relating to client needs and rights are identified is by reference to professional standards. The latter may be codified, as in the work of standard-setting organizations such as the Child Welfare League of America, or generally diffused throughout the professional literature. When workers perceive these standards to be violated by human service organizations, a problem or "performance gap" may then be said to exist.[19]

Generally, these problems confront all practitioners who want to assure that "the right service is delivered to the right client in the right sequence." [20] According to Aiken and his colleagues, the problems men-

[18] C. Wright Mills elaborates the distinctions between "private troubles" and "public issues." See *The Sociological Imagination* (New York: Grove Press, 1961), p. 8.

[19] Zaltman et al. suggest that changes are instigated by a "performance gap"— that is, a discrepancy between what the organization could do by virtue of a goal-related opportunity in its environment and what it actually does in terms of exploiting that opportunity. They do not, however, call attention to the fact that the perception is a subjective one. Performance gaps will be perceived differently by different members of an organization. Gerald Zaltman et al., *Innovations and Organizations* (New York: Wiley, 1973), p. 2.

[20] Michael Aiken et al., *Coordinating Human Services* (San Francisco: Jossey-Bass, 1975), p. 4.

tioned most frequently in the literature are "fragmentation of services, inaccessibility of services, lack of accountability of services, discontinuities in services, wastefulness of resources, and ineffectiveness of services." [21] The litany could be continued at a less general level of abstraction. The agency does not "reach out" to potential clients; its intake procedures are incongruent with client life-styles and actively discourage use by "nonresponsive" persons; in its insensitivity to client definitions of problems, the agency selects those for whom public sympathy is high and "de-selects" the others; it makes referrals for agency rather than client benefit; or it offers one modality to meet all needs.

The problems can of course be as extensive as there are common professional beliefs and values violated by agency policies and programs. The importance of the point is that it directs the attention of practitioners not only to their responsibility to individuals who use the service but to those who, although unserved by the agency, may need its services as well. It also focuses attention beyond the single client and agency to a larger population segment and a broader area of social concern.

Some of the phenomena that we have termed "problems" receive organizational recognition or legitimacy. But organizational legitimacy tends most often to be reserved for three types of problem. One has to do with the maintenance of the organization (e.g., the search for funds is always viewed as a high-priority problem area). Possible exposure of an agency's inability to achieve its mission is another (e.g., unfavorable publicity as a result of substandard care in residential settings will, we can be sure, call forth some attempt at remedy). Finally, threats to the interests of top management of the organization will ordinarily be officially designated as a problem area. Irrespective of their source, however, when the so-called problems receive organizational legitimacy, they are inevitably defined in terms of the organization's value system or as barriers to achieving organizational objectives. [22] It is not minimizing the salience of some of these problems to note that they may or may not have anything to do with the adequacy of services to clients.

The hierarchical authority structure insures that in all but the most extreme cases, problem definition is the prerogative of the organization's administration. While any number of individuals and groups of organizational members may experience situations as problematic, it is solely the task of the administration to "recognize" the situation officially as a problem and hence, by implication, as a situation to be addressed.

Consider, for example, a large community mental health center located in a multiethnic urban setting. The majority of the community residents who come for service are white and middle class. The services they

---

[21] *Ibid.*

[22] This fact of organizational life has important consequences for the change-oriented practicitioner and is explored further in subsequent chapters.

receive are individual counseling, group counseling, and family therapy, services that seem largely to satisfy them. Some professional staff, however, express concern over the fact that those low-income and minority-group clients who come are less interested in clinical services than in assistance with problems in housing, health facilities, and public welfare—that essentially they are requesting advocacy services. Not receiving satisfaction, they tend not to return, and in fact, there are very few minority-group clients currently being served by the agency. These workers express this as a major "problem" for them and the agency. The response of the administration is that the agency's purpose is to provide clinical services, not advocacy services. While it is unfortunate that the agency cannot meet the needs of all community residents, they say, it is not the agency's problem that the needs of some people fall outside the purview of the organization's purposes.

While the organization's administration may pay a "price" (e.g., lowered morale) for not responding to the staff expression of concern, administrators may consider this to be less "costly" than recognizing the problem and having to cope with their notion of the consequences (e.g., a decline in the agency's reputation as a leader in the clinical field). These kinds of events, an aspect of everyday life in the human service organization, are inevitably given both the contradictory imperatives to which the organization must respond and the differential effects of bureaucracy on organizational members.

The options available to the organization's administration with regard to problem resolution may themselves be limited, but they are much greater than those available to low- and middle-level organization staff. Administrators have access to a wide range of organizational resources that can be used for such purposes. They are enabled by the authority system to structure the priorities and activities of others; they are supported by organizational norms that legitimize their attending to problems; and they have organizational sanctions to dispense. In contrast, the options available to lower- and middle-level staff are severely constrained. It is within the parameters of these constraints that we cast our consideration of staff-initiated change.

WORKER RESPONSES TO ORGANIZATIONAL PROBLEMS

People seek to work in the human services field in large measure because of a sense of idealism and commitment to serving the needs of people. What, then, is the impact on them when they believe that agency programs and policies run counter to the needs and rights of those who are presumably supposed to benefit from the service? To some degree, they feel themselves "defined" by the problem and, being new to the field, they may act enthusiastically to effect resolution of the problem. For many, the expectation is that all professionals are similarly oriented to client needs and that administrators who are made aware of a problem will try to remedy it. Thus, they fire off memos, raise the issue at a meeting, or discuss it with their superiors. Following what is likely to be the repeated failures of such direct efforts at problem solving, the new worker begins to realize the extent to which organizational problems are endemic to professional life. Reaction to the stress that this realization generates varies widely with the nature of the organization and with the individual in question. There are, however, a number of responses that do reduce dissonance for the worker.

One is moral indignation. The worker "blames" the corruption of the agency and its administration. If indignation alone is insufficient to assuage his upset, he considers a gamut of action possibilities to express his resentment. At one extreme is the fantasy of expecting wide-ranging basic changes. This fantasy is compelling not only because of the worker's observation that it is needed but because, as the organization continues to frustrate his commitment to service, the worker develops a kind of redemptive investment in radical change. It is as if a fundamental change— be it a basic reorganization of the agency, its elimination, or the removal of a particularly oppressive administrator—will vindicate the worker who feels he has been forced into complicity with the agency's "corrupt" practices.

We use the term "fantasy" here precisely because the notion of an individual or a group of line workers effecting such fundamental changes has a "David and Goliath" quality to it. While it performs the function of keeping the worker psychologically separate from the organization and its deeds, it does not reflect how change in the field takes place. What frequently happens in such morally indignant accommodations is that workers attempt to effect basic changes and fail. The failure is in large measure related to the fact that their ambitious goals overreach their power to bring about the change, as well as to their lack of skill in change practice. The unfortunate consequence is that many of these committed and well-intentioned workers accept their defeat, leave the agency, or adjust and fade from the ranks of those actively concerned with improving human services.

A second response to the dilemma facing committed workers who are critical of the character of their agency's service is to isolate themselves psychologically. Psychological isolation involves separating oneself from the dissonance between the desire for change, on the one hand, and powerlessness to effect change, on the other. These workers become jaded, perform at bare minimum, and look for ways to sabotage the organization. Still others become numb or passive, involve themselves in paperwork, and do precisely as they are told. They either no longer perceive that the organization has problems or are unmoved by the problems that exist. The

the structure of American society, we also believe that when one chooses to attack an organizational difficulty by working for change in that organization, the effort responds to a manifestation of the problem rather than to the problem per se. Only the restructuring of the economic and class structure, as well as the social priorities of American society, would address what we have characterized as the root causes of the majority of organizational problems. Consideration of such a restructuring is not only beyond the scope of this volume but, in our judgment, currently beyond the grasp of human service professionals, individually or collectively.

Organizational Change

We have referred to change without defining the term, much less what we mean by such qualifying adjectives as "modest" or "significant." Since a definition is obligatory, we shall provide one. We recognize, however, that as the frustrations of particular organizational problems lead workers to innovative attempts, a precise definition of change is of small consequence for them. The meaning derives from their concern about its impact. The organization is viewed as altered or not, depending on the extent to which what is now being done represents the workers' commitments more fully than what was done previously. Such a notion suggests that, if not the technical definition, surely the meaning of organizational change is buried in the values and perspective of the observer.

MODIFICATIONS IN PEOPLE, TECHNOLOGY, OR STRUCTURE

Organizational change or innovation ultimately entails modifying the actions and interactions of numbers of organizational participants.[26] These modifications in behavior result from alterations in the people themselves, in the organization's technology, or in its structure. Change may thus be defined as alteration in any of these three elements. Although the goal of all change is the behavior patterns of people, the primary focus of intervention varies among the three variables. In part at least, the particular variable selected will be determined by the change proponent's definition of the source of trouble.

People-Focused Change. People-focused change assumes in some measure that the participants perform unsatisfactorily as the *direct* result of their own insufficiencies. In this view, it is not structural arrangements

---

[26] We use the terms "change" and "innovation" as synonymous in this book, although some organizational theorists distinguish between the two. Our meaning relates to something that is new or different to the unit that adopts the change, rather than to a discovery or invention per se.

that are responsible for inadequate performance (confused role definitions, for example, or a maldistribution of organizational rewards), nor is the problem seen to be caused by the agency's activities. Rather, the activities are viewed as appropriate to the organization's mission, but staff is insufficiently skilled in providing them; or role definitions are seen as clear, but workers are uncertain about how to apply them.

Training and other forms of education are the primary modes of intervention that focus directly on people. These might include ongoing, elaborate, and formal devices, or informal mechanisms such as discussion, appeals to conscience, and sensitivity sessions. A second method of people change is the replacement of present staff or the addition of persons with different competencies, experiences, or qualifications.[27]

While inadequate performance is sometimes a source of organizational difficulty, there is, we believe, a too ready disposition to define organizational problems in terms of the abilities or attitude of incumbents and thus to overemphasize people change. The manifestation of a problem is more obvious than its source, and since most organizational problems are apparent in the behavior of members, other, less visible causes tend to be ignored. For example, a problem may be seen as due to the staff's unwillingness to "change with the times" when, in fact, the difficulty stems from the existence of organizational penalties for workers who introduce new ideas.

People change is the type of change most likely to garner the support of top hierarchies. It is implicitly critical of the organization's personnel rather than the organization's program and structure or its ideology, and is therefore far less controversial. Indeed, changes in people are often encouraged by powerful participants for political reasons since it is often in their interests to give the appearance of dealing with a problem rather than to solve it.[28]

Technological Change. Technological change refers to alterations in the agency's services—the procedures and activities that contribute to organizational output. The range of examples is as large as there are varieties of services and methods of providing them, and the change may be directed to the type of service itself (e.g., a reorientation from individual to community intervention) or to alterations within a particular modality. The magnitude of the change is ordinarily greater in the former instance, but variations in the magnitude of technological change occur in the latter

[27] When upper-level staff are replaced, or when there is a large influx of different types of people (e.g., placing poor people on boards), the change might be characterized as structural as well as person-focused.

[28] As this comment suggests, many relatively minor changes in people, particularly as reflected in their attitudes rather than in their behavior, can be viewed as changes in an organization only by a broad stretching of the definition.

case as well. The change may be as minor, for example, as the replacement of a brief intake interview by a self-administered questionnaire or as major as a basic overhaul of the interviewing process itself.

When the magnitude of the innovations is roughly equal, a technological change is more likely to impact on an organization (and thus draw greater resistance from top-level staff) than a change in people. Slight modifications in the style or competence of the people who comprise the organization may have little appreciable effect on other aspects of the organization. On the other hand, slight changes in agency policy can have far-reaching consequences for agency operations (for example, a minor change in a service can result in many more or different clients seeking the service).

Similarly, changes in technology are less subject to reversal than are changes in people, since they tend to be categorical changes as opposed to changes in degree. Compare, on the one hand, the change in an organizing effort from house-to-house solicitation to making contacts through local community groups with the change in an administrator's way of conducting staff meetings from an authoritarian style to encouraging staff participation. With the person change, the opportunity to backslide into the former authoritarian style is substantial. While it may be significant, the change is a matter of degree. In the case of the technological change, however, once it is implemented, there is no context for reversal. The change is categorical and thus self-stabilizing.

Structural Change. By structure we mean the ways in which the members of an organization are arranged in relation to one another, the prescribed relationships and rules, either formal or informal, that define organizational authority and responsibility. Shifts in patterns of communication, the creation of new roles or the redefinition of current roles, redistributions of rewards and responsibilities, all constitute examples of structural change.[29]

The impact of organizational structure on the behavior of members is often clear, as for example when the application of sanctions to compel a desired behavior directly induces the compliant response. Katz and Kahn note, as a matter of fact, that the authority relations represented by structure are the chief organizational means of controlling human variability.[30] But the effects of structure on behavior may also be subtle and unrecognized. For example, conflicts defined as clashes of personality may really be generated by structural arrangements (e.g., overlapping responsibilities set in motion a struggle for "turf").

[29] For a more detailed discussion of structural change, see Robert Mayer, *Social Planning and Social Change* (Englewood Cliffs, N.J.: Prentice-Hall, 1972).

[30] Daniel Katz and Robert L. Kahn, *The Social Psychology of Organizations* (New York: Wiley, 1966), pp. 79–83.

Changes in structure range on a continuum from slight to major in the same way as do innovations that focus on people or technology. The degree of change is theoretically limitless—from changing the supervisor to whom a single individual reports to total reorganization of the agency. Similarly, structural changes vary in the extent to which they are categorical or a matter of degree. A categorical change in structure, for example, might involve the decision to move the client-eligibility unit of a public service agency from Department X to Department Y, which would make it a self-sustaining change. A structural change reflecting degree, on the other hand, might require the director of Department X to consult with colleagues in Department Y on certain types of eligibility cases, a change that is often subject to informal subversion over time. In any case, however, for reasons discussed below, the impact of changes in structure is typically the most profound, that of changes in technology somewhat less so, and that of changes in people least significant.

CHANGE IMPACT

Keeping in mind that the point of departure for consideration of change is the worker's perception of an organizational problem that compromises his ideological commitments, change impact can be defined as the extent to which the change has the effect of more fully implementing those commitments.[31] It is thus a relative concept. The impact of a change is "significant" or not depending on the expectations and assessments of the perceiver. There is a further complication as well. Not only is the significance of a change difficult to assess per se, but the time frame of the assessment frequently affects one's determination of its significance.

A "minor" change may trigger a "major" one at some future time. Or minor changes may accumulate so that their full significance goes unobserved until late in the process. For example, the introduction of a new elective course in a university would ordinarily be viewed as an insignificant alteration of the curriculum. Assume, however, that over a period of time the course increases in favor. More sections are offered. Subsequently, some faculty decide that the subject matter is sufficiently important to make it a required course. This position is ultimately adopted, and a large number of sections are now organized. Some instructors are retrained to teach the new subject matter, and as the university hires new faculty, one criterion becomes expertise in the hitherto uncovered area. By now a significant change has occurred, but at what point in the process was an observer to assess its significance?

The time dimension in assessing change impact may work in reverse

[31] The narrow focus of this definition has consequences for change perspective that are considered in the following section, on the unanticipated negative consequences of change.

negative consequences. The notion of unanticipated consequences is familiar to the sociologist [33] and is beginning to receive attention in the context of planned change.[34] The notion is clear in its conception but difficult to apply in practice.

Examples of negative consequences of planned change abound in the social welfare field. The separation of social services from income maintenance in the field of public welfare offers a classic case in point. Proponents of separation maintained that when a single caseworker delivers both material and social services, the caseworker has the power of exerting subtle or unrecognized coercion on the client to submit to counseling as a condition of receiving the monthly allotment. The proposed separation of service from the provision of income was intended to put the client in charge of the decision to seek service. Yet as separation was implemented, income maintenance became a clerical function accomplished largely through computerized procedures permitting the client no personal contact with the welfare department. Its result was to reduce still further any influence clients might have had on the way in which they were managed by the welfare bureaucracy.

Anticipating the possible negative consequences of a change is difficult, since it requires that the practitioner accurately picture the nature of affairs in the future *after* the change has been implemented. Nonetheless, it is not impossible if the worker avoids conceptualizing his task too narrowly and is open to positions other than his own.

A view of the larger context in which the change is to be introduced is important. A broad understanding of why things happen as they do within the organization provides some ground for predicting possible outcomes. What, the worker may ask, are the interdependencies between the to-be-changed element of the organization and other elements that may be impacted by the change? What factors might intervene to shape the result in unintended ways? What would be their cost? Nagel and Neef argue that unanticipated consequences can be offset if "one has a reasonably accurate model of the process" in which one intervenes.[35]

Evaluating the positive functions of the status quo is another way of revealing the potential negative consequences of change. Sometimes the enthusiasm of practitioners for the change blurs their vision of the constructive elements in current arrangements. Since planned change begins

[33] See, for example, Paul F. Lazarsfeld and Robert K. Merton, "Studies in Radio and Film Propaganda," *Transactions of the New York Academy of Sciences,* series 2, 6, pp. 58–79.

[34] Alvin W. Gouldner, "Theoretical Requirements of the Applied Social Sciences" in W. Bennis, K. Benne, and R. Chinn, eds., *The Planning of Change,* 2nd ed. (New York: Holt, Rinehart & Winston, 1969), pp. 93–97.

[35] Stuart Nagel and Marian Neef, "Department of Unintended Consequences: Two Examples from the Legal Process," *Policy Analysis* 2, no. 2 (Spring 1976), p. 359.

with the perception of a problem, the worker's thinking tends naturally to fix on negative features of the way things are. But this one-sided view does not allow him to factor in the positive functions of the status quo as well. In the public welfare example noted above, change proponents were so committed to the notion of the separation of social services and income maintenance that they overlooked or ignored significant client advantages in the union of the two functions—e.g., the fact that the relationship of clients with workers allowed clients to influence the amount of material assistance they received as well as to obtain quick redress when mistakes occurred.

Finally, one's opponents in the change effort are important sources of data about possible negative consequences. Because organizational change is a political process, the practitioner tends to perceive opposition to change in political terms. Rather than consider the content of an opponent's argument, the worker frequently attributes lack of support to an undeclared issue of organizational preference or self-interest (which may *also* be an accurate perception) and seeks means of neutralizing the opposition. But frequently the rationale put forward by a vocal opposition contains an important observation, and attending to the substance as well as the politics of one's opponents is an important means of assessing the negative consequences that might accompany the introduction of change.

BORING FROM WITHIN: A VALUE CONTROVERSY

Ethical issues related to organizational change attempts from within are a source of controversy among responsible professionals. The controversy includes such questions as who has the right to initiate change; under what circumstances; in whose interests; with what safeguards or systems of accountability; and who should be included in the change planning. The controversy is most rancorous, however, in regard to "appropriate" and "inappropriate" means of change.

Although we discuss this issue later in the book, in light of the strength of the disagreement, we believe readers have a right to know where we stand at the outset. In addition, the matter is particularly relevant in the case of worker-initiated change. Unlike administrators, who have greater power to implement the changes they desire, practitioners must work through others to transform their ideas into action. If those with the influence to implement ideas look upon them with favor, the task is relatively straightforward, and some of the practice techniques described in the following chapters are not critical to accomplishing a change. But there is frequently a variance of opinion which runs the gamut from administrative indifference to sharp disagreement with worker goals.

When workers have good reason to believe that variance in commitment to a change idea exists, they are confronted with two sources of risk.

First, open efforts to move the change idea may jeopardize the worker's position with superordinates. Second, the worker's activity may jeopardize the change idea since the chances of its adoption are significantly reduced once an administrator formally considers the change and passes negative judgment on it. Faced with these circumstances, the worker can abandon the idea, continue to pursue it openly, or begin to work for the change in a less obtrusive fashion.

It is the last of these options that calls forth the most negative judgments by some professionals. We take the position, however, that under certain circumstances it is not only acceptable but appropriate for a worker to "go underground" in his efforts to effect positive change. Although the position will be criticized by many, we accept responsibility for engaging the controversy.

The core of this controversy is typically argued in the context of "professional accountability." Those critical of our view hold that when an organization member becomes interested in pursuing a particular change idea, it is appropriate to utilize the established mechanisms of organizational problem solving. Such open activity assures that the idea will receive wide exposure. This process, the argument asserts, guarantees that the idea will be thoughtfully evaluated, and the possibility of ill consequences or personal gain on the part of the idea's initiator are thus reduced.

When an individual operates outside such mechanisms, the argument continues, the accountability functions of these mechanisms are obviated. If the worker employs "underground" means to promote his change ideas, he is regarded as assuming that he "knows better." Denying the judgment of his colleagues, he is employing questionable methods to reach what may be naively conceived ends.

But the situation is more complex than this argument suggests. First, the authority structure of the formal organization assures that the worker will possess far fewer resources for influence than the administrator. If one accepts our position that organizational location influences perspective and self-interest, it is reasonable to expect that administrator and worker will frequently disagree on the efficacy of one or another change idea. Yet if the worker restricts himself to the use of the formal organizational problem-solving structure, a structure over which the administrator holds essential control, it follows that such disagreements will be resolved in the direction of those with the greater power, the organization's administration.

Of equal importance is the fact that the use of covert means of influence is pervasive at all levels of organizational life. If the administrator is interested in instituting some form of innovation and believes that he will encounter resistance if he simply implements it in an open way, he will begin to use various unobtrusive means, such as "feeling out" persons to assess their support or opposition, preparing for the introduction of the idea by conducting persuasive preliminary conversations, or linking additional components to the innovation in order to increase its appeal to potential opponents. We question standards that consider this behavior when engaged by the executive simply as an aspect of effective administration, but when engaged by the worker to be an example of "insubordination" or unethical practice.

To deny the legitimacy of the unobtrusive use of influence will not prevent its occurrence. It will be employed in any case, although unrecognized or denied. Indeed, we believe that those who argue most vociferously against the practice often engage in deception—of themselves and others—as they make the argument. Is it not more professionally ethical to recognize the pervasiveness of covert influence in organizational life and to be aware of one's own behavior in regard to its practice? It is only with awareness that the worker can reserve its use for particular circumstances and monitor his practice in the context of self-imposed standards. Many who raise issue in regard to this form of practice may do so less because they object to covert means of influencing per se than because they oppose calling attention to what they believe to be everyday organizational practice. In this view, naming the practice for what it is is the objectionable act rather than the covert behavior itself. Indeed, many who argue the point most vociferously are guilty of using underground means in so arguing.

The critical moral and professional question concerns the conditions that justify the exercise of covert influence and the safeguards employed to present its abuse. We posit three guidelines to an ethical answer.

The first is that unobtrusive means be used only when the problem the worker has identified compromises the needs and rights of clients or potential clients. This position assumes, for one thing, that the worker has substantial familiarity with the problem before he moves to a self-initiated change effort. In view of the complexity of organizational problems, the longer one has coped with a problem and the better documented it is, the greater the likelihood that one will accurately assess its ramifications and develop action alternatives that are both responsive to the difficulty and workable within the organization. A further assumption is that workers can accurately assess client needs and rights, which by and large one would hope to be the case. In this regard, the value of self-determination as well as common sense suggests an additional safeguard. The recipients of a service are quite able to assess its impact on them, and data concerning client judgments about proposed changes are available to the resourceful practitioner. Wherever possible, this information ought to be sought and should serve as a significant determinant of the worker's course of action.

A second major guideline to steer the practitioner in an ethical direction lies in the values of the social work and other human service professions. Although social work values are general and subject to the contradictions noted earlier in this chapter, they do reflect moral imperatives that are important in assessing the efficacy of a self-initiated change idea. Some of these values are a commitment to social equity, the primacy of the welfare of clients, the precedence of professional responsibility over personal interest, worker responsibility for the quality and extent of service provided, respect for the privacy of others, and the responsible use of information gained through professional relationships.[36] Although reasonable people might disagree regarding the application of these values in specific circumstances, they provide boundaries within which to make practice decisions.

The final guideline relates to worker accountability. The first factor in this regard is straightforward. It is that workers should employ unobtrusive measures only when the formal organizational mechanisms have already been exhausted or when, on the basis of past experience, it can be inferred that these formal mechanisms will result in failure.

A further safeguard to maximize accountability is to develop informal consultation relationships with trusted colleagues—both those who see the world in much the same way as the worker and those whose perspectives are different. The latter, of course, are particularly important if one is to avoid the pitfalls of collective misperception. Finally, workers must hold themselves accountable as mature professionals, not only for the virtue of their intentions but also for the consequences of their actions. They must, in other words, be aware as they begin a change effort that they carry responsibility for any negative consequences that flow from it. The only risks that are permissible are risks to themselves, or the risks that clients and colleagues understand and have agreed to share.

Dedicated workers will choose to take the risk, at least for themselves. They are aware that the human service field, characterized by conflicting ideologies and the contradictions inherent in formal organizations, is inevitably beset by problems. Services are too narrowly defined, inadequately developed, and inequitably delivered; people are incompletely served, and too many are not served at all. The effort to solve these problems and the struggle between the progressive and the regressive elements in the human services field are integral elements of its character. Workers either will choose to engage the struggle for progressive change however modest, and by unobtrusive means if necessary; or, by default, will lend support to those aspects of organizational functioning that work at cross-purposes to the interests of clients.

---

[36] These values are extrapolated from the Code of Ethics of the National Association of Social Workers, amended April 11, 1967.

Part I

FORCES AFFECTING STABILITY AND CHANGE

The constraints in planning change, even for more potent groups than human service workers, are considerable. It is seldom that a practitioner, particularly a line worker or middle-level supervisor, "creates" change. More typically, if the worker is skillful enough, he can assess the dynamic set of forces affecting a situation and attempt to channel their impact to move more effectively toward a chosen objective.

Our intent in this part of the book is, first, to sensitize workers to the array of forces that inhibit or impel change. These forces can be viewed as stemming from an organization's environment, its internal structure and process, and the meanings ascribed by organizational participants to environmental and organizational events. We have selected only those ideas that are most accessible to practitioner use and consider only those variables that have a major impact on stability and change. In thus limiting our attention, we run the risk of oversimplifying a complex process. It is a risk worth taking, however, if our restricted vision adds to practice understanding.

Our second intention is to establish a framework for what follows regarding change technology, to place the exploration of what a single worker does in a single agency within a broader context. In a book devoted to practice, the focus is necessarily on interventions of small scale, but such a focus is distorting if it does not incorporate a larger view of process and setting. At the least, the reader is entitled to know the assumptions on which the practice advice to follow is predicated.

The Field of Forces

We draw our core notions about the dynamics of the change process within organizations from the work of Kurt Lewin, since Lewin's field theory [1] conceives of change in a way that is particularly useful for prac-

[1] Lewin Kurt, *Field Theory in Social Science* (New York: Harper & Row, 1951), pp. 188–237.

tice application. According to field theory, the unit of change interest—be it a work group, a department, or an entire organization—is located in a field of countervailing "forces." The unit maintains a given pattern as long as a relative balance of forces is maintained. Thus, stability is seen as a dynamic rather than a static state and is represented by a balance of complementary and opposing forces.

Lewin's "forces" can be thought of as the range of variables which we discuss in the following three chapters. Change occurs when alterations in a force or set of forces begin to generate stress in the balanced system. These forces might be environmental variables, such as changes in funding availability, variables from within the organization, such as a power struggle between competing administrators, or any combination of the multitude of factors that impinge on organizational life. As forces increase or decrease, stress builds. At some point the increase in stress causes a shift that disrupts the system's current state of affairs. Following a period of disequilibrium and readjustment, a new dynamic stability emerges that represents the new balance point of the altered forces.

The force-field conception takes on greater clarity when one thinks in terms of the possibility of a specific change. Stability exists when the "driving forces" (those pressing for the change) are offset by the "restraining forces" (those inhibiting the change). For change to occur, the field of forces must be modified so that the driving forces are increased, the restraining forces reduced, or some combination of both.

The notion is suggestive for practice purposes, since it provides a basis for planning change. Thus, if one is interested in altering an aspect of organizational functioning, he will attempt to influence the force field. This begins with his envisioning an alternate state of affairs, or change goal. With the change goal in mind, the practitioner identifies the driving and restraining forces that respectively appear to support and inhibit movement toward the goal. He then assesses the feasibility of alternate action strategies. Ultimately, he selects a plan which will involve the reduction of the restraining forces, the increase of the driving forces, or both. If successful, the plan will alter the field of forces in the predicted manner, facilitating the desired goal.

Assume, for example, that the director of a hospital social services department is concerned about reports that the patients who attend the hospital's outpatient clinic for low-income community residents are subject to undignified treatment. Following an appraisal of the situation, the practitioner decides that a major element of the problem is the scheduling of patients for clinic hours. They are required to wait long hours before seeing a doctor, and when patients arrive at the clinic, they frequently discover that their appointment has been moved to another time without their having been consulted or notified. Finally, choice of available appointment times is severely restricted, and no attempt is made on the part of the clinic to accommodate the scheduling constraints imposed by the patients' jobs, family responsibilities, and the like.

The practitioner notes that the source of the difficulty involves several components. First, most of the physician time available at the clinic is donated by the doctors. This means that doctors feel less obliged to protect clinic hours when other time pressures arise, and, hence, they frequently cancel clinic time. The service has low prestige and therefore has not received the attention of hospital officials. Funding for this kind of service is minimal, and the clinic is short-staffed relative to its patient load.

The social service director selects as a change goal the establishment and enforcement of a set of scheduling standards for the clinic that will prevent the indignities that currently exist. His task now becomes the identification of forces that mediate toward and against the establishment of this goal. Some of the driving forces he identifies include the standards established by the hospital's funding agency, the fact that complaints have been received from the Community Advisory Board, the recent hiring of a new hospital administrator who has a reputation for being responsive to community concerns, and the pro-patient value system of significant staff members. The restraining forces that he determines are impeding the goal include inadequate reimbursement rates, the low status of the patient population, the volunteer status of the clinic physicians, the fact that many hospital staff feel *themselves* to be mistreated, and the general staff ignorance of the medical consequences of this kind of patient treatment.

The practitioner understands that his goal is beyond the scope of his authority and that in order to alter the situation effectively he has to work through others. In planning to actualize the goal, the social services director has to decide which driving forces might be increased (e.g., by feeding negative information to the funding agency, strengthening the potency of the Community Advisory Board with which he is associated, reaching the new administrator, or forming a coalition of pro-patient staff) and/or which restraining forces might be diminished (e.g., by working for a change in reimbursement arrangements, trying to modify attitudes toward patients, attempting to establish a different arrangement for physician staffing, supporting the grievances of hospital staff, or developing a training program to increase awareness of the impact ill treatment has on patient motivation to seek service as well as on the relationship between physical and psychological factors in illness). Such an effort would obviously require enlisting the aid of colleagues and involves a range of complex practice considerations, discussed in detail in later chapters.

The example is oversimplified and itself raises a series of questions. Since we discuss force-field analysis as an assessment tool in detail in Chapter 5, we shall not deal with those questions at this time. Our aim here is to establish the notion that organizational equilibrium is a balance among forces in dynamic interaction, and that either the predisposing or the restraining forces must be modified for changes in organizational operations to take place.

Unfortunately, field theory does not specify the origins of the forces that press for or retard change, nor is it helpful in assessing their relative potency in determining the point of balance in any current situation. Our discussion of the variables stemming from the environment, internal organizational arrangements, and the perception of participants in the three following chapters is responsive, in some measure, to this deficit.

The Organization and Its Environment

It is a truism of the literature that change in organizations represents their adaptation to external circumstances—that is, that the major impetus for internal change stems from an organization's environment. Systems theory suggests that when environmental factors that are important to the organization's functioning are stable, organizational programs and policies tend to persist over time. When environmental factors shift, the organization either adjusts to the external force, attempts to influence it, or both. Each interaction between an organization and its environment represents a real or potential internal change.

Two environmental factors are often cited as significant. One has to do with the "situational demands" generated by different technologies that impact on an organization's structure.[2] In this view, as technical and market conditions become more complex, the organization has to adjust its structure and processes to maintain or increase its effectiveness. The second factor has to do with the rate of change in the environment, which can be considered a barometer of potential innovation within the organization.[3] Turbulence in the outer world spurs greater internal change, environmental tranquility the reverse.

In Chapter 2, we consider more specifically the forces within the environment that preserve stability and generate change. For the present, we wish to provide a framework for viewing environmental impact. The focus is suggested by the work of Wamsley and Zald, who argue for "political-economic" analysis in the study of organizations. They define political economy as "the interrelation between a political system (a structure of rule) and an economy (a system for producing and exchanging goods and services)."[4] Following their definition, we contend that the environmental

[2] Joan Woodward, *Management and Technology* (London: H.M.S.O., 1958), p. 38.

[3] Tom Burns and G. M. Stalker, *The Management of Innovations* (London: Tavistock, 1961).

[4] Gary Wamsley and Mayer N. Zald, *The Political Economy of Public Organizations* (Lexington, Mass.: D. C. Heath, 1973), p. 17.

forces of most critical significance in explaining organizational processes are political and economic. By "political" we refer to the use of authority and power to affect the values, norms, and goals of a social system. "Economic," in our usage, suggests the means by which social services are provided and the rules and mechanisms that shape their exchange.

Internal Structure and Process

Environmental explanations of internal change are incomplete, since they do not account for the variety of adaptations different organizations make to similar forces in their milieu. So, for example, an exploratory study of seven family agencies in New York City found widely differing responses to the turbulence of the 1960s. Five responded to the renewed societal interest in the poor by changing the amount and type of resources spent on disadvantaged groups, while the programs of two of the agencies were not modified at all.[5] To some degree, this may have been a consequence of differences in their immediate as opposed to the larger environment—that is, differences in the agencies' sources of funding, constituencies, and the like. In part, though, it stemmed from differences in the organizations' internal structures and processes. Factors operating within an organization rather than in its relationship to the environment may thus be responsible for its position in regard to stability and change.

A host of internal variables have been identified as empirical correlates of organizational innovation. One set includes such interrelated economic factors as wealth, size, and the availability of resources. A number of studies conclude that more wealth, larger size, and a greater availability of resources increase an organization's readiness to adopt new patterns of behavior.[6] Another set of characteristics predisposing to innovation are political in nature, including decentralization of organizational structure, breadth of organizational goals, and absence of dominance by a single professional ideology.[7] We deal more fully with some of these factors in Chapter 3.

While political and economic forces in the environment shape organizational structure and process, organizations operate in turn on their environments. In fact, of course, organizations differ in the degree to which they attempt to influence their "organizational set" (i.e., other or-

[5] Gertrude S. Goldberg, *New Directions for the Community Service Society: A Study of Organizational Change,* Columbia University, unpublished doctoral dissertation, 1976, pp. 189–233.

[6] Mohr details the empirical evidence that makes this point. Lawrence Mohr, "Determinants of Innovation in Organizations," *American Political Science Review* 63 (March 1969), p. 112.

[7] *Ibid.*

ganizations with which they interact). At one extreme are those organizations that strive to impinge on and exploit their environment; at the other are those that try to ignore its existence.

Interestingly, there is evidence that an agency's effectiveness is related to the ways in which it interacts with others in its organizational set. A study of twenty-six social service agencies operating in the same environment and with similar organizational characteristics found a high correlation between an organization's effectiveness and the attentiveness of its chief executive to environmental matters, as measured in part by the executive's assessment of the desirability of (1) acting as a buffer for his organization against environmental pressures, (2) stressing informality in interorganizational relations, (3) attempting to influence other organizations, and (4) providing direction to the mutual activities of his own and other organizations through coalition building.[8]

If the environment and the organizational characteristics of these twenty-six agencies were the same, how can we account for the differences in executive outlook? The question is germane to our interest in stability and change since it suggests a further dynamic to explain organizational functioning in addition to the environment and an organization's structure and process—namely, the organization's actors.

The Meanings to Participants

Some organizational actors view the environment as threatening; others observe the same event and define it as creating an opportunity. Similarly, one group of workers sees an agency's supervisory structure—for example, close supervision—as aiding them, while another group reacts to the same behavior as a hindrance. Further, the same actor may view the same circumstance differently at different points in time. Thus, it is not possible to understand organizational dynamics without incorporating into the schema the meaning of environmental and internal-organizational forces to the relevant actors.

How meanings develop is too complex a subject to be dealt with here. We believe that psychologically determinist explanations are overly simple since they ignore the powerful impact of systemic factors on individual behavior. But structurally determinist explanations are inadequate as well. A person's past as well as current experiences mold his perceptions and interpretations; furthermore, individuals fill multiple roles (worker, professional associate, parent, friend, etc.) so that their organizational position is only one source of meaning to them. While the behavior of organiza-

[8] Richard N. Osborn and James G. Hunt, "Environment and Organizational Effectiveness," *Administrative Science Quarterly,* 19 (June 1974), p. 239.

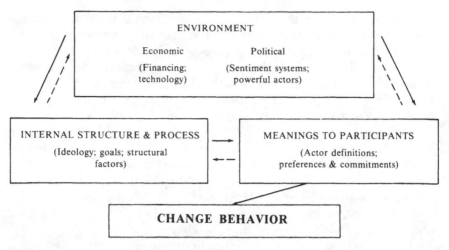

Figure 1. Forces Influencing Stability and Change

tional participants is often shaped by organizational structure, it is also possible to conceive of organizational structure as the outcome of people's attempts to resolve problems.

We therefore agree with Silverman, who argues that the relationship between organizational structure and a changing environment is not mechanical. "Whether a technological innovation is incorporated into an organization will be determined not by an impersonal process whereby the organization 'itself' acts to maximize efficiency." [9] Rather, organizational processes are executed by human activity, which itself is governed by the participants' definition of the situation, their preferences for one or another outcome, and the intensity with which these preferences are held, a subject to which we turn in Chapter 4.

To summarize the discussion—forces from the environment, the most potent of which are political and economic, impact on an organization, pushing it toward or away from change. Organizational structure and process are shaped by these forces and to some extent influence the larger environment in turn. Similarly, the organization's structure and process impinge on the critical actors, either reinforcing or changing the "meaning" of these forces for them. When their definitions shift in ways that suggest new problems or new opportunities, the result is behavior to protect things the way they are or to change them. Figure 1 represents in simplified form this way of conceptualizing the forces that lead to change behavior in organizations. The solid arrows indicate a more powerful impact than the dotted arrows.

[9] David Silverman, *The Theory of Organizations* (New York: Basic Books, 1971), p. 153.

The model of change that these concepts suggest is straightforward. Forces both environmental and internal to the organization interact and impinge on organizational actors. When the meanings for actors concerning opportunity or difficulty are affected, action is likely to follow. Change practice, then, involves a critical assessment of these forces. On the basis of such an analysis relevant forces may be manipulated to maximize their impact on actor perceptions in the direction of desired change goals. We turn, in the following three chapters, to a more specific identification of the most relevant sets of these forces.

2. Economic and Political Forces in the Environment

AN ORGANIZATION'S ENVIRONMENT is that wide arena beyond the organization's boundaries that includes such societal features as economic structure and conditions as well as power arrangements and social climate. Within this general environment are groups, organized and unorganized, some in direct contact with the organization and others not, many of which overlap and shift as they attempt to alter or to accommodate to broad social conditions.

Factors "out in the air" such as recession or boom times and "reactionary" or "progressive" public attitudes are potent influences on the possibility for organizational change. Although their far-reaching nature precludes our considering them here, it is important to mark their significance, particularly because what is "out there" is both intangible and assumed, and therefore its impact may go unnoticed. The attainability of organizational change goals, however, is very much related to the economic system and the state of the economy, since these obviously govern the level of financial support for human services. And what types of programs are permissible is conditioned by the structure of government and dominant political attitudes. Although these forces are hardly amenable to the practitioner's intervention, a "reading" of the organization's macroenvironment can at the least inform the public rationale he offers for desired changes—for example, that a new program will upgrade educational skills, reduce welfare loads, or check juvenile crime.

To map the entire field of social forces that encourage organizational change within this universe requires identification of an impossibly vast range of variables. Even limiting our analysis to economic and political forces does not result in a manageable boundary. We therefore confine our discussion of economic factors to two primary elements, funding and technology, and limit our consideration of political forces to prevailing value systems and the powerful interests that, in direct contact with the organization, shape the conditions of its existence.

available for them. Indeed, workers can sometimes influence practice directions through successful grantsmanship when other interventions would fail. The point is illustrated by the child guidance clinic in which psychodynamically oriented long-term treatment was the only modality offered. A clinic worker was able to interest staff and administration in proffering concrete and advocacy services only after he attracted additional money for the purpose.

Established programs have protectionistic mechanisms in that interests are already staked out and "turf" zealously guarded. Not only do new programs entail unpredictable costs, but the demand that they meet a specified need and that they "work" is always greater than the demands made on established services. In contrast, the mere existence of established programs is often a sufficient justification for their continuance. In times when the availability of funds is rising, the addition of funds for experimentation is possible, whereas during periods of financial constriction, to launch or expand a program requires redistribution of resources. Although the way in which funds are allocated is very often threatening to existent programs, a redistribution of funds is guaranteed to be threatening and, consequently, to provoke resistance. Innovations that necessitate the redistribution of resources thus tend to engender opposition and conflict tactics and require proponents with sufficient power to carry the day.

Often shifts in funding represent neither the addition nor the contraction of the overall amount of money available for social welfare but, rather, its flow from one type of service to another. Under these circumstances, programs are sometimes maintained by revising their formats, if not by altering their activities. Thus, when organizing the poor under the aegis of Community Action agencies came back into disfavor in the late 1960s, some newly developing mental health centers opened storefronts and organized clients as part of the Community Mental Health Act. As shifts take place, the ability to anticipate future program demands becomes an important practice attribute. It is through such ability that organizations increase their capacity to position themselves to receive the funds for new needs and program ideas when these become available.

Funding Sources. Influence is accorded in organizations in direct proportion to one's ability to control the resources the organization most needs to survive and prosper. Money, as a major environmental input, provides funders with a critical source of power to command agency decision making. Change proposals that advance the interests and values of funding sources find strong support, whereas those that impinge negatively on funders engender formidable opposition. To be successful, such innovative proposals minimally require the mobilization of considerable other sources of power. Failing that, their scope must ordinarily be limited so as to be invisible to the givers and getters of funds. On the other hand, the practitioner who obtains a grant, as in the child guidance clinic example above, is likely to increase his overall influence within the agency.

There is a qualification to the conventional wisdom that "he who pays the piper calls the tune," however: he who calls the tune may be tone-deaf. That is, those who dispense funds may not have complete information, nor are they always rational and consistent. They may hold values that encourage them to react to change proposals in other than utilitarian terms. In addition, and most important, funders are subject to the pressures of conflicting interests and reference groups.

Organizations vary substantially in regard to their source of funds. One distinction which has long been considered significant is whether an agency's financing and management are governmental (i.e., public) or private. Traditionally, innovation has been seen as the function of privately funded agencies in contrast to those financed by public monies. Private agencies, it has been held, can afford to be less responsive to political pressures and hence more experimental. Furthermore, since publicly financed programs are accountable to politicians, and politicians must avoid controversy, the public organization is said to eschew change because it is often accompanied by conflict.

There is evidence, however, that this is not in fact the case. Private agencies are as subject to significant political pressures as are public ones. The source of the pressure is different (the businessman-philanthropist rather than the politician), but the effects are quite similar.[2] And in a study of thirty-five instances of planned change, Warren and Hyman found that changes originating under private auspices tended to be arrived at consensually, whereas those under government auspices were overwhelmingly associated with conflict.[3]

Furthermore, the scope of private as opposed to public financing is limited, and it accounts for an ever-shrinking percentage of the human services dollar. This factor inhibits the development of new programs, which, as we noted earlier, are encouraged by the expansion rather than by the redistribution of funds. On the other hand, private agencies may be more flexible than public ones in shaping program goals to meet funding mandates. The functions of public organizations are prescribed by legislation and often leave little room for deviation even when outside funds are available to support growth and change. Whatever the merits of these ar-

[2] Lazarsfeld and Thielens, for example, found no clear-cut differences between the faculties of public and private institutions regarding their perceptions of an increase in political pressure during the McCarthy era of the 1950s. At the public colleges, politicians were most frequently identified as the source of pressure; at the private institutions, it was alumni. Paul Z. Lazersfeld and Wagner Thielens, Jr., *The Academic Mind* (New York: Free Press, 1958), p. 40.

[3] Roland L. Warren and Herbert H. Hyman, "Purposive Community Change in Consensus and Dissensus Situations," in Terry N. Clark, ed., *Community Structure and Decision-Making* (San Francisco: Chandler, 1968), p. 417.

guments, it became clear in the 1960s that private agencies had no monopoly on innovation; if anything, the reverse was true. The trailblazing that took place during that period was performed largely under public auspices.

If the distinction between private and public funding as a change-disposing factor is unclear, the vast expansion of government financing for social services has undoubtedly resulted in power realignments within the private sector. Boards of directors and development departments in the past carried primary responsibility for raising funds (and in many agencies still do). Increasingly, however, the full-time executive cadre has direct access to money, since they are at least as likely as trustees to have the program know-how and political connections necessary to tap public sources. In such cases, influence flows to the executive group. In general, this may be viewed as a predisposing factor for practitioner intervention, since practitioners interact more with agency administrators than with trustees, and interaction enhances influence.[4] Furthermore, the function of executives—to ensure goal achievement as well as organizational maintenance—makes them more responsive to programmatic issues and client concerns than are trustees, whose agency responsibilities tend to be primarily maintaining in nature.

Dependence on Funders. Although all human service agencies are dependent on their environment for funds, there are degrees of dependence among them. Logic suggests that if the environment is a major source of change, dependence on the environment, including funding sources, is more change-disposing than independence. For one thing, organizations are necessarily more susceptible to broad environmental currents as their dependency increases, and they will shift with these currents. Conversely, organizations with a secure funding base are less obliged to consider modifying organizational goals to accommodate outside pressure. Secondly, with greater dependence, there is more impetus for an organization to interact with forces from its environment, including funders, and this makes them more subject to these other influences. Thompson makes the related point that as dependency increases, so too does the difficulty of accomplishing the tasks required of the organization; or, in other words, managing its task environment.[5] The resultant uncertainty leads to search and change behavior.

The degree of an agency's dependence on funding sources cannot be viewed as "good" or "bad" apart from one's evaluation of the content of a change and how it corresponds to environmental forces. Note that during

    [4] Barry E. Collins and Harold Guetzkow, *A Social Psychology of Group Processes for Decision-Making* (New York: Wiley, 1964), pp. 124–26.

    [5] James D. Thompson, *Organizations in Action* (New York: McGraw-Hill, 1967), p. 10.

the 1960s, when the federal government was promoting attention to services to the poor and their participation in decision making, dependence on federal funds might well have been perceived as a positive force by human service workers. At other times, however, the norms and power arrangements of American society have ordinarily not been so responsive to service recipients, and surely not to the most disadvantaged among them. Under these circumstances, the change stimulus generated by financial dependence is likely to be regressive, and funding that is relatively independent of the environment is, of course, preferable.

An organization's dependence on or independence from its funding sources is in large measure related to how its money is raised and allocated. Endowments offer a prime example of a funding pattern that permits an agency to maintain its relative insulation from environmental change stimuli. The change-resistant opportunity afforded by an endowment is illustrated by the experience of the Community Service Society (CSS), the prestigious New York City family agency. While other social agencies reacted to the urban crisis in the 1960s, CSS held fast to its traditional program. One reason, according to a student of the organization's history, was the agency's rich endowment.[6] CSS's need to modify its program was limited by the fact that its finances were independent of external influences, and few outside the agency's board had to be considered in determining how its money was spent. It might be noted parenthetically that when change did come to CSS, it was radical and explosive, and Goldberg suggests that the agency's lack of ongoing accommodation during the decade triggered the explosiveness of that change.[7]

"Purchase of service" contracts, by which public agencies buy services for its clients from private organizations, constitute another funding pattern that reduces dependence. Although such contracts do not altogether limit agency responsibility and can, after all, be renegotiated, accountability is on a case-by-case basis and more difficult to supervise. Although purchase-of-service contracts provide a large portion of the budget of some agencies, they do not include the wide-ranging surveillance that ordinarily accompanies significant financial support.

Other structural arrangements also reduce agency dependence on its funding sources. Sometimes, a third organization is interposed between the service-giving agency and the funder and serves as a buffer. An example is a state department of social services that provides funds to local programs but vests supervisory responsibility in a county authority. The program's latitude is increased by the fact that the county group can only make

[6] Gertrude S. Goldberg, *New Directions for the Community Service Society: A Study of Organizational Change,* Columbia University, unpublished doctoral dissertation, 1976, p. 236.

[7] *Ibid,* pp. 235–36.

level of technological expertise. In this oversimplified analysis, the decisive role technology plays in organizational potency and change becomes clear.

In contrast to the corporate sector, human services organizations are more vulnerable to the power arrangements and prevailing social values in their environment. Agencies are developed by public action to address one or another social problem, be it juvenile delinquency, poverty, or unemployment. Their mandate is to provide service in relationship to the problem as it exists—to rehabilitate the drug addict, find a foster home for the abandoned child, "redirect" juvenile misbehavior. Such mandates are political in that they are determined by power arrangements and prevailing values. In the 1950s the "cause" of juvenile delinquency was considered to be psychological, and the "technology" for its redress involved recreation and counseling. In the 1960s the cause was viewed as social and economic, and the methodology involved developing new opportunities and training for the deviant. In the 1970s the cause was defined as overpermissiveness in dealing with offenders, and the societal mandate was for strict law enforcement and rigorous penalties.

In each of these periods, agencies chartered to "serve" youth elaborated technologies related to the problem definition and the political exigencies of the time. As the mandate shifted, the technology adapted. In other words, the prevailing social climate shaped the technology to be employed rather than the technology independently influencing the direction of the juvenile-serving institutions.

Nevertheless, practitioners must consider how technological developments influence the field of forces to encourage or inhibit specific changes. Three related factors may be especially noted: the organizational stress created by technological developments; the "multiplier effect" of some technological advances; and the contagion that occurs in the field as the result of technological innovation. In each instance, the "fit" between the particular technological development and the desired change determines its pro- or antichange impact. In addition, the characteristics of particular technologies make them more or less amenable as a force for change.

"Inventions," particularly if they are "breakthroughs," generate a high degree of environmental pressure to respond to the "discovery." For example, the addiction-treatment field, which had previously been dominated by psychological approaches, was forced to react to the introduction of methadone maintenance, and the resulting stress generated a high degree of instability. Some agencies welcomed the new technique and began to specialize in dispensing methadone. Others shifted and included methadone among their treatment options. Still others continued as before, and some went out of existence.

Stress of this kind constitutes a pro- or antichange force, depending on the consonance of the technological development with the particular change. We might expect that changes intended to increase clinical resources would be inhibited by instability stemming from methadone's introduction. However, if the goal was to provide for concrete needs (e.g., job training opportunities, health care services, etc.), the same instability might be a force for change.

Some technological advances have a "multiplier effect" in that one new development triggers others. The increasing use of psychotropic drugs such as thorazine provides an example. Such developments were largely responsible for the replacement of long-term hospitalization of of mental patients with a short-term "in and out" approach. Short-term treatment of mental patients, in turn, gave rise to the notion of "deinstitutionalization," which, in its turn, became the goal of other social interventions (e.g., keeping youth out of juvenile custodial institutions or maintaining older adults in their homes). The consequences may be viewed as both good and ill. On the one hand, the use of medication resulted in unstable patients being "dumped" into communities that neither wanted them nor had the necessary supports for maintaining them. On the other hand, the notion of "deinstitutionalization" also resulted in the expansion of creative service patterns (e.g., group homes, halfway houses) and in increasing concern about case accountability for the returning patient, youth, or older adult. Evaluating "deinstitutionalization" is not our point, however. Rather, it is that the correspondence between such social inventions and the change goals of the worker determine its pro- or antichange disposition. Thus, "deinstitutionalization" could provide leverage for practitioners to move their agencies toward community-based practice, while the ready discharge of clients might act as an obstacle to the development of new in-house services.

Human service agencies are vulnerable to program fads and fashions. This may be due to uncertainty about efficacy of service technologies or their limited measurability. Or it may stem from the competition between agencies for a limited resources pie and the premium placed by funders on new ideas. Whatever the reason, contagion appears to take place in the field in response to new service ideas. The juvenile delinquency programs developed as demonstration and research projects during the 1960s offer a case in point. Before the early projects could organize the research that was to be used to evaluate their activities, much less conduct the evaluations themselves, their program ideas had swept across the country. Contagion obviously constitutes a substantial force for change when the new ideas and the worker's change goals are consonant. But contagion can as easily act in the reverse way when consonance is lacking.

Finally, the characteristics of certain technologies may make them more likely to be forces for change, while other technologies inhibit innovation. The more a set of tasks lends itself to standardization, for example, the less open the technology is to practitioner-directed change. Standardized tasks as such. The practitioner must then either retire from the scene or target the norm or value system as the object of the change. Although norm creation is ordinarily inaccessible to practitioner intervention, there are occasions when attempting value change is the only alternative. Rogers illustrates this point in family-planning campaigns in developing countries. Before the 1960s, there was a large-family norm in such countries. Before family-planning methods could be successfully introduced, a small-family norm had to be created. Hence, massive investments were made in communications campaigns to preach the advantages of families with only two children.[13]

SIGNIFICANT ACTORS

All organizations exist in an environment made up of "significant others": supporters, opponents, and quasineutrals with varying interests in the organization. Their viewpoints and the resources for influence that they can bring to bear represent a critical set of forces affecting stability and change.

Significant actors are those individuals or groups who are important to an organization because of their interest in its services and who have the potential or actual ability to influence the organization's direction. The major actors in the human services scenario represent three primary classes of interests: agents of the "public," users, and providers.

Superordinates, Users, and Providers.   The primary participants are, first of all, superordinate bodies, those with responsibility for overseeing the organization's functioning. More often than not, these consist of actors who directly or indirectly pay for or legitimate the service. In the public sector, there may be a complex hierarchy of authority structures, frequently overlapping and at different levels of government. In privately funded agencies, accountability is ordinarily internal to the agency's board of directors, but superordinate funding organizations such as the United Fund also review programs.

In theory, it is the "public," the "taxpayer," or the "community" that accords legitimacy to the agency and supports it financially. The public is ordinarily inattentive, however. It may be aroused in times of crisis or periods of social unrest. A dramatic event or a human interest story may also call public attention to an organizational need or issue. And agencies that represent precarious or tenuous values are closely watched. But by and large, persons who function as the community's agent—the public official, the foundation officer, the philanthropist—yield the power. Since, as we noted earlier, influence is accorded in proportion to one's ability to

---

[13] Everett Rogers, "Social Structure and Social Change," in Gerald Zaltman et al., *Processes and Phenomena of Social Change* (New York: Wiley, 1973), pp. 78–79.

control the resources an organization needs, key in-contact agents of the public-at-large wield considerable power indeed.

The users of a service have more or less impact on the agency depending on how active and organized they are. A dissatisfied client is not ordinarily a "significant other," politically speaking, except in three circumstances. The first is when the dissatisfaction arouses the support of powerful other actors (e.g., the client "gets to" the mayor). Another is when the dissatisfaction has the potential for stimulating broad but latent opposition. The third is when the client's cause is taken up by a representative group of clients. Consumer activism in the health care field exemplifies the latter.

By provider groups we mean those organized groups operating outside the organization itself, such as industry-wide unions and professional associations.[14] They are often motivated by narrow self-interest, and their survival depends on their ability to deliver benefits to members. Occasionally, however, changes that promote the interests of providers converge with the interest of users. For example, the interests of teachers' associations in reduced class size parallel the educational interests of pupils. Furthermore, at least one study has found that membership in a chapter of the National Association of Social Workers *inhibits* the influence of conservatizing social forces on social workers.[15] The influence of provider groups varies depending on a number of factors. The size and cohesiveness of their membership is one factor; the public support they can attract is another. The impact of provider groups on human service agencies also varies with the status of the particular profession within the organization and how central its professionals are to the organization's fulfillment of its function. The influence of provider groups depends as well on the composition and attitudes of internal elites. For example, executives who seek the social approval and professional approbation of their colleagues are likely to be more attentive to the position of professional associations.

Impact on Organizational Change. The impact of these varied interests on organizational change is important in at least two ways. Agencies provide an arena in which superordinate bodies, funding sources, officials, experts, top staff, and sometimes organized client groups vie for the adoption of one or another view. If stability is the result of a balance among forces in dynamic interaction, as we have suggested, an organization's equilibrium is in part the result of accommodation among these often conflicting interests. Positions will be accepted and bargains struck on the basis of the intensity with which views are held and the power the parties perceive themselves as having. But the balance may be a delicate one.

[14] Providers who are internal to the organization are discussed in Chapter 4.

[15] Irwin Epstein, "Organizational Careers, Professionalization, and Social Worker Radicalism," *Social Service Review* 44, no. 2 (June 1970), pp. 123–31.

Views change, and patterns of influence shift. As this occurs, organizational change may be expected. To cite a dramatic example: the increase of client activism in the 1960s and the taxpayer revolt of the 1970s each caused profound alterations in the provision of human services.

Contending interest groups play a second important role in promoting or preventing organizational change. Essentially, they represent the constituency of the organization's leadership. By and large, the latter seek a placid environment, and an important means of accomplishing this is to maintain equilibrium among various interests. Indeed, an executive's view on any specific organizational matter can be inferred with some (if only relative) confidence when one knows how it will impact on powerful others. Innovations that do not impinge on powerful constituents in one way or another have a relatively high degree of success potential. Better still are those innovations that impact positively on the more powerful of them.

Practitioners may not have access to information regarding the views of many of these actors. Sometimes, however, positions can be inferred. For example, the funding source of an addiction services clinic whose policies discouraged the attendance of drug abusers and whose case load was consequently filled with nonabusers might be expected to question these policies. Sometimes, too, sensitive exploration will reveal the stance of powerful actors.

Practitioners are only rarely in a position to modify the views of these interest groups, but we believe that there may be more opportunity to do so in the long term than they ordinarily perceive. Although it is to some extent belied by the experience of the 1960s, there is still some truth in William Form's assertion that "rarely in American history has so little influence been wielded by a group [i.e., social work professionals] that has had so much opportunity to influence. Although the clientele of social work is enormous, it has never been organized to back expanded welfare programs." [16]

Two other characteristics of the relationship between environmental interests and an organization ought to be mentioned as relevant to change propensity. They are: (1) the extent and type of support and opposition in the environment and (2) the attention or inattention paid to the organization by significant others.

Environmental Support and Opposition.   Support in the environment affects change potential depending on its extent and the potency of the supporters and opponents. Widespread public favor and/or a narrow base of influential supporters encourage a more zealous pursuit of organiza-

---

[16] William H. Form, "Social Power and Social Welfare," in Robert Morris, ed., *Centrally Planned Change* (New York: National Association of Social Workers, 1964), p. 87.

tional values. Since this effort is likely to trigger conflict, an organization that perceives itself as having powerful support will be more risk-taking than an organization that does not. On the other hand, support that is mild or of uncertain potency induces caution and thus stability.

Powerful opposition is likely to act as a constricting force on welfare organizations. It generates change toward increased bureaucratization and away from program innovation. Thus the rigidities of the public welfare system undoubtedly stem from the pervasive antagonism toward it. And research regarding a beleaguered community action program showed that extended outer hostility led to an increase in the numbers and influence of instrumental actors (accountants and other supporting staff) at the expense of program people.[17]

Competition within the environment probably acts as the greatest spur to modest organizational change. Our earlier point in reference to the contagiousness of new program ideas is applicable here, since the contagion is at least in part a response to interorganizational rivalry. In this regard, it is ironic that a society that espouses free enterprise and competition as sources of product improvement and consumer benefit does not hold the same values for its service agencies. Yet the principle is the same.

Environmental Attentiveness.   The attention or inattention paid to an organization impacts on change and stability as well. Inattentiveness by superordinate bodies and relevant interest groups acts as a disincentive to agency responsiveness to them—a positive or negative factor depending on one's view of the interests they represent. Inattention allows greater leeway for internal actors to pursue client-oriented though unpopular positions. But it also permits agencies to engage in client exploitation that public attention might otherwise discourage.

Attentiveness itself shifts with time and circumstance. As programs or change proposals become more significant or more expensive, they also become more visible. Inattention gives way too in the face of the interests of a powerful actor or the occurrence of a dramatic event. The impact of visibility as a change force is illustrated by the nursing home scandals in New York City in 1975. An inquiry, spearheaded by a maverick state legislator, drew media attention to deplorable nursing home conditions, the misuse of Medicaid funds, and political collusion in illegal practices. The resulting public furor signaled the rise of an advocacy movement and the improvement of conditions in the homes.

In this chapter we have identified the critical economic and political forces in the environment that affect an organization's stability and

[17] George Brager, *Organization in Crisis: A Study of Commitment and Conflict,* New York University, unpublished doctoral dissertation, 1967.

change—funding, technology, sentiment systems, and powerful interests. Although environmental forces are not accessible to direct practitioner intervention except under special circumstances, they are important in understanding the total field of forces involved in change. Environmental forces predict and precipitate internal changes which the sophisticated practitioner may anticipate and frequently influence in desired directions.

3. Organizational Forces

WE HAVE NOTED THAT, although the environment is a critical influence on organizational stability and change, organizations exposed to comparable external forces may respond differently. The characteristics of organizations intervene between environmental impact and organizational innovation, mediating external stimuli as well as exerting independent influence on an organization's predisposition to change.

In the preceding chapter we viewed environmental forces from two vantage points, the economic and the political. Although economic matters are inevitably political as well, the distinction is a useful one. However, in exploring internal forces for organizational change, the demarcation becomes more tenuous. Although organizational characteristics can also be distinguished as economic (i.e., the system by which an organization produces and exchanges its goods or services) or political (i.e., the distribution of influence as it affects organizational beliefs and sentiments), when change is *planned,* it requires intervention that implies at its core the exercise of influence. For example, structuring tasks in the interests of efficiency is ordinarily seen as an economic matter. But when one seeks to modify the structuring of tasks, it is inevitable that the beliefs and values of relevant participants, their interests, and their respective power positions will come into play.

Three aspects of the organization are particularly important with regard to change—its ideology, goals, and structure. The three are interdependent. Ideology, for example, influences goal setting, which in turn informs agency structure. The reverse is true as well; agency structure shapes the development of an organization's ideology and mission. We discuss the three in turn below and conclude the chapter by noting how the rate and timing of change within organizations affect planned intervention.

Ideology

Ideology—by which we mean a commonly shared, coherent, and intensely held set of beliefs and commitments—is a potent social lever. It shapes self. On the other hand, venerational ideologies, rooted as they are in tradition, are most often found in established, stable, and consequently change-resistant settings.

A second factor is the internal or external focus of the ideology. The more an agency's funding, technology, or belief system is dependent on the environment, the more responsive it is to change currents "out there." Thus, ideologies that require environmental responsiveness will be more change-disposing. Campaign ideologies head the list, since they are particularly vulnerable to changes in the environment related to their issue or social objective. Indeed, if, as one tactician has pointed out, "the action is in the reaction" (i.e., a significant goal of social action is to induce self-defeating behavior by the opponent),[2] then organizations with campaign ideologies are particularly susceptible to change, even those generated by their "enemies."

Client-service ideologies are more environmentally dependent and therefore more change-disposing than process or venerational ideologies. Organizations with a client orientation hold themselves responsible for providing whatever service their clientele appears to need, so that as client populations shift or their needs change, the organization feels compelled to respond. For example, as clients of counterculture service centers began to experiment with "hard" drugs, the centers turned their program attention to include the emerging need.

Another factor is the intensity with which an ideology is held. Individuals who are committed to a particular set of ideas range from those who are open to competing notions to "true believers," for whom the only truth is their own and to whom opposing views are insupportable or evil. The same may be said of organizations. Although all ideologies are intensely held, the intensity varies among organizations. The less the intensity, the less likely that an organization's ideology will serve as a significant impetus for organizational behavior (or change).

It should be noted that a perceived lack of ideology is prized by some persons and organizations. Highly professional agencies with a technical bent, as well as many educational institutions, view ideology pejoratively, as "subjective" and tending to deflect the professionalism of the service or of the teaching/learning enterprise. In reality this may be merely another ideology, reflecting a negative view of someone else's belief systems coupled with the failure to recognize one's own. Nevertheless, innovations in such settings will find acceptance only to the extent that they are defined and perceived as nonideological.

An organization with a dominant ideology (even one that is perceived as nonideological) is vulnerable to *any* innovation that can be defined in terms of the prevailing belief and sentiment systems and is resistant to

[2] Saul D. Alinsky, *Rules for Radicals* (New York: Random House, 1971), p. 136.

any change perceived as counter to its ideology. Thus the organization with a campaign ideology will embrace change that advances its cause or administers a setback to its opponent's; the client-service orientation suggests vulnerability to client need and demand; the organization with a process ideology will respond most readily to refinements and elaboration of its core methodology; and the venerational organization will concern itself with defending its "leadership" position, and its vulnerability will be greatest to those actors whom it perceives to be prestigious.

The matter is not so straightforward as is implied above, however. Many organizations contain a mix of belief systems. Beliefs shift with time, and one or another position may be ascendant at any particular moment. It is interesting to consider the role of developmental factors in the shift. It is possible that over an extended period some organizations, created to solve a social problem (campaign), move to a focus on helping the victims of the problem (client service), then develop a primary interest in the methods used to proffer the service (process), and ultimately come to believe in their unique leadership role (venerational).

A mix of belief systems may also result from diversity among the organization's units. Although these units share superordinate goals (the survival or enhancement of the organization, to mention one) and contribute to the accomplishments of the organization's mission, their organizational environments differ. They have different functions and technologies, different internal needs and external ties, different role systems, and different ways of relating to each other. Consequently, they hold different beliefs and values, with the position of low-power units, or those that are ancillary to major organizational purposes, most likely to diverge from the dominant organizational ideology.[3]

Thus, a change goal may be designed or defined on the basis of a dominant ideology, an agency's mix, or the belief system of particular subunits. The important point is that ideological patronage is exceedingly potent indeed.

Goals

The dynamics we have discussed regarding ideology and innovation apply in large measure to organizational goals and change as well. Connecting an innovation to the mission of the organization is as change-propelling as is linking a change attempt to a validation of an agency's ideology. And as with ideologies, some organizational goals, in their very substance, are

[3] It is probable too that low-power or ancillary professionals in the human services are more likely to espouse client-service ideologies than are dominant organizational groups. Differences of perspective and interest between the organization and the unit are most satisfactorily justified, both to oneself and publicly, on the ground of the primacy of client service.

more change-orienting than others. They presume certain ideational or value underpinnings that predispose to innovation. Thus, agencies that seek client decision making among their objectives or those for which inter-disciplinary collaboration, regardless of profession or rank, is central to goal attainment may implicitly assume values of egalitarianism and hence will be more responsive to influence from lower-ranking participants. Similarly, some goals are more dependent on the environment for their accomplishment, and the organization is more adaptive as a consequence. And like ideology, an organization's goals are qualified by the intensity with which they are held so as to motivate or impede particular change proposals.

Two other sets of organizational dynamics in regard to goals need to be distinguished for change practice purposes. The first set concerns explicit and implicit goals; the second relates to the multiple purposes of organizations.

EXPLICIT AND IMPLICIT GOALS

The formal goals or explicit purposes for an organization's existence are a reference point for several important change-disposing forces. An organization's goals constitute a contract among its constituents, and particularly between the provider of the funds and the governing body or administration of the agency. They indicate the kinds of service the organization will provide, who is eligible to receive service, and, frequently, the social outcome projected as the ultimate result of having offered the service.

These goals in the human services are typically lofty and unattainable. Contrary to cynical observation, they are not lofty because social welfare administrators are inveterate "do-gooders" or "soft-headed" thinkers, unable to specify goals in practicable terms. Rather, an important reason for setting high-minded purposes is to garner support from an environment in which service values are precarious. Human service agencies tend to be caught in a double bind. For example, the demand for accountability and "businesslike" methods is in part a response to the fact that welfare programs typically promise more than they attain. The anomaly is that the public officials who most loudly decry welfare failure and call most zealously for accountability are the ones most likely *not* to vote funds for programs that lack grandiose mission statements.

The survival of social welfare organizations is nevertheless dependent on the continued belief among significant publics that contracted services are being provided adequately and that the organization's goals are competently advanced. Agency administrators are constantly alert to signs in the environment which suggest that the agency's credibility with regard to goal satisfaction is being shaken, and they are equally alert to developments within the organization which—if visible to outsiders—would put such credibility in jeopardy.

An example is provided by the drug-abuse program of a mental hygiene clinic which was able to maintain the statistical count necessary to insure its current level of funding by serving clients who did *not* abuse drugs. Although this policy was in violation of its goal to rehabilitate abusers, the agency ignored this contradiction until exposure by a funding source seemed imminent. It was at this point that a staff member who had been advocating an outreach component and a change in the clinic's treatment protocol found a more receptive hearing. The tension between the agency's objective and the potential perception of a contradictory reality acted as a potent force for change.

Such tension may be augmented by a discrepancy between the agency's manifest and latent purposes. For example, state mental hospitals often assert that treatment is their purpose, although confinement and custody may be the more significant—though unexpressed—objectives.[4] In developing strategies, the change-oriented practitioner must distinguish between manifest and latent purposes and estimate the potency of each. In the instance of the state mental hospital, for example, a worker who wanted to humanize patient care by setting up ward meetings between patients and staff could not assume that the mental health objective of his proposed change would influence other participants. Furthermore, he would have to consider how the change might affect custodial goals so as to assess its feasibility and, if he could, to link the change to the hospital's custodial purposes.

The latent objectives of organizational policy are often obscure, and the worker who innocently assumes agency commitment to its manifest goals may imperil his change idea. Policies that are ineffective, inefficient, or appear to go counter to goal attainment must serve some latent purpose to persist. Unless this purpose is identified, the practitioner acts in the dark.

For example, a worker new to a multidisciplinary family service agency observed that its intake procedure seemed unnecessarily cumbersome. An applicant was seen in intake by a worker for several meetings, following which a dispositional conference was held to formulate a treatment plan. The case was then referred to one of the psychiatrists, psychologists, or social workers, depending on who was deemed most "suitable" to work with the client. The process caused considerable mischief, however, since treatment was delayed for several months, many clients dropped out, the intake material did not always appear as relevant to the assigned therapist as information he would himself obtain, and clients often expressed anger

---

[4] This disparity between manifest purpose and latent function applies not only to organizational goals. The same dynamic exists in regard to procedures, policies, structures, and other aspects of all organizations.

that they had to begin again with a new worker. The agency might have been able to justify the process professionally except for one factor: in almost every instance, the dispositional conference assigned the client on practical grounds to the worker who happened to have space in his case load. The new worker proposed that therapists rotate the intake interviews depending on room in their case loads and that the intake therapist present the material at a dispositional conference for assessment and planning and carry the case unless this was contraindicated by the conference review. What she did not take into account were the latent purposes of the intake process: to "cream off" those clients most likely to accept the agency's type of intervention, and to foster the sense of "professionalism" which the elaborate process engendered on the part of staff. Without that knowledge, her attempt to make the change was hampered.

Many policies that appear to meet an agency's explicit goals may in fact have other compelling but unrecognized reasons for their existence. For example, a strict emphasis on health care in a nursing home facility (e.g., deciding what a patient may or may not eat, whether it is "safe" for a patient to leave the home) seems, on the face of it, to be motivated by concern for the health needs of the older adult client. But it is also possible —since people rarely follow a strict regimen of "what is good for them" and often allow themselves a measure of leeway—that a latent goal of rigid health rules is to avoid the administrative inconvenience incurred by special circumstances or exceptions to policy. Or it may be to control patients, simplify the problems they cause, and thus make it possible to manage them more efficiently.[5]

Most relevant to the current discussion, however, is the fact that one basis for the persistance of latent purposes is their latency itself—that is, the fact that they are not publicly acknowledged or widely understood. In part, this hidden feature enables social units to perform functions that they may feel to be undesirable (e.g., isolating older adults from society and controlling their behavior) but has a socially acceptable rationale (e.g., caring for older-adult health needs). Thus, an agency can have its cake and eat it too. In some measure, then, the exposure of a latent function may threaten the existence of the function. To the extent that an agency implicitly pursues socially unacceptable objectives while avowing socially acceptable ones, a change-producing tension exists.

MULTIPLE PURPOSES

An agency's goals may of course represent a contract, not with a single provider of funds, but with a variety of funding sources; for example, a

---

[5] Goffman has noted that "total institutions" (mental hospitals, prisons, etc.) attempt to control the behavior of inmates by stripping them of their individuality. Erving Goffman, "The Characteristics of Total Institutions," *Symposium on Preventive and Social Psychiatry* (Washington, D.C.: Walter Reed Army Institute of Research, April 1957), pp. 25–29.

community family-service agency might contract with a local school district to provide day-care services, with the county welfare department for homemaker help, with Planned Parenthood for family planning, etc. Its goals would then typically reflect the span of services within its purview. In other words, social agencies have multiple aims more often than not. This is so, as a matter of fact, not only because agencies are pressed to widen their horizons by others in their organizational set, or by their own sense of responsiveness to social need, or even by their desire for aggrandizement. Multiple goals stem as well from the differences in perspective among an organization's internal constituency—its various subunits. As in the case of ideologies, a subsystem may have goals that vary from those of other units or of the agency as a whole.

To the degree that the overall (although multiple) goals of an organization are reinforcing, they produce stability, and only those changes that refine or elaborate the unified set of goals can be considered. More typically, however, these goals are difficult to orchestrate. Moreover, the existence of varying functional subsystems inevitably places the members of these units in competition for goal ascendancy, producing an organizational tension that is a force for initiating innovative proposals.

An organization's ability to compromise differences among goals influences its receptivity to change, as well as the strategies available to the change-oriented worker. When multiple goals are roughly compatible, they may be pursued through mutually supporting actions. One means is by advancing the different goals in sequence; another is by merging them. For example, one unit of a multipurpose agency may define its mission as reaching out to the homebound elderly; another may see its goal as engaging youth in growth-producing activities, including job finding. The two purposes are merged in a program in which youth are hired as companions or helpers to the senior clientele. Adaptations such as these permit staff to aggregate influence through the development of coalitions; thus they serve to encourage change.

In large bureaucratic organizations it is also possible to insulate one goal from another so that potential contradictions are obscured. In such cases, an organization may offer programs that are inconsistent or adopt incompatible innovations, as long as the organization's structure makes it possible to obfuscate the infringement of one goal on the other. Innovation within the Department of Labor in the mid-1960s offers an example of the point. The department, which traditionally offered employment services to the stable working force and employers, was enjoined to shift in part direction to service the needs of the chronically disadvantaged worker. Since providing services to all three of these groups entailed contradictions in policy, manpower programs for the disadvantaged were insulated in a new department. Until such time as this department was firmly established, it would have been unable to ward off threats to its existence from the more traditional and powerful bureaus.

As in the example above, a new program may be insulated from other parts of the organization to protect its integrity. But its isolation may also be used to contain the impact of an innovation on an agency's primary goal. An example is provided by an agency that served a middle-class clientele and was intensely committed to psychodynamically oriented intervention. Induced by environmental forces (e.g., the availability of funds to serve minority poor who were not prime candidates for analytic methods), the agency devised an outreach program in a neighborhood distant from the locus of its major activities. The outreach project was organized as a self-contained unit with limited ties to the central office and limited support from it. It was thus structured almost as if the intention was to prevent the project from contaminating the agency's major activities. In sum, insulating an innovation that is incompatible with other agency goals may be intended either to nurture a change or to retard its development.

A typical accommodation to conflicting goals is through ambiguity, "papering over" the differences among the participants to permit the perception of a commonality of values. Organizations vary on this dimension; some have focused purposes, others are considerably more vague. Professionals decry the lack of clarity, often rightly, since imprecise goals subject an agency to potential confusion of policy, activities at cross-purposes, and ultimate ineffectiveness.

However, goal ambiguity is most advantageous to the *least* powerful members of a unit, since certainty decreases individual license and reduces worker options. The lowest-ranking members of an organization ordinarily have the fewest options and therefore benefit disproportionately from uncertainty. The point may be illustrated by considering the outcome of a struggle over values within any organization. The losers (by definition, the less influential) are ordinarily worse off for the conflict, since the new-found clarity forecloses their position with a finality that could not have existed before the conflict was made explicit. In effect, the precise goals of agencies represent the clarity of their most powerful members.[6]

Organizational Structure

Earlier we identified three structural elements—hierarchy of authority, specialization of task and function, rules and regulations—that inherently create problems for organizations and their staffs. The three also generate significant forces for and against change.

Since every organization has a hierarchy of authority to a greater or lesser degree, it may seem a relatively simple matter to locate who has responsibility for particular decisions. In fact, however, the matter is con-

[6] This point is discussed in George Brager and Harry Specht, *Community Organizing* (New York: Columbia University Press, 1973), p. 141.

siderably more complicated. The "authorized" decision maker may be unconcerned about or inattentive to specific issues. In such an instance, he will have delegated authority to others—or others will have filled the power vacuum created by his inattention. The distinction between formal authority and informal influence is, of course, a well-documented concept in the organizational literature.

Secondly, the nature of the decision, or how it is defined, determines where it is to be located. A procedural matter, for example, requires one decision point whereas a policy change entails another. But the distinction between procedure and policy is often unclear and varies among organizations. Furthermore, the specific content of a decision affects where it is made. Specialization leads to the development of subunits with different functions, but the boundaries between the subunits are not always clear. For example, counseling the ill on the physical and psychological ramifications of their illness might fall within the purview of the nursing staff or of the social-service department in a hospital. The location of a boundary-spanning decision—whether responsibility for making it lies within one unit or another or both together—rests on the ways in which agency tasks are differentiated and coordinated, along with how the issue has been shaped or defined.

The structure of an organization sets the parameters within which this decision-making process takes place. It establishes who may legitimately participate in the decision. It accords some actors resources for influencing the process and withholds influence from others. It shapes the preferences and the commitments of actors and thus who will advocate and who oppose particular decisions and with what intensity. It determines the flow and quality of the information on which interaction takes place. As such, organizational structure encourages or discourages organizational stability and change.

Three variables have received particular attention in the literature of organization change. They are complexity, centralization, and formalization. Each is associated with a structural element mentioned in Chapter 1 (i.e., specialization, hierarchy, and rules, respectively). We shall comment on the three variables below, consider their relationship, and conclude this section with a discussion of how patterns of coordination also affect an agency's predisposition to change.

COMPLEXITY

Citing research done primarily in hospitals and schools, Hage and Aiken postulate that the greater an organization's complexity, the greater the program change.[7] Their indicators of complexity were twofold: the

---

[7] Jerald Hage and Michael Aiken, *Social Change in Complex Organizations* (New York: Random House, 1970), p. 33.

intricacy of the task as measured by the extent of training required to perform it, and the number of diverse occupations within an organization. They reason that highly trained personnel tend to keep abreast of new developments, introduce them into the agency, and thus act as stimulators of program change. Ordinarily too, the more trained a staff, the more they view their profession rather than the agency as a source of identification or career advancement. They can thus afford to be more risk taking, while at the same time the organization is likely to be more accommodating to their input, particularly if their expertise is in short supply.

Thus, organizations whose staffs are more "cosmopolitan" (i.e., professionally as opposed to organizationally oriented) are more receptive to change than agencies in which this is not the case. The point is also suggestive in regard to training programs within organizations (e.g., the "teaching hospital" or student unit within a social agency), since an implicit function of such programs is to "upgrade" the professionalism of their staffs. There is research, for example, supporting the notion that doctors are encouraged to provide high-quality services more by socialization mechanisms such as involvement in student training than by the use of sanctions.[8]

Complexity in an organization (as measured by the number of different occupations it encompasses) leads to program change, according to Hage and Aiken, because it increases the number of perspectives on which decision making is based. In addition, competition among varying specialities provides an incentive to influence the agency in ways congenial to the particular occupation groups. The point is of limited use to practitioners, since the argument is comparative across organizations rather than indicative of the predisposition to change of any particular organization. It is useful, however, when placed in a dynamic context. Over time, as the number of occupations in an organization increases, so too does its amenability to change.

An illustration of this process is found in Charter House, a group home setting we discuss at some length in later chapters.[9] Begun by a priest who opened his apartment to homeless adolescents, the program was unable to meet the needs of all the youths who applied for service. Several domiciles were added, and friends of the priest with connections to the church formed an enlarged staff nucleus. The founders turned to the Department of Social Services for financial support, and the support was forthcoming contingent on Charter House's hiring social workers and psychologists. The consequence of adding clinicians to the religiously oriented staff was

[8] Jerald Hage, *Communication and Organizational Control* (New York: Wiley, 1974), pp. 51–52.

[9] Gay Fiore Shoup, "A Change at Charter House," case record, Columbia University School of Social Work, 1976.

to set off a vigorous competition for ideas, autonomy, and prestige. The result was that Charter House retreated in part from its religious humanitarian philosophy of child-care treatment as it adopted clinically oriented procedures and policies.

There are two major qualifications to the argument that complexity leads to organizational change. The rub, according to Wilson, is that the factors favorably disposing organizations to generate change proposals are precisely those factors that also decrease the likelihood that a given proposal will be adopted. The greater the diversity of tasks, the more a change will affect organization members differently; just as a proposed change will benefit some, it will necessarily constitute a cost to others. Members will protect their investments in the current arrangement, and, in Wilson's view, adoption then requires a more centralized authority than is generally available in organizations marked by task complexity.[10]

The second qualification has to do with the respective power of diverse groups within the organization. As the skill to perform his task entails more training, a practitioner is accorded greater influence. Thus, psychiatrists are more influential than social workers or nurses in shaping mental-health programs. Furthermore, when the task is primary to the achievement of organizational purpose, whatever the degree of training required, its performance brings with it more influence than is accorded to performance of an ancillary task. So, for example, even though social-work tasks require more training than nursing tasks, the nursing staff of a medical facility tends to carry more weight than the social-work personnel in influencing hospital policy.

In other words, although structurally complex organizations may be more predisposing to change than simpler structures, the case may hold only when there is no single dominant profession. Otherwise, the ways in which a change impinges on the most powerful grouping are critical, since only those changes that do not violate the interests of this grouping will be adopted. The point is highly relevant to professionals whose function is ancillary to central organizational goals, as is often the case with many human service professionals. In such instance, a complex structure is likely to be less predisposing to change in areas of specific interest to the ancillary group than a simpler structure dominated by their own profession.

CENTRALIZATION AND FORMALIZATION

Centralization connotes a structure in which decision making is restricted to the top members of the hierarchy. Centralized structures are

[10] James Q. Wilson, "Innovations in Organization: Notes Toward A Theory," in James D. Thompson, ed., *Approaches to Organizational Design* (Pittsburgh: University of Pittsburgh Press, 1966), pp. 202–3.

pyramidal, have "tall" rather than "flat" hierarchical arrangements, with formal and informal power supportive of one another. Formalization refers to the elaboration and enforcement of rules.

According to Hage and Aiken, a high degree of centralization inhibits innovation.[11] For one reason, a small elite is likely to protect its privileges against change, so that innovations that even inferentially threaten the current distribution of rewards are vetoed. Furthermore, decisions are the province of a relative few, and the decision makers develop personal stakes in their choices. Since proposals for change imply criticism, they are avoided, and underlings are evaluated in terms of their loyalty to decisions already made. Finally, centralization limits the free flow of ideas. Small-group research, for example, indicates that hierarchical differentiation impedes free communication, inhibiting the problem-solving capacity of groups.[12] And there is evidence that a high degree of centralization sharply reduces horizontal communication channels, thus isolating units from the stimulation and competition that engender change.[13]

It should be pointed out, however, that the content of an innovation determines the pro- or antichange direction of forces impinging on the change goal. Thus, although centralization is thought generally to inhibit change, modifications that increase the power of the agency's top hierarchy are likely to be encouraged by greater rather than by lesser centralization. Interestingly, one study reports not only that decentralized schools adopted more new programs than centralized ones but that the changes adopted even further increased their decentralization (e.g., they permitted more participation by teachers in decision making).[14]

Hage and Aiken also suggest that the greater the formalization, the less the program change.[15] This is because new programs tend to run afoul of rules; organizational rewards go to those who adhere to "standard operating procedures," so there is less incentive to be innovating; and the greater the job specificity, the less the ambiguity, an element that we have noted is useful in maneuvering a change. At the least, a policy that has been codified is ordinarily more resistant to change than one that, although followed in practice, has not been formally sanctioned. Once again, however, the content of the change is primary. While changes that deviate from standard operating procedures have little likelihood of acceptance in

[11] Hage and Aiken, op. cit., p. 38.

[12] Peter M. Blau and W. Richard Scott, Formal Organizations (San Francisco: Chandler, 1962), pp. 121–28.

[13] Hage, op. cit., pp. 168–69.

[14] Françoise Cillie, Centralization or Decentralization?: A Study in Education Adaptation (New York: Teachers College, Columbia University, 1940). Cited in Hage and Aiken, op. cit., p. 40.

[15] Hage and Aiken, ibid., p. 43.

formal structures, modifications that bring programs into conformance with standard procedures are likely to be embraced.

Centralization and formalization are structural properties that are often found together. Departments of social services, for example, have "tall" structures with rigid hierarchical distinctions, and their tasks are also bounded by formal rules. On the other hand, centralization/formalization and complexity tend to be inversely correlated variables.

COMPLEXITY VS. CENTRALIZATION

In a complex structure, where tasks are intricate and require extensive training, the organization has to count on the creative professional capacities of its staff to attain its objectives. It must relinquish some measure of autonomy to its staff—that is, allow decentralized decision making. Repetitive and predictable tasks, on the other hand, can be effectively controlled through established procedures and supervisory surveillance, and thus lend themselves to centralization/formalization. There is in fact a growing view among administrative theorists that organizational effectiveness depends not on which type of authority distribution is predominant (e.g., centralization or decentralization) but rather on the consistency between the organization's pattern of authority and its task structure (e.g., centralization is more effective when there is a high degree of routinization and decentralization is more effective when tasks are complex).

Although there is a strain toward a "fit" between the two variables, in the disorder of the real world it is unlikely that it follows in any simple pattern. Interestingly, a study of sixteen health and welfare agencies found a relatively high correlation between complexity and program change over a three-year period, whereas the relationship between decentralization and program change, although also positively correlated, was considerably less so.[16]

Structural dimensions are not static but shift with time. One organizational theorist has suggested that organizational conflict is an outcome of the disjuncture between centralization and complexity.[17] That is, as a centralized organization increases in complexity (e.g., through increased specialization, the addition of new departments, the further training of staff), there is an inherent demand by the participants for more autonomy or a "larger slice of the action." Since those who wield power are likely to resist relinquishing their influence, conflict ensues until such time as an accommodation is made and there is either a decline in centralization or a

[16] Jerald Hage and Robert Dewar, "Elite Values Versus Organizational Structure in Predicting Innovation," *Administrative Science Quarterly* 18 (September 1973), p. 285.

[17] Hage, *op. cit.*, p. 99.

retreat from complexity. The Charter House case illustrates the point. As clinical staff was added, increasing Charter House's complexity, there was a press for decision-making perogatives to be lodged with the professional staff (i.e., decreasing centralization). Tensions were heightened, and the agency made accommodations to the demand. The converse also holds true. As a decentralized agency standardizes its operations, there is a strain toward the ingathering of control, with a similar result.

Although we doubt that all organizational conflict can be explained in these terms, the case is nevertheless persuasive for some types of conflict and is suggestive for practice purposes. The fact that receptivity to change increases as an organization's complexity increases or its centralization decreases provides useful data for a practitioner's assessment of the feasibility of a proposed change. That change in one variable encourages change in the other in a predictable direction suggests strategy as well. In some cases it may be desirable to pursue a change, such as winning a more participative decision-making policy, indirectly, by increasing complexity (e.g., through further training or a more specialized division of labor), rather than head-on. The timing of a change attempt may also be suggested, at least in part, by an organization's location in respect to the two structural variables and the direction in which it is moving.

As we indicated earlier, some theorists have argued that while complexity encourages the initiation of change ideas, the adoption of change requires centralized authority. Zaltman and his colleagues maintain that the ideal structure for the generation and initiation of innovative ideas is a complex and decentralized unit (such as a research and development department), with implementation the responsibility of a more hierarchically organized unit (such as a production department).[18]

There is merit in this position. However, although empirical evidence is unavailable, we believe that the character of a proposed change has major bearing on how the complexity/decentralization dimension affects its adoption. For example, changes of lesser scope, which do not require the agreement of diverse units, are more likely to be adopted in a complex, decentralized structure. By eliminating the proposal's need to travel up the hierarchy, decentralization encourages its adoption. Furthermore, when a change does not impinge on the interests of a top hierarchy, it has a better chance in a looser and more diffuse structure. Although such changes will have to be "sold" to upper-ranking participants in any case, there are more potential "buyers" and more opportunity to make the "pitch" in a pluralistic decision-making pattern with more open communication than in a centralized structure.

Our discussion of structure has largely treated the organization as if its structure were a unitary entity, but this is only a partial truth. Organiza-

---

[18] Gerald Zaltman, Robert Duncan, and Jonny Holbeck, *Innovations and Organizations* (New York: Wiley, 1973), p. 146.

tions are, we indicated earlier, composed of interdependent subsystems. Subunits themselves are differentially complex or routinized, centralized or decentralized. Thus, although one can speak of a dominant organizational structure, many organizations are composed of a mix of subsystem structures.

Our comments regarding the relationship between an organization's structure and its predisposition to change hold for the structures of its subsystems as well. Some units are more, some less, receptive to change as a consequence of their tasks and hierarchical patterning. The point is suggestive in regard to where one might route a change attempt in the case of a change whose content spans unit boundaries or is sufficiently flexible to permit a decision regarding whether the change is to be located in one unit rather than another.

PATTERNS OF COORDINATION

The way in which human service agencies coordinate their work is another structural factor influencing change. In large measure, patterns of coordination are shaped by the nature of the tasks necessary to complete an operation or attain a goal. Although the requirements of coordination vary on a number of dimensions, we shall consider here only one of the most change-relevant characteristics: the degree of interdependence inherent in the agency's technology.

Thompson identifies three types of interdependence: pooled, sequential, and reciprocal.[19] Pooled interdependence refers to circumstances where each unit contributes to the organizational effort, but no unit is directly dependent on any other. Although the work of each influences the overall effectiveness of the organization, interaction among them is unnecessary to accomplish their task. Traditional clinical treatment is an example of pooled interdependence in the human services, since the work of each clinician permits him or her to be independent of the work of any other.

In situations of sequential interdependence, one person or unit must act before the work of another person or unit can take place, and unless the second unit acts, the effort of the first may have been wasted. The assembly line is the classic example, but there are instances in the human services as well. Intake interviewing prior to the development of a treatment protocol is one such illustration. A departmental training program is another. In sequential interdependence, there is a need for interaction, though it is often possible to standardize the contact through the use of forms and procedures. The dependence of one person or unit on another is greater than

---

[19] James D. Thompson, *Organizations in Action* (New York: McGraw-Hill, 1967), pp. 54–55.

in pooled interdependence but considerably less than in reciprocal interdependence.

Reciprocal interdependence requires the responsiveness of one person or unit to the other if either is to accomplish its task successfully; as Thompson puts it, the outputs of one become the inputs for the other. Mutual adjustments are necessary; interaction is high; feedback is a major coordinating device; and workers are highly dependent on what other workers do. Milieu therapy, in which all aspects of an organization's environment are supposed to converge to create the treatment result, is an example of reciprocal interdependence.

When workers perform in isolation from one another (pooled interdependence) or when communication is difficult, an individualistic ethic is likely to emerge within the organization. The organization is in a position to emphasize individual rewards (e.g., permit clinical autonomy) in return for administrative control and the workers' disinterest in organizational policy. An individualistic bias may lead workers to overlook both the consequences of organizational arrangements for services to clients and the mutual support that might otherwise be available to them from their colleagues.

Conversely, when workers are more dependent on one another, the circumstances favor the development of collectivist values, norms of loyalty to colleagues, and a heightened sense of group solidarity. Although empirical evidence is scanty, reason suggests that as workers are dependent on one another, the incentive to influence one another also increases.[20] Furthermore, heightened interaction provides opportunities for influence attempts, and the necessity for mutual adjustments encourages trade-offs, a prime currency in the exchange of influence.[21] When technology requires reciprocal interdependence, therefore, organizational predisposition to innovation is maximized. At least one study supports this notion. Zald found that the stimulation of new ideas and attempts to influence were more characteristic of milieu therapy than of traditional treatment approaches.[22]

The discussion to this point has referred only to interdependence among workers and units. But the principle applies to clients as well. When the task requires greater interdependence among clients—as in residential care or community organizing—heightened interaction of clients constitutes a potential force for change, since interaction is a precondition by which relatively powerless individuals may aggregate their

[20] For some workers, the opposite may occur as well. That is, as dependency increases, there may be increased responsiveness to one another, leading to conforming rather than innovative behavior.

[21] See Chapter 4 for a further discussion of this point.

[22] Mayer N. Zald, "Organizational Control Structures in Five Correctional Institutions," in Zald, ed., Social Welfare Institutions (New York: Wiley, 1965), p. 464.

strength. We may speculate, as a matter of fact, that one explanation for the limited responsiveness of so many service organizations to clients is related to the lack of interaction among the service recipients.

The same applies as well to interorganizational exchanges. The technologies of some organizations (for example, advocacy or information and referral services) encourage linkages with others in the organization set, whereas the technologies of other organizations (e.g., child guidance clinics) is neutral in this regard. Although the net benefits derived from interorganizational interaction may be dependent on environmental conditions, all things being equal, organizations with more numerous exchanges are more likely to be receptive to internal change. In part, this is because they gain more accurate perceptions of environmental conditions through the interaction and thus anticipate the adaptations that are in their interest to make. In addition, exposure to new ideas and programs that are already being tested in one organization reduces the risk and uncertainty of adopting it in another.

The significance of coordinating mechanisms in inhibiting or encouraging change directs attention to interface personnel, those who operate at the boundary or point of linkage between internal subunits or between an agency and outside organizations. Research regarding a Teacher Corps effort to introduce educational reform into a number of schools, for example, found that when there was a successful outcome, it stemmed principally from the efforts of team leaders from the public schools and cooperating faculty from the teachers' colleges (i.e., those at the organizational boundary).[23] The tension inherent in an interface location demands special sensitivity, however. Interface personnel are at least in some measure marginal people. One source of their strength—their knowledge and understanding of both groups—is simultaneously a weakness, since it may make them suspect to both. To be perceived as loyal to their own unit as they try to elicit understanding and extract concessions for the out-group, boundary personnel must be talented indeed.

Turbulence and the Perspective of Time

We conclude this chapter by highlighting two issues that overarch the entire life of the agency. The first has to do with stress, which, when it accelerates at a rapid rate, creates turbulence within the organizational field. The second is an issue to which we have already referred in passing: the exigencies of timing.

[23] Ronald G. Corwin, "Strategies for Organizational Innovation," *American Sociological Review* 37 (August 1972), p. 447.

TURBULENCE

The placid organization—one that is immured from environmental pressures and has a high degree of internal homogeneity and harmony— probably does not exist, but as an "ideal type," it represents the most stable of systems. For change to take place, economic or political factors must cause enough discomfort or strain to provide the incentive to pay the costs that innovation entails. Organizations are thus more or less receptive to change depending on the existence of stress in the system.[24] Dalton, reviewing a series of empirical studies regarding administratively directed change, notes that degree of initial stress or tension was associated in almost every instance with the success of the outcome.[25]

The degree of stress within an organization is difficult to define operationally or to measure. That its level varies and that this variance has a significant consequence for organizational change are nevertheless important to note. All organizations manage some degree of tension, and it is through the management of tension that revisions in program and policy are often worked out. Sometimes the stress builds to crisis proportions, and then the crisis acts as a propelling force for change. Wilson suggests that a major reason this is so is that "crises eliminate discrepancies between individual and organizational objectives," so that during times of high stress, as organizational interests supersede those of individuals or subunits, "pulling together" in the interests of the larger collectivity (and thus receptivity to change) is increased.[26]

But crises also often heighten the visibility to outsiders of internal organizational matters and thus inject hitherto inattentive, quiescent, and powerful outside actors into the organization's operations. For these and other reasons, although crises may increase organizational vulnerability to change, they also intensify the influence of external forces and the organization's vulnerability to more powerful actors rather than less powerful ones.

Wilson's point may be qualified further. Crises impinge differently on different sectors of an organization; different perspectives, as well as the differential consequences to these sectors, result in disparate perceptions

----

[24] In this respect organizations are analogous to individuals in treatment. Jerome Frank asserts, for example, that "the importance of emotional distress in the establishment of a fruitful psychotherapeutic relationship is suggested by the fact that the greater the overall degree of expressed distress, as measured by a symptom checklist, the more likely the patient is to remain in treatment, while conversely two of the most difficult categories of patients to treat have nothing in common except lack of distress." Jerome Frank, *Persuasion and Healing* (New York: Schocken, 1963).

[25] Gene W. Dalton, "Influence and Organizational Change," in Gene W. Dalton et al., eds., *Organizational Change and Development* (Homewood, Ill.: Irwin and Dorsey, 1970), pp. 234–37.

[26] Wilson, *op. cit.,* p. 209.

regarding what the organization's interests really are. Thus, crisis can generate internal conflict and extreme stress as well as organizational solidarity; indeed, perhaps more so. Janowitz, for example, concludes, on the basis of his study of the military, that continued exposure to stress weakens solidarity and undermines organizational effectiveness.[27]

When internal conflict gets so out of hand or stress of any kind reaches excessive proportions, the organization may approach a state of such turbulence that day-by-day survival becomes its sole concern. Thus, periods of major disruption or turbulence, while serving to "unfreeze" an organization, are also often accompanied by a high degree of chaos and unpredictability. This is hardly the circumstance in which to consider innovation, and planned change, particularly by lower-ranking members, becomes impossible.[28] The unpredictability of an organization whose rate of change is accelerating at an extreme pace creates a disincentive for practitioner intervention. For one thing, a high measure of unpredictability decreases the likelihood of success and consequently reduces the inducement to make the attempt. For another, in a highly turbulent field, where events can go dizzyingly out of control, the risks of intervention—both to the organization and to the practitioner—increase commensurately. Organizational actors know that it is often the better part of wisdom to wait out a storm.

TIME

We have noted that both assessment and strategy can be sharpened by an analysis of agency structure measured against itself—that is, at one point in time as compared to some prior point. The same may be said for an agency's coordination patterns, which, when modified in one or another direction in this or another year, may indicate its receptivity to particular proposals. Lacking comparative data across numbers of organizations and more operationally available variables, practice requires that comparisons be made of the organization against itself over time. In other words, an organization's history provides a rich store of information with regard to its potential for change.

Two related historical perspectives should be noted. One has to do with "natural forces," ongoing patterns of change and growth that represent a consistent, if often subtle, force *independent of practitioner influence*. For example, one might expect that as an organization matures rules will be codified, precedents will accrue, and patterns of influence will become established. One student of organizations has observed that "natural forces" have resulted in the consistent movement of dominance in

---

[27] Morris Janowitz, *Sociology and the Military Establishment* (New York: Russell Sage, 1959).

[28] The analogy to therapy holds here as well. That is, when the emotional distress is too overwhelming, the individual is often inaccessible to treatment.

hospitals over time, from lay to professional to administrative groups.[29] The identification of these forces offers the practitioner an opportunity to enhance the potency of his effort by relating his change goal to them.

Secondly, perceptions and valuations of the organization's history by organizational actors can be change-disposing in their own right. All organizations have a bank of normative lore or cansensual recollections concerning critical past events. These may be positive recollections or may reflect past trauma, and their accuracy is less significant than the strength with which they are held. But they will be change-inhibiting or disposing depending on the positive or negative associations participants make between agency lore and any current effort. At its simplest level, the fact that a similar change was tried before and failed has major significance for its current chance for success and how one might approach the task. Prior to advancing a change idea, the exploration of an agency's valuations of related past events is required.

Shifts in ideology, goals, or structure provide another example of forces that, over time, may represent organizational disequilibrium, which acts as a further force for change. If the practitioner finds staff demoralized, his ability to mobilize coherent action may be significantly impaired. Shifts in personnel, a factor we have not yet considered, also produce potentially change-disposing disequilibrium. Hasenfeld and English assert, "Typically, major organizational change can be initiated only after executive substitution, whereby the new executive serves as a change agent or mobilizes support for change efforts."[30] Although in our view this is an overstatement, the fresh perspective of the executive-newcomer, his freedom from onus for inadequate organizational conditions, and his stake in placing his own stamp on the organization do introduce a dynamic for change. As might be expected, a study of administrative succession in the public schools found that superintendents promoted from within place emphasis on system maintenance, whereas those recruited from outside the system are more change-oriented.[31]

Newly hired practitioners bring a similarly fresh outlook and interest in change and may thus become members of a change coalition. They are considerably more vulnerable than old-timers, however, and, except for those in top hierarchical positions, do not ordinarily possess significant resources for influencing (since resources tend to accrue with tenure). Unfortunately for successful innovation, as their tenure grows, practitioners

[29] Charles Perrow, "The Analysis of Goals in Complex Organizations," *American Sociological Review* 26 (December 1961), pp. 854–66.

[30] Yeheskel Hasenfeld and Richard A. English, eds., *Human Service Organizations* (Ann Arbor: University of Michigan Press, 1974), p. 681.

[31] R. O. Carlson, "Succession and Performance Among School Superintendents," in Hasenfeld and English, *ibid.*, pp. 192–94.

become simultaneously more able to influence the organization and less energetic in the pursuit of change.

In the matter of timing, however, the most important point is neither the organization's history nor its shifting currents. For the practitioner, where the organization *is* at any moment with regard to the possibility of change is the critically significant variable. The elements referred to in this chapter may be fixed at one moment in time, shift almost imperceptibly at another, and become dramatically altered at still another. Noticing and appreciating these changing organizational characteristics so that one can decide to defer action or to "seize the moment" take refined practice skill.

4. Participant Interests and Influence

ORGANIZATIONS "SENSE" their environments with internal mechanisms. Environmental pressures are felt indirectly as they impinge on an organization's structure and are transmitted through the demands of its members.[1] Whatever environmental and organizational forces are at play, organizational change is *executed by people* whose action is governed by the meaning these forces have for them, their preferences for one or another outcome, and the intensity with which these preferences are held.

An example will highlight the point. The Monrad Community Mental Health Center, located in a private hospital, offered a variety of inpatient and outpatient services. Although its hospitalization services accommodated approximately ten day patients (i.e., clients who spent their day at the hospital but lived at home) and the center also offered an extensive lounge program for former patients, no program was offered specifically to people who were more impaired than the typical outpatients but yet did not require hospitalization. In effect, day patients fell between the cracks of the inpatient and outpatient departments. A mental health worker within the hospitalization services viewed this as a serious gap in the center's array of services. After considering a number of alternate solutions, he concluded that a day hospital was the most appropriate and feasible remedy.[2]

Strong environmental forces were at work in regard to the potential change. Monrad had received a sharp reduction in its federal community mental health grant, and the grant was ultimately to be phased out. This, combined with a mandate that the center expand its catchment area, highlighted the need for additional revenue. In addition, during a periodic inspection visit, officials from the National Institute of Mental Health, one of

[1] James Q. Wilson, "Innovation in Organization: Notes Toward a Theory," in James D. Thompson, ed., *Approaches to Organizational Design* (Pittsburgh: University of Pittsburgh Press, 1966), p. 198.

[2] Alan Boyer, "A Change at the Monrad Community Mental Health Center," unpublished paper, 1977.

the agency's superordinate bodies, had criticized the center for not having a day hospital.

Internal organizational forces also played a role in influencing the possibility for change. Reorganization was being planned in reaction to the reduction in funds and the increase in potential clientele. The center's tradition as a leader in the community mental health field and its ideological commitment to preventive services were two other elements. Further, mental health professionals from many disciplines were employed by the center, and thus the agency's structure, which was high in complexity and low in formalization, encouraged the introduction of new ideas.

But these environmental and organizational forces had different meanings for different actors, and in planning a change, the mental health worker had to consider the varying preferences and commitments of these participants. Thus the executive of the center was likely to respond favorably. A day hospital would provide the center with additional revenue (i.e., third-party payments), support the policies of the funding sources, and be consistent with the agency's process ideology. But the commitments of Dr. N., in charge of hospitalization services, and Dr. B., in charge of the outpatient department which included the lounge program, were uncertain. Both of them were concerned about how the pending reorganization would affect their departments, and their reaction to the day hospital would depend on whether it was administratively located in hospitalization services or the outpatient department. Finally, the reactions of staff were likely to be mixed, some in favor and some opposed. The center had a discontented staff which felt that the difficulty of their work with severely regressed patients was unrecognized by the center hierarchy. Their preferences were likely to be strongly influenced by their estimate of what the establishment of a day hospital would mean to their jobs (e.g., what were their chances for transfer to a potentially more satisfying assignment? would present inpatient staff be reduced?). In sum, forces generated by the participants' definition of what the change would mean to them were a primary source of data for the Monrad worker.

As our example suggests, the actual or potential stance of organizational actors, as well as the basis for it, is essential information for a change attempt. Are organizational members likely to be for the content of the change idea, against it, or neutral? On what grounds? How intensely will they favor or oppose the change, and what resources will they be prepared to use to support or resist it? When these factors can be inferred prior to taking action, the chance for a successful outcome is enhanced.

The meanings participants ascribe to events—and thus their reaction to particular changes—stem from a variety of factors. Organizational role is one. Multiple statuses are another factor. Thus, the drug counselor who is also an ex-addict may have a different definition of the same organizational problem and espouse a different solution than the drug counselor who has never been an addict although both occupy the status of drug counselor. Social class, ethnicity, and culture are also significant sources of an actor's definition of events. Past and present life experiences, both inside and outside the organization, also generate values, goals, and expectations among organizational participants.[3]

The factors that shape the meanings to participants of organizational issues are thus varied and complex. None, however, is a more potent basis for predicting an actor's reaction to a change idea, in our judgment, than his organizational self-interest. We therefore devote the first half of this chapter to a discussion of the concept. We then turn to an exploration of the participants' resources for influencing. Although interests are major determinants of an actor's preferences, the intensity with which preferences are held is in part shaped by the actor's ability to reach his goals—in other words, by the amount of influence he has. Resources for influence also significantly affect whether a participant will act in regard to his commitments and how effectively he can do so. They are therefore central to the success or failure of any change attempt.

Organizational Self-Interest

The importance of self-interest in determining behavior is an obvious concept, although how people define and experience self-interest sometimes obscures the way in which it works. Participants tend to function in organizations so that watching out for their interests is integrated with other considerations (e.g., their value system and sense of professional responsibility). Furthermore, committed professionals tend to regard their own interests as synonymous with the organization's. Thus, while an administrator might judge his staff's effort to reduce their case load as self-serving, the workers may perceive these efforts as organizationally enhancing, perhaps by permitting them to offer a higher-quality service because of more realistic time demands. The converse is true as well. The administrator defends a stable case load because he believes it will maintain the integrity of the program in the face of powerful challenges, whereas the workers might view his effort as personally advantageous, because challenging outside forces might jeopardize *his* position. In each of these instances the actors' views are genuinely held because they experience their own self-interests as harmonious with other organizational, professional, and value concerns.

Broadly, self-interest can be taken to mean anything an actor wants, such as more leisure time, more satisfaction from the exercise of his skills, improved interpersonal relations, and the like. On closer consideration, we have selected three components of self-interest that appear to be especially

[3] For a detailed discussion of this point, see David Silverman, *The Theory of Organizations* (New York: Basic Books, 1971).

significant as predictors of the reaction participants will exhibit to organizational events. These are the actor's autonomy or power, his share of organizational resources, and his accrual of prestige.

THREE MAJOR COMPONENTS OF SELF-INTEREST

In exploring the major factors that we believe constitute an actor's self-interest, we make a central assumption about attitudes and behavior: people strive to reduce uncertainty; they fear the unknown, and unpredictability constitutes an inherent threat. Actors in organizations feel the desire to reduce uncertainty in part because they are realistically dependent on organizations for their livelihood. Another reason is that the work ethic is disproportionately significant in our value system, and one's work often serves to define one's self. Reducing uncertainty in organizational life reduces the threat that these critical needs will go unmet.

Organizational members can accomplish the reduction of uncertainty in two ways. One is by abdicating responsibility for making any decision at all; the other is by obtaining control over aspects of the setting that might serve as pathways to the unknown. In the first instance, the individual seeks certainty by becoming a cog in the organizational wheel, embracing routine and defining the demands of others as his own desires. This results in what has been called a production-line mentality, where the individual relinquishes responsibility for independent judgment and performs his work by strict adherence to the rule book.

At the other extreme is the effort to acquire and exercise as much autonomy as can be managed. Although these two adaptations seem mutually exclusive, this is not quite the case since people may choose one or another depending on different organizational circumstances. However, seeking autonomy is the more commonly preferred accommodation among professionals than the first. Developing invisibility within the organization is one way professionals protect themselves against encroachment. Another is attempting to control the content and context of their job—that is, by increasing their influence over the surrounding environment. Whatever the form, however, autonomy, control, and power constitute the pillars of professional self-interest and as such will be fiercely protected when challenged. Because of how the actor under assault experiences the issue, the self-interest underlying such a defense will tend to be obscured by his assumption of a public stance reflecting commonly shared values, the benefits to the organization, or the needs of others. Nevertheless, we believe that self-interest is likely to be at the root of the matter.

The press for autonomy and control may be seen as a major cause of what has been described as professional "role creation" [4] and is sometimes pejoratively called professional imperialism. By broadening the boundaries

---

[4] Rue Bucher and Joan Stelling, "Characteristics of Professional Organizations," *Journal of Health and Social Behavior* 10 (March 1969), pp. 12–14.

of their province, professionals seek to limit their dependence on other groups, particularly in areas of undependability or unpredictability. School social workers and school psychologists, for example, may vie for roles that involve them in classroom observation and management. Although not officially within their function, the classroom role increases their interaction with children and teachers, ensuring the likelihood of their receiving a steady flow of individual cases. Further, it reduces their dependence on guidance counselors for referring pupils to them and moves them closer to the center of the school enterprise. They thus incorporate tasks that are subsidiary to their core practice but that contribute to their mission, and they thereby win greater control over their operations.[5]

This also helps to explain why the allocation of resources by organizations among subunits and members is a second major element of self-interest for participants. The more resources one has, the more control one has over one's operations. This is the case from both economic and political vantage points. A larger budget provides leeway to accommodate various programs and service claims. And an increase in staff or budget makes for greater impact on the organization as a whole, enhancing the ability to influence organizational policy. In a study of a medical school, for example, Bucher observes that the size of the department and the extent to which it is designated as important are "clear contributions" to the power of its staff.[6] Expansion thereby both increases a department's control over its activities and helps it get a further "up" in the next round of negotiations for resource distribution.

Since resources accrue power and are commodities in limited supply, competition for their acquisition is inevitable. It is precisely the protection of these interests that encourages encroachment on the interests of others and is responsible for many attempts to change organizations—whether, as in a social agency, the competition among staff is over funds and personnel or, as in a university, it is over the number of student-consumers or course offerings. And this dynamic is responsible for the resistance to change as well.

A third major component of self-interest relates to one's place in the sun—that is, to the maintenance or enhancement of the participant's self-esteem or the esteem in which he is held by others. Apart from the satisfaction that flows from approbation, acquiring prestige is, as Thompson notes, the "cheapest" way of acquiring power, for if one finds it prestigious to exchange with another, the latter has gained a measure of influence

[5] Thompson makes a telling argument regarding an organization's need for certainty as well. James D. Thompson, *Organizations in Action* (New York: McGraw-Hill, 1967), p. 10.

[6] Rue Bucher, "Social Process and Power in a Medical School," in Mayer N. Zald, ed., *Power in Organizations* (Nashville, Tenn.: Vanderbilt University Press, 1970), p. 35.

without making any commitments in return.[7] Innovations that, even inferentially, dispute an actor's expertise, expose his actions to question or criticism, or create uncertainty about what is required to demonstrate his competence to others are seen as challenges to the actor's interests.

In sum, autonomy and influence, the acquisition of resources, and prestige are interdependent elements that make up an actor's central organizational self-interest. Although these components serve expressive functions, if they act primarily to decrease uncertainty and to expand one's control over his organizational destiny, as we have argued, they constitute a rational response to unpredictable or limiting circumstances. To view them in this way is to view them nonpejoratively, as something to be expected of rational actors. But rational or not, these elements delineate the inner boundaries of an actor's "turf," that area which individuals and subunits struggle to protect or expand. As such, they can largely predict the preferences and commitments of participants in response to a change idea.

DETERMINING THE SELF-INTEREST OF PARTICIPANTS

The self-interest of a participant can in part be inferred from his organizational role, particularly his hierarchical location, the tasks he performs, and the units to which he belongs. Participants of different ranks, performing different tasks, and belonging to different departments face different constellations of issues and consequently have different preferences, commitments, and opportunities in regard to change.

Location in the Hierarchy. Hierarchical location imposes a unique set of concerns. An elite cadre is responsible for the overall functioning of an organization. Their structural accountability makes it more likely that they see the organization "whole." The higher up in the hierarchy they are, the more diverse the elements they must accommodate in making decisions.[8] This dynamic helps to explain the relative "conservatism" of upper-ranking members compared to lower-ranking ones and their apparent unwillingness to take "appropriate" risks. On the one hand, decisions that have broad and uncertain organizational consequences or are highly visible are made cautiously. On the other hand, his overall perspective leads the administrator to downgrade the importance of decisions that affect only one department or program. When those decisions, however important to the specific department, cost something in time or energy for the administrator to make, his disinterest is often apparent.

[7] Thompson, *op. cit.*, p. 33. Thompson's argument relates to organizations, and he cites a study of a voluntary hospital in which the creation of a favorable image to its salient publics was an important way in which the hospital controlled dependency. But the point is relevant to individuals and subunits as well.

[8] Robert K. Merton, *Social Theory and Social Structure,* enlarged ed. (New York: Free Press, 1968), p. 272.

Because they are responsible for the total organization, executives have less stake in the struggle among individuals or subunits over the distribution of influence, prestige, or resources. They can be counted on to react to the substantive content of the conflict more than can the competitors. Furthermore, the executive group may not only *want* to protect their authority but *need* to do so in order to fulfill their organizational responsibilities. Thus, participatory management, frequently advanced in the management literature as a constructive tool, has not been widely embraced, in part at least because administrators are loath to relinquish the authority that their accountability requires.

Upper-ranking staff need to balance the divergent organizational interests that impinge on them. As might be expected, they will be more responsive to their superordinates than to their subordinates, but it would be a mistake to assume that this always holds. For example, the manager of a decentralized unit may be more willing to accommodate the desires of his staff than the dictums of a central office administration because he "lives with" staff, or he is protected by civil service regulations, or for other reasons. Such was the case in even so authoritarian a setting as a large city welfare department, where a welfare administrator ignored his immediate superior's view in favor of his caseworkers' positions. An executive's need to balance the demands of diverse constituencies—and his prior history in doing so—often pinpoints the appropriate entry point in a change attempt.[9] As we noted in Chapter 2, one of the ways in which administrators assure themselves of successful "balancing" is through the maintenance of organizational calm. It is in their interests to "keep the peace."

More than other actors, administrators are uniquely responsible for satisfying external constituencies, and their need to manage these constituencies gives them a different stake in the content of new ideas than the practitioner, whose interests tend to be oriented internally. In the tension between satisfying external constituents and meeting professional standards, the needs of the former are likely to take precedence. Admittedly, the executive who is also a professional is more likely to choose maintaining high-quality services over accommodating external pressures than the executive who is not. One reason for this, in addition to professional socialization, is that the former's career interests interlock with those of the profession, adding another constituency to take into account. But apolitical workers who expect the tension to be resolved usually in favor of professionalism are probably guilty of projecting their own lower-ranking set of perceptions without sufficiently crediting inherent executive interests. Thus, one psychologist was surprised to find his appeal unpersuasive when he sought to use the inadequacy of services as the basis for persuading his

---

[9] We discuss the practice implications of this point in Chapter 8.

psychiatrist-administrator to intervene in the agency's satellite drug clinic. Subsequently, however, when his argument centered on the clinic's falling case load (a circumstance that made the agency vulnerable to outside criticism and possible funding problems), he was able to obtain administrative action.

In light of the administrator's need to balance divergent internal interests and satisfy external forces, we need to qualify our earlier statement that executives tend to respond substantively when subordinates differ. Substance is likely to be sacrificed when the contending parties are differentially ascendant and one has more trading power than the other. Further, when the executive's decision has consequences for the esteem in which he and the organization are held, his reaction to the substance of an issue may yield to these personal and organizational interests.

Finally, as one moves up the hierarchy, commitment to the organization's ideology, goals, and maintenance requirements increases. So for example, in radical organizations, upper-level staff are *more* radical than lower-level workers, a point sometimes overlooked by structurally blind practitioners who expect a correlation between radicalism and lower rank.[10] Executives are more likely to define themselves and to be defined by the organization they head than are line staff. The well-being of an agency redounds more to the credit of its executive staff than to that of other participants. Executives are thus more likely than others to perceive their personal well-being as congruent with the organization's. In other words, organizationally salient interests are more likely to inform decisions the further up in the hierarchy an actor goes.

Task. The actor's task, or the function he serves within the organization, is another guide to self-interest. Individuals evaluate change proposals largely in terms of how the proposals impinge on the tasks they perform. Innovations that reduce surveillance, increase available resources, or enhance the value in which the tasks are held will generally be embraced by those who are affected in that way, whereas changes that threaten the reverse will generally be resisted.

An illustration is provided by the change effort of a young practitioner at Charter House. This group home setting, we noted in the previous chapter, was geared to a religious-humanitarian "love-care" ethic of

---

[10] This argument is supported by a study conducted at Mobilization for Youth, a community action project. High scorers on an index of commitment to agency values regarded as radical (e.g., that social protest was an effective social-action strategy for the poor) varied with agency rank. Thus, 48.1 percent of the executive staff fell in the highest commitment group, whereas only 39.4 percent of the supervisory staff and 26.1 percent of the line staff evidenced high commitment to the agency's "activist" posture. George Brager, "Commitment and Conflict in a Normative Organization," *American Sociological Review* 34, no. 4 (August 1969), pp. 482–91.

child care. It held as a major tenet that if we (the child-care staff) love you (the adolescent), we expect you to love us in return. No formal policy or criteria for discharge existed at Charter House. Child-care staff who believed a child to be "unloving" could recommend discharge to the priest-director, who, in the worker's experience, had never refused a child-care staff member's request. The worker's hope was to protect the adolescents from the results of idiosyncratic judgments. Consequently, her change notion was to develop more explicit criteria for discharge and to institute a committee procedure or "fair hearing" in which the social service department and the child's social worker would contribute significant data on the basis of which to make discharge decisions. Because of the tasks they performed, it could be anticipated that the child-care staff would resist the diminution in their autonomy inherent in her idea. The clinical staff—for the reverse reason—could be expected to constitute her natural allies. Furthermore, it could be inferred that the director and some of his key associates (who were clergymen and nuns) were unlikely to embrace her idea, since it would enhance the image of expertise and hence the prestige of the clinicians and their value to the agency. The advance in importance of one professional group is often associated with the falling off of the importance of another. The planning for change at Charter House had to be based on an understanding of the task-impelled interests of the respective parties.[11]

The significance of tasks as a source of support or resistance depends of course on the net influence of those who perform the tasks—that is, the amount of influence they have relative to the amount the innovator has. Professional "pecking orders" and sensitivity to the "place" of one profession as opposed to another are illustrated in the Charter House example and are prevalent issues in multiprofessional (or multipurpose) agencies. As suggested earlier, professional groups seek to define and control the boundaries of their province, yet the work of each often must coordinate with the work of others. Inevitably this creates conditions for the encroachment by one professional group on another, thereby generating struggle between them. In settings such as these, there is likely to be special sensitivity to the ways in which potential innovations impinge on professional standing. Unfortunately for the social worker, social work is more often than not on the lower rungs of the prestige and power ladder in multiprofessional settings.

Subunit Membership. We have implied that organizational participants define their interests in terms of the prosperity of their subsystems, but the point should be made explicit. The Hawthorne studies first brought to the literature of organizations a fact that workers have always known

---

[11] Gay Fiore Shoup, "A Change at Charter House," case record, Columbia University School of Social Work, 1976.

intuitively—people who work closely together are more likely to develop close relationships, with attendant values and norms, than are people with less frequent on-the-job contact.[12] It is also true that people who share a common profession, even without close working ties, develop a common identification or "professional identity." Organizational decisions often similarly affect individuals belonging to the same profession or subunit (e.g., *all* child-care workers at Charter House faced a loss in autonomy, and *all* clerics would lose prestige to the clinicians if the change were adopted). To the extent that this is so, the interests of individuals and their subsystem *are* the same.

Subsystem membership independently influences member interest, however. Members often identify their welfare with that of the group even when the two are not directly related. They see the function of their unit as right and just and experience challenges to it in moral rather than substantive terms. Furthermore, since group norms are powerful regulators of behavior, members who violate prevailing norms pay a high cost for doing so—for example, the risk of losing influence in the unit or the esteem of their colleagues. Loyalty arrangements (i.e., that a member must not challenge another member's position in public or reveal the unit's "dirty linen" to outsiders) are among the most critical in predicting the commitments actors will or will not make in support or opposition to a proposed plan.

This is not to say, of course, that individual interests may not supersede subunit interests. Nor, as a matter of fact, is rank or task as uniformly predictive as may have thus far been suggested.

As we indicated at the start of this chapter, it is the view of the participant regarding what an action means to him that is the crucial determinant of his response. Thus, whether an innovation is or is not in accord with the rank, task, or subunit interests of actors is less important than how it is *perceived* by them. And the perceptions may well diverge from what outsiders judge to be the reality. For one thing, the perceptions of participants may be discrepant or conflicting depending on variables mentioned earlier (e.g., social class, ethnicity, personal life events, and the like). For another, only incomplete or imperfect information may be available to the parties. Exposure to a change effort of a similar character (whether it turned out well or badly) can also affect the current perception. Furthermore, relationship with the innovator—whether it is characteried by admiration and trust or dislike and suspicion—may color one's perception of the innovation and of its impact on one's interests. So too may the judgments of significant others.

Even if the importance of objective reality in shaping perceptions were absolute, however, the relationship between self-interest and the organiza-

---

[12] F. J. Roethlisberger and William Dickson, *Management and the Worker* (Cambridge, Mass.: Harvard University Press, 1939).

tional elements cited earlier would need further qualification, for self-interest is a multifaceted variable.

INTERESTS AND VALUES

People have multiple, overlapping, and even conflicting interests. An actor's values frequently complicate his choices and commitments as well. Inferring an actor's interests from his organizational role is confounded by these elements.

Personal vs. Role Interests.   Practitioners might expect that a change idea which challenges the autonomy, share of resources, or prestige attendant on performing a particular role will be opposed by those occupying the role. This is a safe assumption according to our earlier generalization. But organizational role may be secondary to the personal interests of some actors. They may, for example, be on their way up and out of the agency, in which case they may support or oppose an innovation on the basis of future personal interests rather than current role interests. Or they may be attuned to nonorganizational reference groups (e.g., the attitudes of professional friends on issues of "principle").

Role interests increase in importance relative to personal ones as an organization increases in salience for the actors. But even in the case of administrators, for whom organizational salience is greatest, the correlation is in no way complete. The psychiatrist-administrator of a mental health clinic who is also in private practice, for example, may place his interests in the latter above his interests in the clinic. He may then gladly relinquish a measure of control to an assistant in return for more time to devote to his private practice.

Individual vs. Group Interests.   A further element to confound the assessment of interests is the tension between the interests of the individual and those of the group. If a practitioner automatically assumes that role interests are universalistic and that actions that increase the autonomy, resources, and esteem of incumbents in a role benefit *all* those who occupy the role, he will overlook the particularistic benefits (or costs) to individuals in the role. Individuals often reap rewards from a specific innovation that transcend their role interests or the interests of the units to which they belong, and which thus affect their attitudes. The proposed change in discharge policy at Charter House, for example, would have reduced the autonomy of the child-care staff, and it therefore appears safe to assume the staff's opposition to the proposal. But for some child-care staff, other benefits might intervene, resulting in a contrary stand; for example, those workers who were interested in further training and viewed a "professional" orientation as prestigious.

Differences of interest between an individual and his membership group can result in distorting the definition of group interests, so that the group acts contrary to its welfare. This occurs when an individual or elite is sufficiently powerful to influence the definition of the situation. McCleery reports this dynamic in a study of change within a prison.[13] A new administration had introduced sweeping and humanitarian reforms which deprived the guards of some of the authority they had exercised under the old regime. Although they had used their authority capriciously and at times brutally, the guards had worked out a system of accommodation with inmate leaders, who kept the other prisoners in line in return for special privileges. This accommodation was disrupted by the policy changes. Although the new decision-making apparatus was more equitable and humane and therefore in the prisoners' interests, it was not advantageous to their leaders, and prisoner resistance erupted.

Other Multiple Interests.   Multiple interests may be involved even when personal-vs.-role or individual-vs.-group interests are not at issue. Many events simultaneously include both positive and negative consequences to the interests of an actor. Heightening the visibility of a program, for example, can result in both a loss of autonomy for the actor and an increase in esteem.

A study of innovation in the public schools by Gross and his colleagues is suggestive of how such ambivalence sometimes gets resolved. The change called for a redefinition of teacher role—away from the traditional emphasis on the content of learning to a primary focus on students' interests by means of self-contained, open classrooms. Teachers who perceived negative consequences for themselves in organizing an open classroom were willing to go along with the innovation when they saw *some* positive effects in the change as well. Only those teachers who perceived nothing positive to balance their negative assessment actively resisted the change.[14]

Values.   It is important to note that self-interest is not the only motivator of preference and commitment. We have singled it out because professionals, discomfited by the concept, tend to see the pursuit of self-interest as a violation of professional norms and thus neglect its primacy. But personal and professional values also act to constrain or encourage change behavior, depending on the issue in question. By and large, we agree with Lazersfeld and Thielens that belief and sentiment systems result

[13] Richard H. McCleery, *Policy Change in Prison Management* (East Lansing: Michigan State University Press, 1957).

[14] Neal Gross et al., *Implementing Organizational Innovations* (New York: Basic Books, 1971), p. 143.

from self-interest, selective perception, and processes of mutual reinforcement.[15] To a considerable degree, values serve to invest one's interests with moral justification.

But that is not the whole story. Values play a mediating function when interests are in conflict. Whether the actor will risk the loss of autonomy that might be incurred by making his program visible or will opt for the potential increase in his esteem depends in part on his value system—i.e., whether he prizes autonomy or esteem more highly.

People may also act on values that conflict with their interests. Values stem from accumulated experience as well as from one's current organizational role. Furthermore, the importance to an actor of approbation from an external reference group may transcend his concern for his immediate organizational interest. An example of differing accommodations to the conflict between interests and values is provided by the conflicting stance of two law offices, both subunits of professionally directed antipoverty programs. Each required support from "liberal" city administrations and received funds from the same federal office. While one legal staff was zealously innovating on behalf of its impoverished clientele, even though its policy brought the ire of important public officials, the other followed a more cautious and traditional line. The difference between them cannot be explained in structural or even political terms; essentially, it had to do with the different value commitments of the legal directors and their antipoverty program executives. Values and even personality factors (such as the propensity for risk taking), then, add further complexity to organizational behavior.

In sum, although we view the self-interest of actors as a potent determinant of their reaction to change proposals, the concept can be used only as a basis for tentative inferences which require further testing and possible revision. Actors, sometimes intuitively and sometimes explicitly, weigh the costs and benefits to their interests of one or another response. Since the values of individuals differ, one can speak only of the possibility that a particular set of net benefits over costs will provide the incentive for a specific behavior. Practitioners may be comforted by the fact that the very complexities that make such assessment difficult also contribute to the strains and ambivalences that make internal change more possible.

Resources for Influence

An actor's perception of his self-interest is a major determinant of his response to a change proposal, and the intensity of his commitment is an indicator of the resources he will bring to his support or opposition to the change. But resources can be committed only to the extent that they are

[15] Paul Lazersfeld and Walter Thielens, *The Academic Mind* (New York: Free Press, 1958).

available. An understanding of one's own resources as well as those of potential proponents and opponents is therefore necessary, not only to inform a practitioner's judgment about whether to move ahead or not, but about *how* to do so as well. The content and scope of potential innovations vary with the influence of the innovators, and the generation and maximization of resources for influence are critical tasks.

Resources for influence are those properties of individuals or groups that enhance the ability of the actors to get others to think, feel, or behave in a desired way.[16] Influence may be exercised through shared norms and acceptance of another's right to command (authority); by trading money, gratitude, or deference in return for the desired conduct (exchange); or through compliance stemming from the actual or potential use of sanctions (power). That is, resources are anything that can be used as an incentive or disincentive by one actor in relation to another to increase the probability of an outcome desired by the first actor.

Some resources have already been identified in our previous discussion of economic and political factors in the environment and organization. We have noted, for example, that command of funding is a critical source of organizational influence, as is control over values and norms. Similarly, actors who have a constituency, either one that is large and cohesive or one composed of prestigious and resource-rich actors, can dominate an organization. Our prior comments about rank and task, though their focus was self-interest, are also suggestive in this regard. Clearly, the higher one's rank, the more rewards and punishments one has available to induce compliance by others: responsibility for hiring and firing, promotions, assignments, evaluations, references, and the like. An agency's authority system grants a further resource: legality or legitimacy. When commands are defined as legal or legitimate, other resources are not required to induce compliance. As a matter of fact, the major access to organizational change for lower-ranking members is to influence the behavior of higher-ranking actors, whether by educating, persuading, maneuvering, or pressuring the formal decision makers.

RESOURCES OF LOWER-RANKING PARTICIPANTS

Our primary interest here is in the resources that lower-level participants can use to influence organizational decision making.[17] They fall

[16] We hope, in using this inclusive definition, to avoid the conflicting concepts in the literature on power. For practice purposes, distinctions between authority, exchange, and power are at best only partially relevant, since each features one or another means of "getting others to think, feel, or behave in a desired way"—in short, of influencing them. Our use of the concepts of authority, exchange, and power is taken from definitions in Peter Bachrach and Morton S. Baratz, *Power and Poverty* (New York: Oxford University Press, 1970).

[17] For an extensive discussion of resources for influencing available to low-ranking participants, see George Brager and Harry Specht, *Community Organizing* (New York: Columbia University Press, 1973), pp. 239–58.

into two categories: those that stem from the structure of systems (e.g., the position and function of participants) and those having to do with the attributes of individuals (e.g., expertise). Resources are often interdependent in that having one enhances the quality of another, and there is considerable overlap among those resources that might be defined as structural and those that stem primarily from the characteristics of individual actors. Thus, the latter are more or less usable depending on the actors' location on the stage where the action takes place. And similarly, one's position in an organization can lead to the development of personal resources or provide the circumstances for making them visible.

Structural Resources.   As we have suggested, resources are unequally distributed, and an actor's location in the structure in large measure defines his opportunities for influencing. Participants who have been given authority and legitimacy to work in particular areas are advantaged in this respect. There are two other structurally determined resources that should be noted: access to information and control of communication.

Organizational decision making can hardly take place without information on which to base the decision, and information is differentially available depending on an organization's structure. Trustees must rely on executives for the organizational intelligence on which their policymaking is based. To the extent that the gap between trustee and executive in access to intelligence is wide—as in large, complex, geographically far-flung organizations—the executive's ascendancy is enhanced. Similarly, the disparity between the executive and the staff in such agencies increases the power of workers vis-à-vis their supervisors. That is, the workers are likely to have and the supervisors are likely to need information about the agency. Indeed, to the degree that upper- or middle-level ranks need the information in order to perform *their* tasks creditably, their dependency on the information holders is increased. In addition, participants with access to information have considerable potential for exerting influence through selecting or withholding information, providing accurate or ambiguous information, or otherwise adapting data to the purpose at hand. One's access to information thus not only increases others' dependency, which is central to influencing, but also provides one with the opportunity for making the impact on the organization invisible.

A closely related and similarly determined resource has to do with the actor's location in the communication system. When participants control access to important others or serve as links between groups, the resource can be a potent one. Thus people who can open or close doors (e.g., the boss's secretary) may have little authority but considerable influence. And those who serve as links between persons or groups are in a position to interpret each to the other. In acting as gatekeepers for the flow of information, a practitioner can segregate audiences, share information differentially, or shift its emphasis. This occurs unconsciously as well as consciously, since people often color information to their advantage even without being aware of it. Interests are thus made to appear similar or dissimilar almost as the communicator's wish and skill dictate. The concept holds for the executive interpreting staff positions to trustees and the reverse, for supervisors acting as middlemen between top managers and lower ranks, and for line staff defining client reactions to administration and administrative policy to clients.

Whether it is through rank or function, access to information, control of communication, or even personal attributes, the actor who is in a position to grant favors is in a good position indeed. When a practitioner extends himself beyond the requirements of the job to aid or accommodate organizational policy or participants, he has incurred an obligation, since reciprocity is the expected norm.[18] The favors granted yesterday are the credits redeemable tomorrow. Whatever may be its moral sanction, politically speaking, it is better to give than to receive.

Individual Resources. Some resources are potentially available for use by individuals regardless of structure. Among them are knowledge and expertise, social appeal, social rewards, shared norms and collegial relationships, energy, tenure, and the backing of solidary groups.

It has been noted that professionals control their dependence on a given system by creating and maintaining a favorable impression of their "product" in the eyes of a salient public.[19] Through expertise, or apparent expertise, they accrue the prestige that enhances their opportunity to obtain compliance. Furthermore, to the extent that organizational decision making requires technical know-how, the expert who has this know-how can make demands on the organization in turn. Thus, an expert on health care policy who is familiar with actual and pending legislation and understands funding-source requirements is in a position to exert considerable leverage on the direction of a health-maintenance organization which employs him. Expertise may be used against an agency (or agency policy) as well. A well-documented statement which challenges current policy has internal utility that may be persuasive to some decision makers. Public exposure may also be implied or threatened, or information "leaked" to influential sources.

Social appeal is another individual attribute with influence potential. The more socially attractive a person is, the more likely others are to seek his approval or recognition, and therefore the more likely that he can in-

[18] Alvin Gouldner, "The Norm of Reciprocity," *American Sociological Review* 25 (April 1960), pp. 161–78.

[19] Francine F. Rabinovitz, *City Policies and Planning* (New York: Atherton, 1969), p. 121.

fluence their behavior.[20] Bucher observes in a study of a medical school that the *assessed stature* of individual faculty members was an important source of power, since it affected their ability to persuade or negotiate successfully. The following qualities entered into the assessment of stature: the quality of the faculty member's work; "whether or not he appears to be 'smart' or clear thinking; whether he is a decent human being . . . ; whether he has good judgment; and whether he 'pulls his load.' " Finally, his outside reputation was another factor in his ascendancy in faculty politics.[21] The qualities described are as relevant to the professional in a social agency as to one in an academic institution and appear to combine the attributes of personal appeal and competence within the notion of "stature."

Social appeal supports or enhances other resources for influence. For example, as persons are seen as appealing, the social rewards they have to dispense become more valued. Furthermore, social appeal—or informal leadership, as it may otherwise be called—is important in gaining peer participation in both pro- or antichange alliances.

Every individual has social rewards to dispense: gratitude, deference, recognition, approval. As in all influence attempts, these rewards are effective or not depending on both the person and the position of the dispenser (the gratitude and approval of an executive are ordinarily more valued than those of a low-ranking worker) and on the desire or need of the recipient for the social reward.

Another source of influence is the sharing of values and social relations with decision makers. What has been called the "old-boy network" comes into being when actors have worked together in other settings over a long period of time and have developed common identification and sentiments. Such a network is often observable in the federal bureaucracy, the army, and among alumni of the same institution or workplace; it was marked among Peace Corps volunteers whose common membership led them to share their "connections" with one another in the years following their membership in the Corps.

For lower-ranking human service workers, the sharing of professional norms and the development of professional relationships operate similarly, if less potently. Whatever their respective ranks, professionals share a common set of sentiments and develop a common identity. The point ought not be overstated, since there may be varying identities and contradictory sentiment systems—for example, among different specializations within professions. Nevertheless, values that are pervasive within the profession or which are jointly held by actors can be used in a bargaining proc-

[20] David Mechanic, "Sources of Power and Lower Participants in Complex Organizations," in William Cooper et al., eds., *New Perspectives in Organizational Research* (New York: Wiley, 1964), pp. 145–46.

[21] Bucher, *op. cit.*, p. 29.

ess or invoked as persuaders. Although an appeal to mutually shared sentiments is ordinarily insufficient to resolve a major issue, it can tip a noncritical decision in one direction or the other. The social-work norm of self-determination, for example, though it is perhaps observed more in the breach than in the practice, has nevertheless been used effectively by practitioners to advance client interests.

Professional commonality may be a source of staff influence with an executive. This resource is limited by the inherent tensions that exist between ranks; for example, the executive's need to manage the organization vs. the staff's interest in functioning autonomously. Nevertheless, an executive who seeks the approbation of his professional colleagues is vulnerable to this source of influence. For professional commonality to be useful, however, workers must be willing to concede that the administrator too can be a "good professional." Workers who see hierarchical distinctions as "class warfare," so that upper ranks can do no right, relinquish the leverage available in professional commonality as a resource.

Energy is a resource that, in concert with the others cited, can serve to take up the slack that exists in most influence systems. The less the effort expended or the attention paid to a subject by high-ranking persons, the more the power of low-ranking ones. Energy refers to the assertion, persistence, and amount of activity invested in an influence attempt. Sometimes assertion takes the form of an effort to redefine a situation; that is, the usual norms flowing from prestige or position are ignored in favor of other standards on which to base the "right" to influence. Persistence has the advantage of dramatizing the importance of an issue to a worker, and may so "wear down" a decision maker that granting the worker's request may cost him less than the worker's continued tenacity. Energy, as manifest through active participation, is particularly useful in redressing balances of power when, as often occurs, persons with significant influence limit their concern to "critical" as opposed to "routine" decisions (though organizations run by routine).

Tenure, the length of time a participant has been with an organization, is another source of influence. There are a number of reasons why this is so: the identification of the long-tenured member with the agency and his loyalty to it are less subject to challenge; his historical perspective may be critical to the way the change is designed; his established place permits greater risk-taking; he is likely to have developed relationships which can be called upon or to have granted favors for which he can exact repayment; and he may make use of precedents with more legitimacy. Furthermore, the long-tenured member knows the agency's rules, those which circumvent other rules, and their differential application depending on circumstances. In contentious situations, such an actor is decidedly advantaged over others. Perhaps most important, the longer a practitioner has been with an organization, the more thoroughly he knows its decision-making structure, formal and informal; therefore he knows how best to route and manage a change attempt.

The single most powerful resource available to low-ranking members is their potential solidarity. The practitioner who has developed a constituency among his colleagues has created a rich resource. As we implied earlier, influence and dependency go in tandem, since a person who is dependent on another is subject to that other's influence. Clearly, then, an organization is more likely to be dependent on a group of its workers than on any single one of them. A case in point is the reaction of the welfare center manager, mentioned earlier in this chapter, who deferred to the position of his staff when they were aroused and cohesively organized, even at the cost of incurring his own superordinate's displeasure. But the notion is obvious enough not to need belaboring. A first step for those who would change agency procedures or policies is to find other persons with whom action can be effected. It is in the forging of such coalitions, either informally (as in a caucus or through a grapevine) or formally structured (as in a duly constituted committee), that a position on a given change is mobilized into a process.

It would help, both theoretically and practically, if one could assign some relative value to the various resources for influencing. If we were able to assert, for example, that money is more or less powerful than a constituency, how much more powerful it is, and under what circumstances, this would increase our understanding of the influence of actors and of the net influence of some actors over others.

Some rough approximations can be made of a resource's value based on its characteristics. For example, resources vary with regard to their generality; that is, some are highly specific to a particular situation while others are more general and therefore more exchangeable. Using generality as the criterion, Clark found that money had the highest "buying power" in his inventory of resources, followed in order by knowledge, popularity, and social access to leaders.[22] Money and knowledge are also high on Clark's list of those resources that are *directly* convertible into influence.[23] But the designations are and must remain gross ones because the potency of any resource is situation-specific. In a subsequent section, we indicate some of the criteria by which their value can be approximated.

REPUTATION AND ACCESS

Thus far we have discussed resources for influencing as if they were commodities in the actual possession of respective actors. Often of course

[22] Terry N. Clark, *Community Structure and Decision-Making* (San Francisco: Chandler, 1968), p. 60.
[23] *Ibid.*, p. 63.

they are. But for the purposes of influencing change, the *reputation* for having resources or access to them may be as significant. In assessing the feasibility and strategy of change, therefore, the worker must consider not only resources directly in his own possession and in the possession of potential proponents and opponents but also their reputation for having resources or access to them. Each of these conditions has an impact on change attempts.

When someone is believed to be influential, others are likely to accord him that influence, whether or not he in fact has the requisite resources. Perceived as having resources which can be used to exchange or reward and punish, the reputed influential can win the day without having to use sanctions. Thus, the staff member who is believed to have a constituency will have the same impact on organizational decision making as the member who actually has one—or almost the same, since this is not the whole story. As long as the practitioner does not have to use the resource (i.e., his "bluff" is not called), his influence is secure. If exchange or actual sanctioning is required, however, his position deteriorates rapidly. He is revealed as resourceless, to be ignored at will. This takes place under two circumstances. One is when meeting the practitioner's demands is more costly to a target than the threat of a sanction. The other occurs when the issue is pursued so vigorously that the door to graceful retreat has been closed.

The implications of these points are obvious but considerable. They suggest (1) that practitioners need to seek to enhance their reputation for having, or having access to, resources for influence; (2) that, to the extent possible, the reputation must be concerted with the type of innovation being sought—that is, the issue must not be so costly for the target to accede to that he is tempted to call the worker's bluff; and (3) that reputedly resource-rich but actually resource-poor actors must not press their case more aggressively than their resources or the target's tolerance allows.[24]

Similarly, access to a resource is almost as good as the resource itself. As a matter of fact, the major way in which low-ranking workers garner influence is through aggregating their own modest resources by forming coalitions with actors of similar organizational interest. In generating additional resources, however, practitioners must be mindful that this often involves them in a further trade—with a subsequent price to pay. Thus, if A wishes to influence B and requires the intercession of C, he puts himself in C's debt, a debt whose significance is directly related to the importance of C's contribution. He must therefore weigh the importance to him of using C against its cost to him in future payments. So, for example, one executive whose agency budget was contingent on the approval of a public

---

[24] We make this point in the context of seeking the successful adoption of a specific change. It is recognized that there are occasions when assertion serves other purposes and is therefore appropriate.

official had access to a trustee on his board to whom the official owed a favor. Since the trustee's position on a number of significant issues was, from the director's viewpoint, anticlient and using his help would have substantially increased the trustee's influence on board decision making, the executive sought other means of access to the official. With considerable effort, he successfully located other, more neutral persons who could deliver the official's approval. He had decided, however, that if his other ("cheaper") resources had not worked, he would have had to have risked the payment entailed in using the trustee. In other words, although access to a resource may be as potent a resource as the resource itself, it entails a cost that practitioners must measure.

THE CONVERSION OF RESOURCES TO USE

Mere possession of resources, the reputation for having them, or access to them do not mean that one can use them effectively. The value of a resource is correlated with its value to the party to be influenced; that is, the resource must be something the target wants or wants to avoid, and the actor must be able to afford to expend it.

One criterion by which the usefulness of a resource may be estimated, then, is its centrality or criticality to the target. How important to the individual's or organization's functioning is the resource at any particular moment in time? Access to funding sources, for example, is a more valuable resource during times of financial constriction than financial expansion, and agency officials will accede more influence to the practitioner with funding access during such periods. If the funds can be used to support central agency goals—for example, to hire more clinicians in a traditional psychiatric setting—rather than programs that are less central to its purposes—for example, to develop a case aide component—the resource increases in significance still further. A second criterion has to do with its availability in the marketplace. For example, an actor's expertise may make a significant contribution to agency operation, but if the expertise is generally available from others, its use in influencing is limited.

Whether the actor can afford to use the resources is a third factor. Will it cost more to him to grant or withhold than the influence attempt is worth? For example, a group of social-work students whose work produced money for an agency (through third-party payments) believed that their production of income provided them with leverage in influencing agency policy. To use the resource in a direct influence attempt, however, would have required that they threaten to withhold their services. To do so would have entailed great risk to them, and it was obvious that they were not prepared to take the risk for the change that they had in mind. Their resources were in that case nonconvertible.

Finally, the resource and the behavior to be induced must be in rough balance. That is, the resource must be worth enough so that the target is willing to pay the asking price. The dynamic is similar to a commercial transaction. To effect a purchase, an article must be available for sale and sufficiently valuable to the purchaser for him to meet the seller's price. No purchase will take place if the article is desired but priced too high.

To gain support for a policy change, the practitioner must have something to offer that the other values (e.g., the goal of the change, support for an issue in the other's interests, recognition, camaraderie, professional self-esteem, etc.) and values enough to take the desired action despite the cost in time, energy, ruffled feathers, etc. Much, then, depends on the impact of the innovation and the action required to support it. For example, for a colleague to spread the word to friends about the desirability of a noncontroversial organizational change costs little, and the practitioner's gratitude may be sufficient to effect the "purchase." As the change issue becomes more debatable, however, or the required actions more taxing, the cost may be too high for resources such as gratitude or camaraderie. In other words, in assessing his resources, one must estimate their value or utility to the other in the context of what he wishes the other to do.

There is an important difference between a commercial transaction and an influence attempt, however. In a commercial transaction, payment for benefits received is more assured: money changes hands, a contract is drawn, the commerce has legal sanction. In influencing, on the other hand, the terms are often vague and payments are typically deferred. Trust is thus a requirement of the exchange. If a practitioner seeks a colleague's assistance in one matter by implicitly offering to support him on another, the colleague must trust that the support will be proferred when the time comes. Ambiguity is intrinsic to such transactions since these "contracts" have to be negotiated with indirection or they risk violating the professional norm that professionals act on issues solely on the basis of merit. In this context, the worker's "tact" in contracting and his credibility are additional resources.

Frequently, particularly in adversarial situations, agreements are made that are vague, ultimately "misunderstood," or withdrawn when the circumstances change. In any long-range relationship, such behavior is self-defeating since it violates trust and endangers credibility, consequences which make future negotiations uncertain at best.

We have focused on two major elements regarding participants in this chapter: their self-interest and therefore their preferences and commitments on an issue and the resources for influencing that they command and thus the likelihood that they will act on their preferences. An understanding of each provides significant clues regarding who is likely to support a particular change idea, who oppose it, and who remain neutral, as well as the scope of the support or opposition and its location within the organization. Furthermore, it directs attention to the efficacy of the potential reaction—the extent to which proponents, opponents, and neutrals might be influential in advancing, impeding, or ignoring the change attempt. It is perhaps belaboring the obvious to suggest that, prior to taking action, informed practice requires this assessment.

The requisite information is only partially accessible, however. This is the case for practitioners of all hierarchical levels, but particularly so for low-ranking workers. And were the data more complete, knowledge of organizational theory is so limited that evaluation of the data would itself be imperfect. Wilson observes that material incentives are the cornerstone of the economy precisely because they have numerical values (money prices) assigned to them.[25] Once nonmaterial values such as interests and influence are introduced, they cannot be calculated precisely. Practice cannot wait on precision, however, and all that may be asked of the practitioner is that he appraise these factors as systematically and sensitively as possible. It is to the matter of initial assessment that we turn in Part II.

---

[25] Wilson, *op. cit.,* p. 205.

Part II

INITIAL ASSESSMENT

Planned organizational change begins when an individual experiences a tension between things as they are and things as he would like them to be. The actor considers a range of issues relating to the problem and subsequently judges it either unsolvable or amenable to change. Possible solutions are sounded out with trusted others, and a change idea is launched. The idea is debated and revised as various forces impinge on it until the organization is committed to a course of action. Once adopted, the change idea is actualized and, following a trial period, becomes an integral part of the organization's functioning. Planned organizational change is thus a series of events flowing through time—in other words, a process.

We have selected five phases to characterize the process: (1) initial assessment, (2) preinitiation, (3) initiation, (4) implementation, and (5) institutionalization. Part II of this book is devoted to a discussion of the first phase.

Initial assessment, in our definition, is that phase of the change process in which the discrepancy between the actual and the desired state of affairs is recognized and some notions of what can be done about it are formulated. Relevant data are collected and organized, disciplined consideration is given to whether a change is feasible (and if so, *what* change), and a decision is made about attempting a remedy—matters that are discussed in Chapter 5. If the decision is positive, further appraisal is necessary regarding specific courses of action. The worker must consider the tactics he will use to advance the change, along with the role to be played by both clients and himself. These issues are discussed in Chapter 6.

We qualify the notion of assessment with the word "initial," because assessment is in fact required from the beginning of the process until the end. Indeed, the notion of steps is itself artificial, since one stage inevitably interrelates with the next. An ebb and flow occurs, with constant movement back and forth between one step and another. We focus on these artificial phases largely in order to highlight in logical sequence those elements in the change process that are most relevant to practice. Thus, although assessment takes place throughout a change effort, it is useful to note at the start the factors to be considered during an initial planning period, since much of what is done at the beginning of a process shapes its character later on.

5. Analyzing the Forces for Change

PROFESSIONAL PROBLEM SOLVING is characterized in part by the consideration of relevant alternatives and conscious selection from among them on the basis of understanding and knowledge.[1] In social work, assessment has tended to focus either on the service needs of specific individuals and groups or on the technical aspects of services and systems affecting categories of clients. While these are significant areas of professional activity, we believe that a set of concerns that might be called "political"—including the tasks of identifying potential opposition and support, negotiating an exchange of rewards, and the like—is no less important although it has been largely neglected.[2]

The politically oriented data required for organizational change purposes are especially difficult to obtain and appraise. Much of the information is uncertain or incomplete, and the wide assortment of the data further complicates the task. Information regarding dissimilar entities, at different levels of abstraction, having different direct or indirect impact on a change must be equated and weighed. Such disparate categories of data as the acceptance of or hostility toward the organization by its environment, the agency's structural constraints and opportunities, the interests of various individual participants, and the like must be integrated to allow even a tentative and approximate prediction about whether and how practitioner intervention will influence change.

Force-Field Analysis

Several devices for organizing data have been developed by behavioral scientists for practitioner use,[3] but, as noted in the introduction to Part I,

---

[1] This paraphrases the argument of Allen Pincus and Anne Minahan, in *Social Work Practice: Model and Method* (Itasca, Ill.: Peacock, 1973).

[2] While the technology is significantly different from that presented in this book, the field of organizational development represents an important trend in professional concern with issues of organizational change. See Richard Beckhard, *Organizational Development: Strategies and Models* (Reading, Mass.: Addison-Wesley, 1969).

[3] Harvey A. Hornstein et al., *Social Intervention* (New York: Free Press, 1971), pp. 531–52.

we believe that the most useful conceptual tool for organizational change purposes is Kurt Lewin's force-field analysis.[4] Force-field analysis is a construct, at once both simple and comprehensive, that enables the practitioner to organize information in terms of its relevance for change. After the data have been considered in the context of a particular change goal, force-field analysis aids in highlighting areas of uncertainty, determining the feasibility of the change, and evaluating alternate interventions.

A brief summary of Lewin's ideas bears repeating. At the heart of his "field theory" is the conception that stability within a social system is a *dynamic* rather than a static condition. Seeming stability among the elements of social systems is, in this view, the result of opposing and countervailing "forces" that continuously operate to produce what we *experience* as stability. Change occurs when the forces shift, thus causing a disruption in the system's equilibrium.

Lewin called the systematic identification of opposing forces a "force-field analysis." In analyzing a field of forces, a range of variables is identified which have a probability of influencing the preferences of significant organizational participants with respect to the desired change. Some of these variables constitute *driving forces* which, when increased, alter preferences in such a way that organizational participants act to support the planned change. Other variables constitute *restraining forces* which, when increased, reinforce an actor's commitment to the status quo or move him to resist the change; conversely, when decreased, they modify actor behavior in the direction of the desired change. By means of a force-field analysis, a practitioner can identify the range of driving and restraining forces critical to his goal and assess the interventions necessary to move them in the desired direction. The emphasis of this chapter is on the use of the analysis as a means of organizing data so as to permit educated— though necessarily tentative and approximate—predictions regarding the likelihood that a given organizational innovation will gain acceptance. Consideration of potential interventions is reserved for Chapter 6.

A number of steps are necessary to construct a force-field analysis in sufficient detail to guide the initial planning of a change. First, a change goal must be specified to deal with the problem or set of problems the worker hopes to solve. A second task is to identify those actors who are critical to achievement of the chosen goal. The worker is then able to specify the driving and restraining forces as they impinge on the relevant actors. Finally, he has to evaluate each of these forces in terms of their change-disposing characteristics. We detail each of these four steps in the following sections. First, however, we look at the matter of data collection, since the validity of the analysis depends on the accuracy of the information on which it is based.

---

[4] Kurt Lewin, *Field Theory in Social Science* (New York: Harper & Row, 1951).

Collecting Data

Since one is ultimately concerned about how organizational actors will behave with reference to a change proposal, the focus of data collection is on the meaning a potential change has for the relevant participants. In Chapter 4 we suggested that inferences can be drawn about an actor's preferences on the basis of his interests, that informed speculation is possible regarding the intensity of commitment for or against a potential proposal, and that initial judgments can be made about the influence respective parties have or might be willing to commit to affect an outcome. But these are only inferences, informed speculations, and initial judgments. They need to be researched, "felt out," probed, and revised before they become a foundation for action. The practitioner must engage in a search, employing the full range of information sources to which he has access.

The breadth of relevant information is wide indeed. As one gathers data, it is necessary to move from the general to the specific, increasingly narrowing the range of information that has special significance. The worker must also try to gather information in ways that will not commit him to a course of action until his change goals and strategies are well formulated.

Important sources of data are frequently a matter of record, an open file within the organization, and they may commit the worker to little more than the time they take to read. Statements of organizational mission and agency promotional material fall into this category and reflect what agency directors believe will impress significant publics. Past and present funding proposals are similarly representative of the agency's administration "putting its best foot forward" and may also be descriptive of program characteristics relevant to a particular change. Program evaluations, whether done internally or by outside researchers for reasons unrelated to the change, may reveal agency vulnerabilities related to the change proposal. They are often an excellent source of political information as well.

Administrative material is also useful. Annual budgets reflecting patterns of change over time highlight developmental trends and suggest the relative power positions of different actors and units. Personnel practice codes reveal a number of potentially important issues: formal authority arrangements, patterns of accountability, and sources of task ambiguity. Finally, policy manuals indicate not only the agency's rules but also which policies are in disuse and which rules are differentially applied depending on whether it is in someone's interest to apply or ignore them (and whose interest that is!). As a matter of fact, a critical element of information is the extent to which there are significant inconsistencies between the agency's self-descriptions and the agency's practice.

Another source of data useful in refining initial assumptions is the prior behavior of various organizational participants. Much can be gleaned from their past comments on organizational matters, the values they have espoused, and the positions they have taken. Further, generalizations can be drawn from patterns of an actor's associations within and outside the organization, his position on issues relevant to the change effort, instances of his creativity concerning change issues, and the degree of risk-taking he has demonstrated (and on which issues).

Observation at meetings is often a useful way of collecting relevant political data. In the meeting format those who possess a high degree of functional power tend to stand out. They are not necessarily the same actors who hold formal authority in the setting. High-power actors tend to talk more than others, their communications include more influence attempts, and they more often win their way.[5]

Another means of organizational assessment is to listen for complaints. They often pinpoint an organization's malfunctioning, or at least illuminate the bases of dissatisfaction, and therefore are revealing of possible forces for change. Similar data can be inferred by assessing what appear to be sources of difficulty workers experience in performing their jobs. In the same vein, expressions of hope, aspiration, or vocal "daydreaming" about how things might be are often reflective of potential actor interest in change. In listening to complaints or aspirations, however, sensitivity is required to distinguish between what people would *like* to happen and what they believe they have a right to *expect* to happen.[6] They are more likely to act in the latter instance than in the former.

These methods require no more of the practitioner than that he observe, listen, and hear. When observation is not possible or yields insufficient data, however, one must become more active in the exploration. The refinements of skill which are required to ask the right question and recognize the right leads in organizational practice are similar to those required in effective interviewing in social work, although the unit of attention is different and the information to be gathered is more politically sensitive. For this reason, the practitioner will try to obtain perspectives from a number of different sources before he draws a conclusion.

An illustration of active exploration, as well as of the risk inherent in this type of interviewing, is provided by the mental health worker from the Monrad Community Mental Health Center, to whom we referred in the previous chapter (pp. 80–81). The worker's goal, it will be recalled, was the development of a day hospital, and he was uncertain regarding the position Dr. N., the director of hospitalization services, might take. He

[5] Barry E. Collings and Harold Guetzkow, *A Social Psychology of Group Processes for Decision-Making* (New York: Wiley, 1964), p. 154.

[6] David Silverman, *The Theory of Organizations* (New York: Basic Books, 1971), p. 158.

used the occasion of a drive home from a conference to explore the matter with his friend Robert, who was also a trusted confidant of Dr. N.

> I began to discuss Robert's relationship with the Director of Hospitalization Services. Robert mentioned that he felt close to Dr. N., who trusted Robert's advice. He said that Dr. N. was concerned about the Center Director's plans for reorganization and how this might affect Hospitalization Services. I asked Robert what he thought Dr. N. would do, and he answered that Dr. N. was always looking for a new job in the event that he might suffer a loss in power.
>
> I asked him about the workshops we had attended. Did he feel that it was a good conference? He wondered why I was asking him so many questions. I said that I was curious if there were presentations from other psychiatric institutions about programs that we might use at Monrad. He said, "You mean a Day Hospital?" I responded affirmatively, and asked what he thought. He said that it seemed like a good idea from both a clinical and an administrative standpoint. Did he think Dr. N. would go for it? Robert answered that he might; it was hard to know. I asked how he would suggest I proceed. He said, "You need to plant seeds," and agreed that he would water them for me.[7]

The Monrad worker revealed his change interests in the interview, although he seems not to have intended to do so at the start. Because of his relationship with Robert and the positive nature of the latter's replies, the worker could move beyond exploration to forming an alliance. As workers begin active exploration, however, they also run the risk that they will reveal their change plans before they have sufficiently prepared for the effort. Depending on their audience, therefore, they must be circumspect in what they reveal. Had it been necessary for the worker to conceal his plans, he might have conducted the same conversation with Robert in segments that were extended over time, thus not arousing Robert's curiosity regarding a potentially hidden agenda. Practitioners must choose carefully—as did the Monrad worker—from whom they elicit information and opinion. The general rule of thumb is to go to friends first, neutrals next, and unknowns with decision-making authority last.

One other point is worth noting. The Monrad worker was well along in his thinking before he consulted with Robert. He had identified an agency problem that impinged negatively on a group of clients—the fact that day patients "fell between the cracks" of the impatient and outpatient departments—and had formulated a solution, the establishment of a day hospital. This highlights the fact that data collection, although logically a beginning step, continues throughout the change process and that exploration ultimately engages the worker in a series of actions and reactions,

---

[7] Alan Boyer, "Change at the Monrad Community Mental Health Center," unpublished paper, 1977.

requiring further information, then action again, and so on. As we have noted, the same dynamic is true of assessment as well. Our discussion of the procedures in constructing a force field requires that we "stop time" to explicate the concepts, but we do not mean to imply that practitioners can do similarly.

The Change Goal

The force-field analysis starts when the worker has defined a change goal which has emerged from his identification of a problem in current practice. In conceptualizing a goal, elements are added or eliminated, behavior altered, or circumstances rearranged so that some future state of affairs is imagined which "solves" the problem.

Analysis is necessary, of course, prior to fixing upon even an approximate goal. In practice, analysis varies in the degree to which alternative goals are systematically addressed or emerge "intuitively" from long association with the problem. Ordinarily, some alternatives are dismissed out of hand as impractical or ineffective. This leaves a range of goals with varying potential for solving the problem and at the same time being acceptable to the organization. Force-field analysis might be employed at any point in this process of goal development (i.e., whenever the worker has an approximate notion regarding what he would like to achieve) or it may be used more than once to help him choose among alternate possibilities.

An example will make the point clearer. A worker in the social services department of a Veteran's Administration hospital identified as a problem the fact that patients had inordinate difficulty in obtaining welfare assistance. In addition to welfare-system obstacles, there were a number of internal reasons for the problem. The social service department of the hospital was unfamiliar with the application procedures; the social workers in the department were disinterested in the task, viewing treatment as a more appropriate call on their time; and the hospital itself was overly "tender" in its concern for how a sister public agency might view its pressing for patient interests too assertively.

One program in particular, the hospital's substance-abuse program, seemed a veritable Catch 22 to the worker. The inpatient phase of the program did not permit patients to leave their locked ward for thirty days, following which they were discharged and subsequently seen as outpatients. But many needed welfare assistance to begin on the day of discharge, so that they could find a place to stay, have money to tide them over until they could get a job, etc. This required that they apply in person—but because of their lockup, they could not do so in advance. Hence, they were unable to obtain the immediate help they needed. Unfortunately for her ability to have an impact on the problem, the worker did not have an assignment relating to the substance-abuse program. How to proceed?

The choice of goals was virtually limitless, and the worker had to begin to sort them out in a time-conserving way. Some goals were not even considered because they were patently overambitious. For example, as a Veteran's Administration line worker, the practitioner could not hope to reform welfare assistance policies, though this was clearly necessary, nor could she even expect to mobilize higher-ranking hospital officials to engage in a campaign for more sympathetic attention to their veteran clients. Typically, then, these goals did not even occur to her.[8] It is true that some workers think of taking on "the world" even when they are aware of the inevitability of failure. This approach, however, probably has more to do with powerful ideological or personal commitments than with an immediate goal such as helping the hospital and its substance-abuse patients. Such an approach often serves more to buttress the worker's idealism than to accomplish a specific outcome.

There was another range of goals, less ambitious than the first, which she did consider, but these were discarded relatively quickly as impossible to attain. The V.A. worker did not need a force-field analysis to know, for example, that a transfer of the substance-abuse program from the hospital's Department of Psychiatry to another department more responsive to patients' concrete needs was not within her grasp, although she believed that such a transfer would increase attention to their nonpsychological life problems.

It was as the worker developed potentially realistic goals—goals that were only as ambitious as the resources for influence she could muster to achieve them—that the force-field analysis became a valuable device. The V.A. worker's initial notions were twofold: (1) to work toward allowing substance-abuse patients to receive passes to leave the hospital at least one week prior to discharge in order to establish their welfare eligibility before resuming residence in the community, and (2) to ensure that all patients were adequately prepared for the welfare application process (i.e., knowing what questions to anticipate, what forms to bring). So that staff could better serve their clients, her secondary goal required the preparation of a manual on welfare procedures for staff use.

As she examined the driving and restraining forces for each of her goals, the worker realized that her wish to permit patients to obtain passes prior to discharge was *at that time* doomed to failure. Two major restraining forces were her own lack of legitimacy (she had no assignment in the

---

[8] A disclaimer is necessary. We are describing the process as we believe it happens and indeed as we believe it must. We are not prescribing the procedure, however.

substance-abuse program) and her lack of connections with staff in or relevant to the program.

Even so modest a goal as developing a manual posed significant restraining forces which might not be subject to reduction, as well as driving forces whose increase was uncertain. On balance, however, her assessment in this instance was to try, an attempt that was successfully accomplished. Significantly, her decision to work on the manual served to increase her own resources for influencing and thus to decrease some of the restraining forces that had prevented movement on the policy in regard to patients receiving passes. She developed a reputation as an expert in the welfare area, thereby legitimating her attention to welfare issues anywhere in the organization, and she also developed a close relationship with the social worker in charge of the substance-abuse program through contacts necessitated by working on the manual. In effect, the force-field analysis helped the practitioner to successfully engage a modest change effort and then to apply the acquired resources to take on a larger task.

There are several characteristics of goals which affect the likelihood of their adoption [9] and which must, therefore, be considered as the practitioner explores alternate possibilities. First, the more radical the goal— that is, the more it departs from common practice in the organization— the more difficult it will be to move to adoption. Conversely, the more a goal reflects current values, the easier it is to win support for it. A goal's complexity also affects the likelihood of acceptance. Innovations that require highly technical operations or call for coordinating the efforts of various specialities are, for obvious reasons, more difficult to attain than less complex innovations.

Relatedness to the problem to be solved is another characteristic of goals. The more directly a goal impinges on a generally recognized problem and the more obvious are its advantages over current practice, the easier it is to win its adoption. Goal relatedness is dependent on how the problem in question is experienced by other participants, but it has another aspect as well. When a goal's impact on a problem is immediate and direct, the goal is easier to implement after it has been adopted (see Chapter 9).

The issues of scope and reversibility are also important. The broader is the scope of a change goal, the more widespread is its impact on other organizational actors, and the larger the number of levels or functional subgroupings that must approve it; hence, the more resistance one might expect. Conversely, the more likely it is that the goal can be implemented on a limited basis or that its implementation can be reversed if necessary (as in a demonstration project, for example), the greater are its chances of

---

[9] Some of these concepts are detailed in Gerald Zaltman et al., *Innovations and Organizations* (New York: Wiley, 1973), Chapter 1.

acceptance. Finally, goal attainment is enhanced if the implementation of a goal requires a lesser use of scarce resources.

Keeping this range of goal characteristics in mind, the practitioner must attempt to refine his change notion into a goal (or goals) which can be operationalized. In the Veteran's Administration example, the worker's concern about the difficulty encountered by substance-abuse patients was translated into concrete conceptions of specific changes. Both the idea of obtaining a policy change that would allow patients to receive passes and the notion of developing a welfare-procedures manual were precise and specific, in contrast, for example, to a more global and nonoperational concern of "helping the substance-abuse patients deal with the welfare problem." The more specific the goal and the more it can be cast in operational terms, the more useful the force-field analysis becomes in determining its feasibility.

Similarly, goals often have to be partialized to allow effective intervention. A goal may be partialized by reducing its scope, thus reducing the number of people involved in or affected by its adoption. Or the content of the goal may be divided into developmental components (e.g., a two-, three-, or four-step process). In the previous example, the worker partialized the goal into two components. The development of a welfare manual was useful in its own right, but it also greatly increased the likelihood that the other component—obtaining a change in hospital policy concerning passes for the patients—would subsequently be accepted.

Once a goal has been considered with regard to its ambitiousness and defined operationally, the concern of the assessment process is then to locate the individual or group of individuals who have the influence to effect the goal and to identify the set of forces which, when altered, will modify the "meanings" of organizational events for the critical organizational actors so that the desired change will be supported. Thus, the initial assessment question once the goal has been determined is "What alterations in meanings for which organizational actors will result in the behavior changes that are necessary to effect the desired change goal?"

Critical and Facilitating Actors

For any change effort there is an individual or group of individuals who *must* support the effort in order for it to become a reality. "Critical actors" for a given change effort may include the agency administrator, the worker's peer group, or a supervisor who, if convinced of the efficacy of the change goal, *will be able to effect its adoption.* In any organization, the critical actors for a particular change effort will shift depending on the change being considered.

The critical actor is located by asking the question: "Who (or what group) has the power to deliver my change if he perceives it to be in his own or the organization's interest to do so?" Typically, though not inevitably, this is the individual who has administrative responsibility for the area of the organization affected.

We distinguish here between those who have the power to put a change into effect (the critical actors) and those who might be called facilitators. The latter are participants of two types. There are, first, those whose approval must be obtained before the matter reaches the attention of critical actors. (In some instances, to be sure, they are hardly facilitators in the sense that they may need to be circumvented to gain the notice of a critical actor.) The second category of facilitating actors are those whose approval, disapproval, or neutrality has a decisive impact on critical actors.

For example, in the case of Charter House, which we have discussed in prior chapters, the critical actor was the agency's priest-director, since only he had the authority to revise the discharge policy. But the practitioner who sought the change needed the approval of the social services department before the issue could even reach the director for his consideration. It was also clear that, because of the informal influence arrangements at Charter House (i.e., the long and close association of the director and child-care staff), the director would not approve a change if there was strong opposition from the child-care workers. In this case, the facilitating actors were the social-service and child-care staffs, or, more precisely, informal leaders and opinion setters within the two groups.

It is important both to distinguish between critical and facilitating actors and to recognize the part each plays in the change process. In large measure, critical actors are easier to identify since ordinarily they have responsibility for the area affected by the change. It is sometimes true that their authority is unclear or has eroded over time to be replaced by a less clear "common law." But who the critical actors are is ordinarily apparent to organizational participants after a minimum of exploration of the agency's authority system. The identity of facilitating actors, particularly those without formal influence (e.g., the child-care workers), requires more subtle exploration and understanding of the organization's dynamics. Since they influence the critical actors, however, the feasibility of the change and the actions that must be taken in pursuing it are importantly determined by the correct identification of facilitators as well as critical actors.

Who becomes the critical actor for one's change effort is partly a function of the nature of the change goal and partly a function of the structural characteristics of the organization in question. With regard to structure, our discussion in Chapter 3 is germane. The more complex the organization, the more likely it is that the critical actors will be numerous. As the task structure becomes more complex and the range of different professionals increases, the resulting interdependent responsibility necessitates collaborative decision making. By the same token, the more formalized and centralized the organization structure, the fewer critical actors one would expect to be involved in any given change effort.

Identification of the critical actors is also influenced by the nature of the change goal. Consider, for example, the situation where a change goal turns out to involve a critical actor who seems inalterably opposed to the change. It is possible to alter the goal so that it focuses on an aspect of the problem that is outside the purview of the nonsupportive critical actor and related to a critical actor who is more open to the effort. Perhaps more common is the situation where a worker enjoys high credibility with a particular agency official and consciously tailors the change effort so that it directly relates to this official's area of concern. In this situation the change is designed to have the "built-in" support of a critical actor.

In the Monrad case, for example, the worker developed his goal so that the proposed day hospital would be located administratively within hospitalization services rather than the organization's outpatient department. Among other reasons, he did so because of his greater access to Dr. N., the head of hospitalization services, than to Dr. B., the chief of the outpatient department. Another reason was his awareness that Dr. N. was more sensitive than Dr. B. to matters relating to his department's influence within the center and would be more assertive in pursuing the department's interests.

DEVELOPING THE "BALANCE SHEET" AND ANALYZING FORCE ATTRIBUTES

The force-field analysis proceeds with the elaboration of a "balance sheet" of forces, driving forces on one side and restraining forces on the other, as well as a specification of the actor or actors upon whom they are presumed to have an effect (Figure 2). In Part I we considered variables that influence organizational change—those elements of the environment and the organization, as well as the interests and influence of participants, that act as driving and restraining forces. The task for the worker at this stage of change planning is to translate these general ideas into a listing of particular forces that appear directly or indirectly to influence the preferences of relevant organizational actors with respect to the change goal.

The listing of forces must be as specific as possible. While a variable such as "the organization's ideology" may seem to be a driving or restraining force, it is too general to suggest interventions that might increase or decrease the force. Identification of a specific aspect of the ideology and of the particular actor or set of actors on whom it impinges is required to provide the necessary focus for practice efforts. Thus, the worker might note instead that "the executive director's belief in preventive rather than

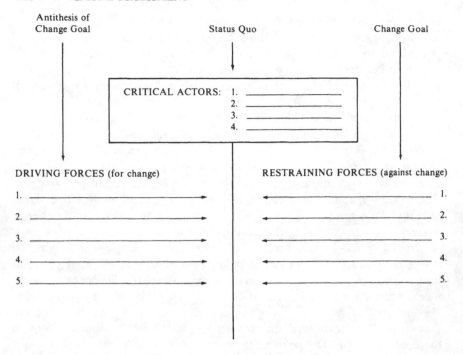

Figure 2. The Field of Forces[10]

treatment services and his commitment to increasing services to a low-income clientele" are driving or restraining forces, depending on the nature of the worker's goal.

To illustrate how this balance sheet is developed, we review some of the forces that influenced the Charter House worker's change effort. It will be recalled that the critical actor at Charter House was the priest-director, and that the worker's change effort involved revision of the existent informal discharge policy, which in effect enabled child-care staff to recommend discharge without substantive grounds and ensured that such recommendations would be approved. The worker's goal was to develop specific criteria for discharge and to involve the clinical staff in a broadly constituted case committee to pass on discharge recommendations.

A partial list will serve to indicate the range of driving forces: (1) The city's Bureau of Child Welfare, a major funding source, mandated the use

10 The figure oversimplifies the relationship of forces to critical actor; unrepresented is the fact that all forces do not affect critical actors equally. While some forces (e.g., strong consumer pressure or threats to continued funding) are so significant that they will have an impact on nearly all relevant actors, many forces (e.g., actor self-interest) affect critical actors differentially. In diagramming the force field, readers may find it useful to note which critical actors are affected by particular driving and restraining forces. Occasionally, the same variable will operate as a driving force for one actor and a restraining force for another.

of clinicians and was concerned with the maintenance of "standards" in its constituent residential settings. In light of the bureau's funding significance, this was a driving force for the critical actor. (2) The humanistic mission of the agency and staff led to an emphasis on the quality rather than the quantity of care. A proposal that improved quality of care would be predisposed to acceptance. (3) The absence of a definitive discharge policy created a vacuum which a new policy could fill, and the informality of the agency's rule system reduced the probability of fixed positions on the part of many participants. (4) The projected goal would have the effect of increasing the influence of the director of social services, and this self-interest feature was likely to move the director to support the change. (5) The idiosyncratic nature of current discharge decision making ignored the individual needs of the adolescents, violating the professional values of the clinical staff. It might thus be assumed that the clinical staff, an important set of facilitating actors, would support the proposal. (6) The change in policy would increase the esteem in which clinicians were held by increasing their importance within Charter House. This suggested that it would be in the clinicians' interests to support the proposal. (7) Child-care workers used the help of clinicians in handling difficult client behavior, and to the extent that they perceived themselves as dependent on clinical staff, their responsiveness to the clinicians' wishes might be anticipated.

Counterbalancing these forces were the restraining forces. Five may be noted: (1) The Bureau of Child Welfare was tentative in its relations with the city's major religious groupings and consequently granted latitude to many of its constituent agencies. This had the potential effect of blunting the possible impact of the bureau's professional orientation. (2) The love-care ethic that infused Charter House equated professionalism with a bureaucratic environment that was unloving and indifferent to clients. This would predispose the actors who shared the ethic (primarily the child-care staff and some of the administrators) to respond adversely to proposals that had a "professional standards" rationale. (3) A number of executives shared the nonclinical orientation of other organizational actors. This orientation was a restraining force since the proposal would be supported by clinical staff and involved clinical criteria. (4) An increase in professional influence posed a threat to the influence and esteem of the religiously oriented staff. Such staff might well associate any increase in the influence of clinicians with a decrease in their own influence. (5) The current discharge policy allowed child-care staff to control "acting out" children, thus enhancing their autonomy. The worker therefore expected the child-care staff to resist a proposal that reduced their autonomy in this area. Other restraining forces were at work as well, but these suffice to illustrate what might be included in a force-field balance sheet.

It may be noted that these forces conform to the environmental, organizational, and participant variables discussed in Part I. It ought to be clear as well that the interests and values of organizational actors can serve simultaneously as driving and restraining forces. For example, the need of the child-care workers for help from clinicians was a driving force, and their presumed desire for autonomy was a restraining force. Often a force field will incorporate a variable on both the driving and restraining sides simultaneously, since the variable may impinge on an actor's interests and commitments in conflicting ways. Similarly, the role of factors external to the organization may reflect two-sidedness on the balance sheet. As is the case with actor interests, the impact of a given external variable upon the change proposal in both a driving and a restraining fashion typically has to do with different aspects of the same variable. In the above example, the Bureau of Child Welfare's mandate of professionalism vs. its responsiveness to the religious community illustrates the point. The fact that these "ambivalences" exist offers potential leverage to practitioner change efforts. We refer here to the fact that each force, even if it simply involves a different aspect of the same variable, theoretically holds the potential for being increased and/or decreased.

Since the purpose of the initial assessment is the collection and evaluation of data in order to develop a strategy for the accomplishment of the change effort, once one has identified the range of probable forces related to the change, he is faced with the question of which forces to influence and in what fashion We approach this question through a closer look at the attributes of the driving and restraining forces. Three are particularly important for practice purposes: (1) the forces' amenability to change, (2) their potency, and (3) their consistency.

AMENABILITY TO CHANGE

Amenability to change refers to a force's potential for modification, particularly the likelihood that the worker will be able to alter it—to increase it if the force is a driving force, or to decrease it if it is a restraining force. Forces may be amenable to worker influence directly or through the intercession of others (e.g., at Charter House, either the worker or other social service staff might become the primary actors in reducing pejorative judgments of professionalism). An objective fact may be involved in altering the force, or the modification may entail perception of that fact (e.g., the attention of the Bureau of Child Welfare to maintaining standards might be increased or the priest-director's perception of the bureau's interest in standards might be heightened). Since the concern of the force field is the reaction of critical or facilitating actors, for purposes of assessing a force's amenability to influence, changes in objective reality and in the perception of that reality may be equally relevant. Furthermore, a force may be increasing or decreasing as a result of "natural" (other than practitioner-initiated) causes—for example, if the Bureau of Child Welfare's interest in standards was increasing independently of the Charter House worker. A naturally increasing or decreasing force is as good as (indeed, sometimes better than) a worker-influenced force and therefore should be assessed as amenable to change.

It is difficult to generalize about criteria for determining the amenability of a particular force to worker influence because it is dependent on variables specific to the situation at the time of the initial assessment. Broadly, however, it is determined by the interaction of the nature of the forces and the resources for influence to which the worker has access.[11]

Our discussion of goals earlier in this chapter suggests some of the characteristics of forces that affect their amenability to change (e.g., the extent to which an increase or a decrease in the force will bring it into conformity with current values or practice, whether its modification requires the action of a few or many actors, etc.). Most significant, however, is the fact that a force is most amenable to worker influence when the proposed modification supports the interests of critical and facilitating actors—or when it may be made to *seem* in their interests. When changes are consistent with the interests of those who must take action or are perceived to be so, the less threatening the changes will be and the less resistance they will induce. Conversely, the more threatening the change is or is perceived to be, the more resistance. And the greater the resistance is, the more power, or resources for influence, that must be brought to bear by the practitioner. In other words, the characteristic of the force and the worker's resources for influence vary in tandem and, in their interaction, determine a force's amenability to worker influence.

Although it can be only approximate, an estimate must be made with regard to the probability that the force will increase or decrease as a result of the worker's efforts or of independent "natural" causes. On the basis of the worker's exploration, his experience with similar matters in the past, and his evaluation of the resources at his disposal compared to the resources of potential opponents, forces may be judged on a continuum from "high" to "low" in amenability to worker influence.[12] Thus, the Charter House worker defined the forces generated by the child-care workers as high in amenability to her influence; that is, their need for clinical assistance might be increased and the threat to the child-care worker's autonomy might be reduced. On the other hand, she deemed it beyond her resources to decrease the nonclinical orientation of the top executives.

If the worker cannot make the judgment of "high" or "low" amenability with relative assurance, he must consider the force's amenability to his influence "uncertain." The "uncertain" determination has implications which will be discussed later.

[11] See Chapter 4 for a discussion of a worker's resources for influence.

[12] For purposes of decision making, we categorize forces as only "high" or "low." The "moderate" range must be judged to be either "higher than low" or "lower than high," thus facilitating a dichotomous judgment.

On the basis of his judgments concerning the attributes of forces, the practitioner has implicitly assessed the critical characteristics of the forces with regard to their usefulness and dependability in service of his desired goal. His estimate of their strength is advanced by an understanding of the categories into which they fall. There are three types: (1) working forces (i.e., potentially usable forces that the practitioner can try to increase or decrease or can otherwise count on to advance his goal); (2) framing forces (i.e., those that structure the change arena but are not directly useful in moving the goal); and (3) unpredictable forces (i.e., those that represent the measure of uncertainty or turbulence in pursuing the change).

WORKING FORCES

We define working forces as those that have been judged moderate to high in amenability to worker influence, potency, and consistency, and are thus the variables in the force field that can be put to use in a change attempt. The Charter House worker, as we found, deemed a reduction of the threat to the autonomy of child-care staff amenable to her influence and potent in its effect on moving her change in discharge policy, and she had no reason to question the force's consistency. Clearly, then, this was a working force.

Occasionally one finds a working force in his force field that is independently increasing or decreasing *and* is also judged to be potent and consistent. Even though the increase or decrease in the force is due to some factor other than worker intervention, since it is potent and consistent, it can be counted on nonetheless. If, for example, the Bureau of Child Welfare had been increasing its insistence on maintaining professional standards in its residential institutions independently of the worker's intervention, it might have had a significant impact on how the Charter House director would respond to the inclusion of clinicians in discharge planning and would thus constitute such a force. Other examples might be an increase in community good will as a new agency develops or a decrease in staff resistance to new forms of service as the merits of the new forms become clearer through the experience of related institutions.

There are also some occasions when a force is high in amenability to influence and consistency but low in its impact on the goal (potency), but the worker decides to try to influence it nevertheless. One such case is when there are a significant number of low-potency forces which, in accumulation, could have an impact on the change goal. The other is when there is little cost to the worker in intervening, other forces are not manipulable, and the low-potency force constitutes a step in the direction of his ultimate goal, albeit a short step.

The likelihood that a practitioner will reach the desired goal is directly related to the strength of working forces relative to his goal. Ordinarily, as workers assess a force's attributes, they are also implicitly considering the actions they might take to influence it. However, once a force has been defined as a working force, a systematic exploration of how to proceed and which strategies will be most effective becomes possible, since working forces constitute the core of a change strategy. The greater the percentage of working forces in the force field, the more likely is the practitioner to be successful.

FRAMING FORCES

Framing forces structure the field within which the change takes place. They provide a predictable context for the worker's efforts but cannot contribute independently to the accomplishment of the goal. They are, in our definition, forces that are high in consistency and low in amenability to change.[13]

Let's assume that a practitioner has informally scanned his organization and believes it possible to initiate a particular change. If the force field he develops involves only framing forces, the change is unlikely to occur since the forces are not manipulable and therefore offer no opportunity for worker intervention.

Framing forces may, however, be a dependent resource for change. When a force field is composed *mostly* of framing forces but there are driving or restraining forces that are amenable to change, the likelihood of movement toward the goal is increased due to the imbalance resulting from changes in these driving or restraining forces. The goal-directed pressure of a framing force on the "driving" side of the force field will no longer be so strongly opposed if a working force on the restraining side is reduced.

An example will make the point more sharply. Let us imagine that the Bureau of Child Welfare's interest in professional standards was neither increasing nor decreasing. Imagine too that it was not subject to worker modification. High in consistency and low in amenability to influence, it represents a framing force. But suppose, further, that one of the restraining forces in the situation—for example, the Charter House administration's nonclinical orientation—was reduced. In such a case, it is possible that the bureau's interest in professionalism might now affect the Charter House director in such a way as to advance the cause of the discharge-policy change. Although the bureau's position in itself was not amenable to the

---

[13] From a practice viewpoint, the potency of framing forces is somewhat hypothetical. Although a framing force could have a major impact on a change goal *if* it increased or decreased, intervention is ruled out with regard to that particular force by definition since framing forces are both consistent and not amenable to influence.

worker's influence and remained stable, a decrease in the nonclinical orientation on the part of Charter House directors might well move them to accept the bureau's standards and, by extension, the worker's goal.

In sum, framing forces structure the change arena and in isolation do not influence the accomplishment of a goal. When located in a field that includes some forces that can be modified, however, framing forces can contribute to goal achievement.

UNPREDICTABLE FORCES

We refer to forces of two types as unpredictable. The first are those that have been designated "uncertain" on any of the three attributes (i.e., amenability to change, potency, or consistency). The second are forces that have been ranked "low" on consistency (i.e., any force, however high in amenability to influence or potency, that the practitioner has reason to believe is unstable).

Where the attributes of the forces are uncertain, the practitioner may need to collect further information before he moves ahead. Indeed, one of the advantages of force-field analysis is that it impels a narrowing of the worker's focus to areas about which additional data must be gathered. Sometimes, too, when the amenability to change, potency, or consistency of a force is unknown, the worker is required to "test the waters" in order to glean the information he needs before he can make the decision to move on his goal. He would do well in such a case to proceed circumspectly, however.

Uncertainty is, of course, a fact of organizational life, and planning and decision making in the context of uncertainty have received considerable attention in the organization literature.[14] Nevertheless, for the practitioner who has exhausted the information available to him and remains uncertain after "testing the waters," a high degree of unpredictability puts the feasibility of his change and the advisability of proceeding into question. The greater the uncertainty, the less he is depending on skill and the more he is trusting to luck. In some change efforts, where the stakes are low for either the worker or the organization, this may be all right. Even here, however, there is some risk since a series of failed attempts has consequences for the judgments others will make about the practitioner's technical competence, political acumen, or both. When the stakes are high, on the other hand, ignorance of the major dynamics related to a proposed change poses too great a risk to proceed. Thus, when a significant percentage of the data related to his scheme has eluded the practitioner's assessment, it may be the better part of wisdom to revise the goal, postpone the effort until a more thorough assessment can be completed, or signifi-

---

[14] James G. March and Herbert Simon, *Organizations* (New York: Wiley, 1958).

cantly extend the timetable, hoping that with the passage of time the field will alter sufficiently to make critical data available for assessment.

When the unpredictable forces represent a judgment of low consistency, the practitioner is provided with an index of the degree of turbulence in the system. A large number of such unpredictable forces augers ill for a successful change. As noted in Chapter 3, in an extremely turbulent setting it is unlikely that one can mobilize and maintain support for a planned change. And the more turbulent the setting, the greater may be the risk to both the worker and the organization of pursuing a change. A force field characterized by substantial instability or turbulence is thus not conducive to planned innovation.

To summarize: by going through the steps of force-field analysis—

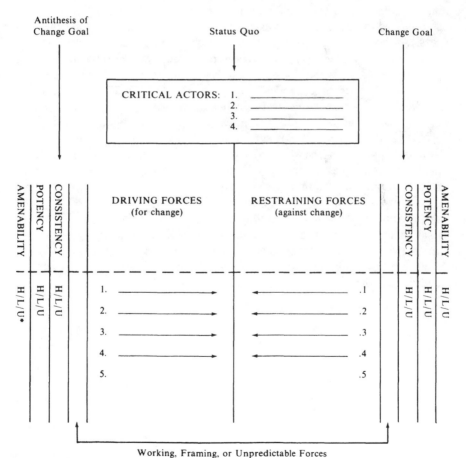

Working, Framing, or Unpredictable Forces

*High, Low, Uncertain.

Figure 3. The Force Field Analysis

choosing a realistic goal, identifying the critical actors to accomplish that goal, listing the driving forces for and the restraining forces against, evaluating each force from the standpoint of its amenability to change, potency, and consistency (summarized in Figure 3), and then weighing the number and strength of working forces, as well as the potential impact of framing forces and the degree of unpredictability in the system—the practitioner can estimate his chances of success in seeking a particular goal.

It ought to be underscored, however, that the estimate will be a rough approximation; he will know, in other words, only whether his effort is "in the ball park." This is the case because force-field analysis attempts to systematize data that are at best incomplete or only partially systematic. Its usefulness is considerable but is also limited. For one thing, our current knowledge does not allow the full development and refinement of the variables employed in the tool. For another, the worker gains fuller understanding of the variables only as he starts his attempt to influence the process. As in all human processes, it is wise to anticipate the unexpected, and continuous re-evaluation is therefore necessary. Force-field analysis provides a significant theoretical starting point, however, and offers vast potential since its precision will increase with continued use, advancing knowledge, and refinements in practice skill.

In addition to its applicability in estimating the likelihood of success of a change attempt, the device offers a number of other advantages. Practitioners who invest the time and thoughtfulness in constructing a force field gain considerably greater understanding of the *overall* situation they face (i.e., the interrelations among discrete variables in the system) than if they had not done so. With continued use, workers also develop a *way of thinking,* a politically "conscious use of self," which adds to their tactical acumen in both current and future efforts. Finally, the analysis sharpens their focus on next steps. It allows the search for alternatives in regard to intervening to increase or decrease working forces, the subject to which we turn in the next chapter.

6. The Choice of Tactics

ONCE THE PRACTITIONER concludes the assessment activities outlined in the previous chapter, he has arrived at a rough approximation of the goal's susceptibility to intervention and has identified those forces that, if increased or decreased, might accomplish the change. The initital assessment is not complete, however. He must still determine a course of action, the specific ways by which to increase driving forces and/or reduce restraining ones. In so doing, he must face a number of issues of a theoretical, practical, and ideological nature. Theoretically, there are questions of the fit between alternative interventions and organizational circumstances. Practically, the costs and benefits of engaging the effort must be assessed. Ideologically, concerns such as the role of clients in the change attempt must be weighed. It is only after considering issues such as these that the practitioner is prepared to move on the change.

Let us consider an example. A social worker employed by a prestigious psychiatric institute was transferred to a long-standing research unit investigating the role of metabolic factors in the treatment of affective disorders. The problem, as she defined it, was the gross insensitivity of the attending staff to patient needs, manifest in the minimal interaction between the two groups, the overt expression of hostility by staff to patients, staff unwillingness to share information with patients concerning their course of treatment, and the prescription of medication with harmful side effects. The worker noted that nurses spent most of their time in a restricted "for staff only" section. One patient who was extremely anxious about impending shock treatments was never informed that the scheduled treatments had been cancelled. Another patient's loss of weight was ignored until the patient was unable to walk. Ward activities were rarely scheduled, and little use was made of the institute's activities for which patients were eligible, such as its occupational therapy program. In the worker's judgment, two feasible goals were the establishment of regular meetings between patients and staff and the institution of a recreational group program. She viewed these goals as important but beginning steps in dealing with the problem.

The worker's analysis included a number of driving and restraining forces, but we shall mention only three of the latter. The routinized nature of the nurses' job resulted in both frustration and boredom—with a consequent reduction in humanistic concerns. A second restraining force was the disinterest of the medical director of the unit in anything other than research; he largely absented himself from unit operations. Finally, the patients were themselves fearful, lethargic, and submissive.

Assuming that these forces were both amenable to intervention and high in potency, the worker then had to select which one to begin to try to influence or whether to try influencing all three simultaneously. She also had to decide what action or set of actions would most effectively influence a particular force. For example, intervening to reduce the frustration and boredom of the nursing staff with their routinized work offers a wide range of action possibilities. A few that the worker actually tried are (1) highlighting the uniqueness and importance of the research conducted on the ward; (2) role-modeling an enthusiastic approach to her own job through participating with patients on the ward and subsequently relaying to the nurses some of the amusing and sad things she had heard from patients; (3) interesting the nurses in the psychodynamic and interactive causes of illness, both informally and through reports on patients' life histories in case conferences; (4) soliciting the nurses' judgment regarding nonmedical interventions with the patients; and (5) choosing a sympathetic and sensitive nurse to co-lead a therapy group with her. Had the organizational context been different, her interventions would probably have taken other forms. For example, with greater authority for unit operations, a number of other options would have been available to her, such as revising the nurses' job load.

The institute worker also had other decisions to make before she completed her initial assessment. For instance, she not only had to assess the most effective means of increasing the medical director's attention to nonresearch issues, but it was also necessary to consider the risks to herself in selecting a set of actions to influence this force. Similarly, she had to weigh whether and how to involve the clients, taking into account their potential contribution to the change, their right to participate in the effort or *not* to participate, the potential risk to them, and the like.[1] We address these theoretical, practical, and ideological issues in the sections that follow.

The Range of Tactics

A tactic, as we use the word, is the means by which the practitioner attempts to increase or decrease working forces.[2] Earlier we said that a

[1] This example is drawn from Laura Rubenstein, "Innovation at the Institute," unpublished paper, 1977.

[2] Although it might be esthetically pleasing to some social workers to substitute a less professionally charged word, our decision to use "tactics" has been made with

modification in the field of forces causes change within the organization by means of its impact on critical organizational actors. But although the aim of any change effort is ultimately to influence the critical actor or actors, action to modify a working force may be intended to move a wide range of organizational participants (i.e., the critical actors themselves, facilitators, potential allies, or opponents). The focus of the influence attempt is referred to in this chapter as the target actor.

By the word "tactic," we mean to convey short-range and specific behaviors. Although the word is often used interchangeably with strategy, the two are distinguishable. "Strategy" refers to the theory or set of ideas that informs the goal of a change effort, moving it from problem to proposed solution. It also refers to the linking of tactics together into a longer-range game plan. Strategy may thus be said to integrate a consideration regarding *what* to do about a problem with a concern regarding *how* to go about doing it.

Viewed in this way, any change has two levels of consideration. The primary level is the goal of the desired change—the modification in organizational functioning which the worker hopes to effect. The secondary level includes the objective of the worker's effort with regard to *each* working force. Since the effort to increase or decrease a working force involves change activities on the part of the worker or his colleagues, each such effort—or tactic—necessarily constitutes a subgoal.

COLLABORATIVE, CAMPAIGN, AND CONTEST TACTICS

Tactics fall broadly into three modes of intervention, ranging on a continuum from those marked by cooperation to those entailing conflict and pressure. They are (1) collaborative tactics, (2) campaign tactics, and (3) contest tactics.[3]

Collaborative tactics are characterized by open communication. Problems tend to be stated as such rather than as solutions, information regarding the perspectives of both parties is widely shared, and a climate of tentativeness typifies the interaction. Collaborative tactics include problem solving, joint action, education, and mild persuasion, each involving a more or less active attempt to influence another party. From the perspective of the worker who is seeking the change, problem solving involves working with the target actors in the search for data, ideas, resources, or models that best fulfill criteria that both parties have agreed constitute a

---

forethought. Words like "intervention" and "method" are more professionally acceptable, but they do not connote the political components inherent in attempts to influence organizational change as does "tactic."

[3] This discussion of a typology of tactics and their relationship to goals, resources, and relationships is a summarized and extensively modified version of the discussion in George Brager and Harry Specht, *Community Organizing* (New York: Columbia University Press, 1973), pp. 261–75.

"solution." While problem solving often embodies some division of labor, the parties have ordinarily agreed that the allocation of tasks is not only equitable but most appropriate to reach their common goals. Joint action denotes teamwork involving the parties in a set of activities. Similar to problem solving, it is distinguished by its connotation of cooperation in the implementation of actions related to moving the change rather than the emphasis on search that defines problem solving.

Education refers to the sharing of knowledge or perceptions which the practitioner has acquired through training or through activities which have provided him with information or insights not available to the target actors. In the educative mode, the worker is not attempting to *convince* the other actors—he simply wishes to *inform*. Finally, in mild persuasion, he is attempting to convince the other party, largely through the spontaneous expression of ideas and arguments.

Although the various collaborative interventions are conceptually distinct, they are in fact interdependent and ordinarily overlap in practice. It may be noted, for example, that in one form or another the institute worker employed all of these forms of collaborative tactics in her interventions with the nurses.

Campaign tactics fall at the midpoint of the continuum between collaborative and conflict tactics and contain some elements of both. They include "hard" persuasion, political maneuvering, bargaining and negotiation, and mild coercion.

"Hard" persuasion involves advocating a position through a presentation designed to appeal to the particular interests and sensitivities of the target actor. Omission or commission may be involved, and the practitioner consciously selects the facts, values, and emotional content inherent in his argument so as to be most convincing to his audience.

Political maneuvering implies manipulating others. As distinct from problem solving, which is characterized by open communication, political maneuvering entails the *appearance* of sharing. Although it is not limited to covert worker activity, the covert exercise of influence is most often an intrinsic aspect of the tactic. Thus, when the worker at the institute helped clients to express their latent dissatisfaction and suggested that they press for community meetings, she engaged in political maneuvering, since she did not identify the idea as her own with institute staff or inform them that she had been involved in the clients' effort.

Bargaining and negotiation involve the sequential exchange of resources, sanctions, accommodation, and rewards, with the intent of reaching some mutually acceptable position regarding whatever happens to be at issue. The exchange may be implicit or explicit, but it ordinarily takes place through making requests or demands, arguing them, and then conceding and accepting some part of the other's position. Bargaining and negotiation perhaps most clearly epitomize the set of tactics that balance cooperative and competitive elements. On the one hand, goodwill and trust are often necessary for successful negotiation (e.g., the worker who relates to the interests of other parties, is consistent in his dealings with them, and understands that cooperativeness begets cooperation successfully manages one aspect of the exchange). On the other hand, it also requires a clear and determined fix on what one hopes to achieve although the achievement is often at the other's expense (e.g., deciding on a "bottom line" or point beyond which one will not go and downgrading the other's position).

Mild coercion, the last on our list of campaign tactics, refers to the mobilization of pressure and/or negative sanctions directed toward the target actor to impel his acceptance of a particular goal. Often, in mild coercion, the worker who has organized the effort tries to avoid taking public accountability for the campaign.

Contest tactics carry coercion a considerable distance further, involving public conflict and pressure. They include virulent clashes of position (through "no holds barred" debate and public manifestos), the violation of normative behavior (e.g., moving out of the bounds of organizationally "proper" behavior by means of protest activities such as demonstrations), and, in the extreme, the violation of legal norms (e.g., halting operations by sitting in).

The case of the institute worker's change may again be used as an example. The medical director had administered the metabolic unit for ten years, and it might be safely assumed that he was aware of but disinterested in the indignities patients suffered. To increase his attention to ward operations in a humanist direction could have been accomplished only by pressure—for example, through formally complaining to the institute's funding source, organizing patients and their families for protest action, attracting the intercession of politically powerful outsiders, and the like.

For reasons that are apparent, contest tactics are rarely used in practice related to internal organizational change and are therefore not elaborated in this volume.[4] They are included both to elucidate the full range of theoretically possible interventions and also, as we shall note later in the chapter, to point up how the tactical constraints under which the worker typically operates may force him to seek options that he would otherwise find unattractive.

The choice of collaborative, campaign, or contest interventions must be considered as the worker approaches the task of increasing or decreasing a particular working force. The major touchstone is how the target actors

---

[4] There is considerable literature on contest tactics. For three examples, see Saul Alinsky, *Rules for Radicals* (New York: Random House, 1971); Martin Oppenheimer, *The Urban Guerilla* (Chicago: Quadrangle, 1969); and Gene Sharp, *Exploring Non-Violent Alternatives* (Boston: Porter Sargent, 1970).

and related others will be affected by the tactic's selection relative to the worker's goal.

Variables in the Selection of Tactics

A basic criterion in selecting a tactic, and the most obvious one, has to do with the commonality or divergence in the goals of the worker and the target actor. A second consideration relates to their respective resources for influencing and how particular resources predispose the use of particular tactics. Thirdly, the relationship of the worker and the target may be an important determinant of tactic selection. Finally, there is the question of restraint in the choice of tactic; that is, the consequence of choosing a lesser rather than more extreme form of intervention when both might be effective.

GOAL COMMONALITY AND DIVERGENCE

Each working force—as well as the goal of the change effort—involves an issue or set of issues that hold potential significance to the target actors. To the extent that those issues are perceived by both worker and target to be congruent with the worker's intervention, there will be consensus between the actors. In its purest form, this kind of relationship is what Deutsch calls pure cooperation or "promotive interdependence." According to him, promotive interdependence occurs when "participants are so linked that any participant can attain his goal if, and only if, the others with whom he is linked can attain theirs." [5] In the nomenclature of game theory, the circumstance is a win-win game: for one party to win, the other party must win as well. Because the situation is perceived by both parties to involve commonality of purpose, the choice of intervention is collaborative, and the worker will engage in problem solving, teamwork, education, or mild persuasion.

In some situations the parties experience a problem with extreme disparity and disagree substantially on the goal. Goals that seriously challenge the influence and autonomy, share of resources, or self-esteem of the target actor—*if they are engaged in this form*—will call forth a response of sharp dissensus. Deutsch refers to this relationship as "contrident interdependence." In its purest form, a participant can attain his goal if, and only if, the others with whom he is engaged cannot attain their goals.[6] In other words, for one party to win, the other must lose (a zero-sum or win-lose game). Since the critical actor in our definition is the individual

---

[5] Morton Deutsch, *The Resolution of Conflict: Constructive and Destructive Processes* (New Haven: Yale University Press, 1973), p. 20.
[6] *Ibid.*

who holds the power to move the change, it is unlikely that he will act to institute a change that is antithetical to his goals unless extreme pressure is applied. The tactical choice, then, is contest.

The clash of position and violation of normative behavior inherent in contest interventions pose tremendous risk for the practitioner, however. If he openly engages in contest tactics, thereby defying both the elaborate set of norms organizations develop and the formal authority structure that enforces them, he will at least be defined as "disloyal" and at worst will court dismissal. The dilemma this situation raises is familiar to the seasoned practitioner. "Do I support the status quo and preserve my position and credibility, or do I engage the issue and possibly jeopardize both my interests and my future effectiveness?" The dilemma is resolved in a variety of ways, but a common solution is to maintain the *appearance* of norm adherence while in fact beginning to engage in political maneuvering—that is, selecting a campaign tactic instead.

Most organizational problems generate goals that fall somewhere between those that are commonly shared and those that participants find extremely disparate. They include some elements that run counter to what the target actor perceives to be congruent with his interests and values and some elements supportive of his interests, and the interaction is thus comprised of both cooperative and competitive elements. In this circumstance, each party may accept the validity of some significant percentage of the other's goal. The aim of the worker is then to maximize the extent to which the outcome reflects his interests while not compromising the interests of the target actor to such an extent that he will disengage and choose not to support the effort. This type of situation might be called a "mixed" game. The response of the parties to the effort is neither goal consensus nor dissensus but what might be termed goal difference. *If the change is engaged in this form,* the mode of intervention is campaign, and the worker will persuade, maneuver, negotiate, and perhaps exercise mild coercion.

We have emphasized that it is the *perception* of goal commonality or divergence that conditions the actor's responses and therefore the use of a particular tactic. One aspect of the point should be underscored. Our reference is to the perception of *both* parties, worker and target. If, for example, the worker defines a situation as a win-win game when it is perceived by the target as a win-lose, the choice of collaborative tactics is likely to be ineffective. Conversely, if the worker sees it as win-lose and engages in campaign or even contest interventions, he risks alienating a target actor who views the circumstance as a win-win and who might otherwise have gone along with the effort.

Since what binds organizations together are common interests and shared values, we suspect that there may be many more occasions in which the win-win game is operative than are ordinarily perceived by organizational participants. Difference is more emotionally charged and therefore more visible than agreement, and, further, short-range differences tend to becloud longer-range commonalities. Indeed, this is one of the implicit assumptions of the organizational development field. Inherent in its ideology is the notion that the overriding nature of a common purpose shared by all organizational participants must be recognized and acted on.[7] As a consequence, organizational development methodology emphasizes collaborative tactics—improving intergroup collaboration, opening communication systems, and the like.

The problem is that although its major objective is to "improve the organization's ability to achieve its mission goals," [8] organizational development underestimates the consequence of the fact that an organization's "mission goals" are more often than not the goals of *some* of its members, the most powerful ones, and that intergroup collaboration and an open communication system, however valuable they may sometimes be, are predicated on a universally shared perception of goal commonality. When the game is mixed or win-lose, the techniques of organizational development become less potent in effecting change.

As we have said, a win-win situation may be (and often is) perceived by one of the parties as win-lose. In such an instance, the outcome for *both* parties is likely to be less satisfactory than if it had been defined accurately as win-win by both. In short, both lose something in the misdefinition. However, when one party defines the situation as win-win, thus engaging in collaborative tactics, while the other actor perceives it as a mixed game, thus moving to campaign interventions, the advantage lies with the latter. He is, in effect, putting the more active influence attempt to work.

Most organization change attempts involve a wide variety of participants—some whose goals are congruent with the worker's and some whose interests are widely divergent. The game is thus ordinarily a mixed one, and the choice of tactics will therefore range along the continuum. Other factors than goal commonality or divergence also come into play.

RESOURCES FOR INFLUENCING

The resources for influence available to the worker and the possible sanctions that may be used against him—for example, the resources of

[7] Thus one leader in the organizational development field, citing the characteristics of effective organizations, suggests that one criterion is that there is a shared value, and management strategy to support it, of trying to help each person (or unit) in the organization maintain his (or its) integrity and uniqueness in an interdependent environment. Richard Beckhard, *Organizational Development* (Reading, Mass.: Addison-Wesley, 1969), p. 11.

[8] *Ibid.,* p. 15.

potential opposition—also play a considerable role in determining tactics. In other words, the choice of interventions must take into account the respective power of the worker and the target actor.

The point is obvious enough. Its implications may be overlooked, however, particularly in regard to the dialectic nature of any change attempt. In selecting a tactic, the worker must anticipate what response is possible or likely as he plans his course of action. He might consider, for example, whether his actions will arouse potentially strong opposition, whereas, if he acted differently, the opposition would remain dormant. Or he might consider the opposite tactic—acting in ways to provoke a self-defeating overreaction from opponents. In dynamic situations, retaliation is always possible, and he thus must take into account what counterresources target actors can bring to bear and be ready with alternate reactions if these resources are employed.

Collaborative tactics tend to be used not only when there is goal commonality but often when a mutually recognized parity in power exists. Problem solving, teamwork, and education lend themselves to situations in which neither party can work its will on the other without undue cost. At the other end of the continuum, contest tactics are employed when power relations between the parties meet one of two circumstances. The first is when their respective power positions are not clear to both of them. Conflict serves the function of testing the relative strength of contenders; it would be avoided as too costly if either party recognized the ascendancy of the other.[9] The second circumstance is when there is a major discrepancy in power between a weak contending actor and a strong target *and* the contender is beyond the reach of the target's retaliation. If the contender were perceived as being as rich in resources as the target, he would have less need to throw potent resources into the fray. In this instance, conflict tactics are used not so much to indicate strength as to generate further support (i.e., to increase the contender's resources). The rub for organizational practitioners, of course, is that they are not beyond the reach of retaliation of more potent target actors. And the risk to them is intensified by the fact that, since they are part of the system, their use of contest tactics is subject to high visibility. These factors explain why outsiders can challenge organizations with a purity of "principle" and militance which are ordinarily unavailable to the internal agent.

The resources available to middle- and low-ranking workers are ordinarily modest in comparison to those available to organizational decision makers. The practitioner who tries to influence critical or facilitating actors—those with more power than he—through collaborative tactics can do so only when there is perceived goal commonality *or* when he can

[9] Lewis Coser, *Functions of Social Conflict* (New York: Free Press, 1966), pp. 133–37.

count on the sufferance of the target actors. And, as we suggested earlier, were he to employ contest tactics because goal dissensus dictated such intervention, the cost to him and his effort would probably be prohibitive. Thus, when there is goal difference between the worker and a more powerful target actor, the worker cannot expect a collaborative response, and contest tactics are generally unavailable to him. The success of his attempt to provide internal change will then depend in some significant measure on his use of campaign tactics.

Resources influence the choice of intervention in other ways as well. Certain tactics either require or are enhanced by particular resources that may or may not be available to the practitioner. Problem solving, for example, will be most effective when skill in fact-finding or research is an integral part of the intervention. This suggests that such resources as expertise and access to information may be critical to success. On the other hand, one cannot use protest or demonstration tactics effectively without the resources of a sizable and organized constituency.

Sometimes the matter does not have to do with whether the practitioner has the appropriate resources available but with the consequences that employing one or another tactic will have on how he is perceived. For example, groups develop particular tactical styles because of the resources available to them, and then the style becomes fixed in the group's culture. But often more than culture is at issue. The group may need to maintain the style to protect the image it has developed (for example, probity in the case of professional agencies or militance in the case of cause-oriented organizations).

Individuals need to uphold an image too and will choose a particular tactic with that in mind. How the worker is perceived will greatly affect his ability to garner support. If he has successfully established his organizational position through the use of such resources as knowledge, the granting of favors, or social rewards, he will rely on these resources to advance whatever change goals he has in mind. On the other hand, if he has come to be defined as an organizational deviant—labeled "troublemaker," "radical," or the like—his causes become tainted unless he has powerful other resources to invest. For to be influential, the organizational deviant must have the resources to impose such influence. Organizational politics are such that a worker may choose this course. The shop steward of a strong union is an example. Even though he is in a low-power position within the formal authority structure, the steward does enjoy an institutional power base which secures his influence in matters he chooses to engage. The position institutionalizes an adversary relationship, however, and hence results in his being deprived of the information and influence available to those who are seen as "trustworthy." The pragmatic need to pay conscious attention to one's image will cause the practitioner to think carefully before he selects a tactic that will affect others' perceptions in such a way as to jeopardize their future support.[10]

RELATIONSHIPS

The practitioner's relationship with the target actor and others is another factor that influences the choice of tactic. The past experience of worker and target with one another is a significant dynamic. Having engaged in prior interaction, each party has expectations regarding the interests and behavior of the other.[11] The target actor's perception of the worker's current goal will be colored by their past interaction. If the interaction has been close, differences in points of view may be viewed as minimal, whereas if the relationship has been distant or unfriendly, even commonalities may be perceived with suspicion. The practitioner's understanding of this point importantly shapes the presentation of his ideas to those he hopes to influence.

On the other hand, the practitioner may make the mistake—on the basis of past close or distant relations—of presuming a reaction by the target actor that may not be accurate. The practitioner might, in this instance, perceive his goal as dissimilar to the target's when in fact it meets the latter's interests. Or he could react the other way around, assuming similarity because of past agreement when their objectives are really in conflict. As we have noted, these perceptions of goal consensus or dissensus are central determinants of the methods used to affect a working force.

Even were perceptions of their respective interests not to be so influenced, the relationship of the parties shapes tactic selection in other ways. In the case where there is goal difference but in which a close relationship also exists, the worker might select a cooperative stance with the target actor. Their friendly relations make campaign or contest interventions unacceptable, because the change issue is not so important as the character of the relationship. Furthermore, the cooperative stance may garner the actor's support because of the mutuality in the relationship with the worker, whereas a campaign intervention might be alienating.

[10] We do not mean to suggest that the perceptions of others are the primary factor that should influence tactic selection. Such a view would compromise the worker's personal and professional integrity. We mean only to indicate that image management, along with a host of other factors, has consequences for both the worker's future relationships and his change effectiveness.

[11] Deutsch notes that the number and strength of cooperative bonds (e.g., superordinate goals, mutually facilitating interests, common allegiances and values) enhance present cooperation while "experiences of failure and disillusionment in attempts to cooperate make it unlikely." Morton Deutsch, "Conflicts: Productive and Destructive," *Journal of Social Issues* 25, no. 1 (January 1969), p. 27.

A converse circumstance also occurs, although probably less frequently. That is, the relationship between worker and target may be so strained or competitive that one or the other has a greater stake in maintaining social distance than in coming together around a mutual interest. Whereas the worker would ordinarily engage the common interest cooperatively, in this instance he might judge that either overt or covert campaign tactics were called for.

Our final comment about the impact of relationship on tactic is to underscore the matter of the worker's image, to which we referred above. Any practice decision to influence a force must be weighed against its consequences to the worker's reputation within the organization—not only in regard to the target actor but to others important to him as well. There are occasions when a worker is unconcerned about how a particularly effective tactic might bear on his relations with the target. But if the action could impinge negatively on how his superordinates—or his friends—view him, the practitioner might choose to forego the immediate advantage of the tactic for their more positive definitions.

THE PRINCIPLE OF PARSIMONY

Tactic selection must take into account how the mildness or strength of a particular intervention influences the change process. The rules of theory building and the wisdom of practice share a common principle, the principle of parsimony. The social scientist who is attempting to develop an explanation for what appear to be patterns in collected data is advised to begin by testing the simplest notion he can think of to explain the assembled observations. If the hypothesis is proven inadequate, he progresses in degrees of elaboration until he finds the explanation that best fits the data. Similarly, the practitioner confronted with a problem who is in the process of selecting a tactic is advised to begin his deliberations with the most modest tactic that might conceivably do the job. If persuasion will work, for example, it is unsound to pursue the goal by mounting a coercive effort. Only when experience or cold judgment suggests that mild methods are inappropriate would a more extreme method be considered.

There are a number of practice reasons why this is so. Most simply, a more extreme intervention entails greater effort on the worker's part, and many change attempts founder on their energy expenditure and the worker's "running out of steam." Furthermore, the more extreme choice may lead others to suspect that the practitioner is not interested in the change so much as in satisfying his own psychological needs for dominance or rebellion against authority. Sometimes the extreme choice does reflect the search for psychic satisfaction. In psychologically oriented professions, however, there is a tendency to interpret political acts in psychological terms with insufficient discrimination. Indeed, in many nonpsychologically oriented organizations as well, there is a double standard, one for the worker promoting change and another for the worker who is more conforming. Practitioners who experience the phenomenon of being judged by a harsher set of criteria than is employed in regard to others are often surprised by the vehemence of some reactions to their activity. Selecting the lesser tactic before choosing a more extreme one will not prevent such reactions, but it is one way of minimizing them.

The principle of parsimony is most important when the practitioner requires third-party support for his change effort. He must appear reasonable and responsible to that party, or at least be able to present an effective public case to explain whatever "unreasonableness" is required. "Jumping the process"—that is, violating the protocol that prescribes that mild actions precede extreme ones—can endanger a good cause.

The Covert Component of Tactics

Covert activity can be part of all modes of intervention, although to varying degrees. It raises a number of significant issues and, as we noted earlier in Chapter 1 of this book, is a particular source of controversy among human service professionals. We believe that responsibility requires explication of the subject, however, since the place of covert behavior in tactical selection is neglected in the literature or addressed in obscure ways.

Covert behavior refers to the worker's attempt to influence target actors in an unobtrusive or disguised way. At the very least, it involves some arrangement of reality for effect (as in persuasion) or an incomplete representation of relevant information (e.g., omission and exaggeration). Covert behavior ranges along a continuum of concealment and selective representation, and at its outer extreme it entails outright fabrication. These are acts of different orders of morality, some more violative of sensibilities than others, but all are covert.

We wish to put aside moral considerations for a moment, however, in order to consider the part covert behavior would play in the practice of change were ethics not an issue. In such case, the use of unobtrusive or disguised activity would vary with such factors as goal commonality, resources, and relationships, discussed in the prior section. Figure 4 illustrates the matter graphically.

Although the chart is oversimplified for the sake of clarity, it summarizes our earlier arguments and reflects the essential relationships among the variables. Thus, collaborative tactics are effective when there is goal consensus, parity of power between the parties (or power is not at issue), relatively close relationships, and—for just these reasons—a minimum of covert activity. In the case of the institute practitioner, for example, interventions with the nurse who co-led the patient therapy group

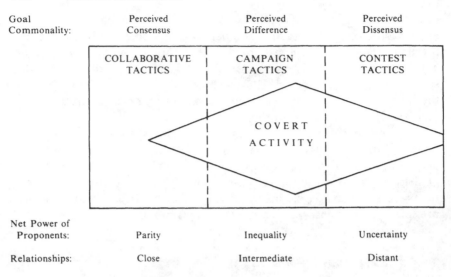

| Goal Commonality: | Perceived Consensus | Perceived Difference | Perceived Dissensus |

Figure 4. Factors Influencing the Selection of Tactics

were marked by collaboration. Like the worker, the co-leader felt that patients were insensitively treated, and the two planned together to move toward instituting community meetings and other ward activities. They not only shared common goals, but they also had equal say and status in their joint activity, and their relationship was close. Thus, all of the variables converged to determine collaborative tactics.

Campaign interventions, as we have said, grow out of goal differences, and there is ordinarily less trust between the parties than collaboration requires. Some degree of covert behavior is inherent in most campaign tactics, and as disparity in power between the actors rises, so too does the use of surreptitious methods.[12] In our institute example, the worker and staff nurses were engaged in a mixed game. Both held some goals in common, and the working force cited earlier in the chapter (to decrease routinization in the nurses' role so as to reduce their boredom) is a clear instance of this commonality. It thus called for collaborative tactics, which she followed. The worker's goal of conducting community meetings was not widely shared among the nurses, however, and in regard to this objective, the power of the nurses to endorse or veto the plan was paramount. Further, the worker's relationships with many of the nurses were best characterized as intermediate, neither close nor distant. Once again, the convergence of variables is clear, and campaign tactics represented an effective set of interventions. Thus, her work with the clients to request of

[12] Powerful proponents *may* exercise covert influence but do not *need* to in order to attain their objectives.

the nurses that community meetings be established was made to seem like an independent client action rather than one that she had helped them devise. (It should be noted that those nurses with whom she had a trusting relationship were taken into her confidence, as in the case of her co-leader.)

Contest tactics involve goal dissensus, social distance is ordinarily high, and the contestants flex their muscles either to build their own strength or to test their respective power positions. Because the conflict is intense, it tends to be public, and there is some mix of overt and covert behavior.

When the practitioner's goals are in agreement with those of critical actors and there is not significant opposition within the organization, collaborative tactics are effective and covert behavior is minimal. Such a circumstance, however, is rare. More often, workers who are committed to clients' rights and needs will engage problems that generate goal differences with influential others. However, it would be unusual indeed for an organization to support overt campaigns or contests waged by subordinates to alter the positions of senior organizational staff. In the institute example, the most potent working force was the disinterest of the medical director. The wide difference between his major concerns (research) and the worker's (humane treatment of patients), the gulf in their respective power positions, and the social distance between them all suggest the choice of contest tactics. And indeed the tactics mentioned earlier as possibilities (i.e., a protest statement to funding sources, organized pressure from patients and families, etc.) fall into the contest category. Although these are appropriate as a set of tactics, the institute worker would have had to have been willing to risk her job to engage in them.

Thus, even in the unlikely event that a lower-ranking practitioner had the resources to launch an effective campaign, his use of the resources would be inhibited by his reluctance to expose himself. We are led to conclude that success for the committed practitioner will depend, in some measure, on his use of tactics that incorporate a covert component.

Whatever moral judgments one might make, two elements of covert behavior are so widely practiced as to be hardly noticed. One has to do with influencing the perceptions of others toward oneself, the second with influencing perceptions about one's position. Goffman has argued that the basic underlying theme of all interaction is the desire of each participant to guide and control the response made by others present.[13] In practice terms, this suggests that the worker will attempt to influence the judgments that target actors make about him. On the basis of his understanding of the target actor's values and attitudes, the practitioner tries to effect a perception of commonality between himself and the other or an image of himself

[13] Erving Goffman, *The Presentation of Self in Everyday Life* (New York: Doubleday, Anchor Books, 1959), pp. 3–4.

as competent, committed, sharing, or whatever set of characteristics he judges will capture the target actor's respect.[14]

Positions are influenced covertly by the selective presentation of material to relevant actors. The worker's image is enhanced by highlighting those elements designed to appeal to the target actor and downplaying those elements that will not. He may attempt to influence the people with whom the target actor will or will not interact. Those favoring the change or with information to support it will be encouraged to communicate with the target actor while an attempt is made to challenge the credibility of those in opposition. In formal interaction, one volunteers information of a favorable nature and shares less positive components only on direct inquiry.[15] Similarly, the flow of written material is often selectively presented. If a worker is attempting to create a positive view of a particular project or effort, positive material is widely distributed and negative material is either screened or "sanitized" in such a way that its impact is lessened.

Although tactics such as withholding information, exaggerating, and distorting are seen as violations of the professional norm of openness, they are not of the same moral order as major misrepresentation or falsification, which we believe to be proscribed on ethical grounds. Nevertheless, one must ask whether or not violating even the norm of openness is beyond the bounds of respectable professional conduct. The answer, in our judgment is that these behaviors represent a course of action that is both ethically and professionally appropriate *under certain circumstances*.

Professional norms and standards of conduct presume universal adherence. When a profession assumes a commitment to serve the interests of its client group to the best of its ability, it is expected that this commitment will be followed by agency director and line worker alike. Yet organizations look different from the top than from the bottom, and it is often the case that the weight of institutional responsibility moderates idealism, replacing a concern for the interests of clients with a concern for the survival of the organization or the maintenance of one's position. When agency officials ignore the needs of clients or abuse the social purpose of the agency in deference to personal or organizational preoccupations, and when the worker has attempted more modest means of promoting change, the use of covert methods with such individuals in the interest of a neglected and powerless constituency is not only ethical but may be professionally prescribed.[16]

---

[14] We discuss "practitioner positioning" in more detail in Chapter 7.

[15] These points can be qualified in a number of ways but our interest here is illustrative rather than suggestive of effective intervention.

[16] We do not mean to imply that virtue, in our view, always rests with the worker. There are many instances when line staff are guilty of abuse of responsibility and client commitment as well, but this is not relevant to our present consideration.

We consider, then, the use of covert tactics appropriate when *all* of the following three conditions are present. (1) Agency officials are ignoring either the needs of clients or the mission of the agency in service of more parochial or personal interests. This condition has two related components and *both* must obtain for covert action to be acceptable. The first involves the neglect of constituent interests and the second involves preoccupation with personal interests. If the administrator is *only* neglectful, open discussion may be sufficient. If he is responsive to client interests and *in addition* attentive to personal concerns, covert methods cannot be justified since his primary professional responsibilities are being fulfilled. (2) The worker cannot tap legitimate sources of influence without seriously jeopardizing himself, his clients, or his colleagues. (3) Overt means have either been attempted and failed or experience suggests that they are not feasible. It is only, we judge, when those in seats of organizational power have abrogated the interests of their clients and staff that we would counsel their staff to exercise influence without the full awareness of or consultation with the powerful.

This position involves the danger that the lens through which the behavior of upper-ranking members is viewed may be distorted by lower-rank perspectives (i.e., the administrator may be acting on the basis of information available only to him, or the worker's reactions may stem more from personal acrimony than client commitment). Since the professionally legitimate bases for covert activity are adherence to professional norms of client primacy and the stated social purposes of the agency, the worker who makes the judgment by himself displays a self-assurance that may fall short of wisdom.

As we had suggested in Chapter 1, the worker's clients offer one way for him to test his views; that is, he proceeds on the basis of client perspectives and definitions of how the organizational problem impinges on them. Another means is the use of confidants. While there are reasons for caution in discussing one's plans, the practitioner is well advised to share his deliberations with trusted colleagues before launching a covert campaign. To the extent that these colleagues fill different roles and functions within the organization the worker's perspective will be broadened, but in any case, consultation provides him with the added assurance that respected others share his view and will support his actions.

Tactical effectiveness is also an issue in covert campaigns since workers who engage in such behavior risk being perceived by the target actor as harboring hidden agendas or as being "untrustworthy"—and what is worse, may seriously weaken their credibility through the organization. It is therefore critical from a pragmatic (as well as ethical) point of view that the practitioner not treat those with whom he has close personal relations as targets of covert influence attempts. Further, our earlier injunction that covert behavior is justified only when other means of influence are unavailable has its pragmatic side as well. The principle of parsimony applies particularly here. The frequency and extent of covert behavior must be limited to the necessary minimum. The worker who has followed these principles may, finally, handle covert behavior in a sufficiently obscure and graceful way so that the "benefit of the doubt" would cause most to suspend negative judgment.

Worker Costs and Benefits

We have made passing reference in this chapter to some of the potential consequences to the practitioner in choosing one or another tactic. It is important to consider the issue centrally, however, since our intent in this volume is to help practitioners to innovate in the clients' interest *and* to survive within an organization as well. To take the point a step further, our concern is not only with the practitioners' survival but also with their long-range effectiveness as change agents within human services agencies. This requires that the choice of tactic take into account the costs and benefits to the worker himself.

Earlier we indicated that self-interest was a powerful determinant of the meanings ascribed by actors to organizational events. Although it may be comforting to suggest that such a motivation affects others more than ourselves, self-congratulation is hardly in order. Thus, we do not exempt the change-oriented practitioner from attention to his own interests any more than we would other organizational participants. The goal the worker has chosen and the means he uses to pursue it (i.e., his tactics) are undoubtedly predicated on how both impinge on his organizational role and function.

We hope that the worker who puts the practice principles developed in this volume to use will do so to meet client needs. However, we recognize that, like any set of techniques, these principles can be misused—put to the service of worker self-protection or aggrandizement more than to client benefit. Although worker and client interests are often similar, their interests also frequently diverge. When they do, we believe it is important to face the issue squarely. There is greater comfort in trying to rationalize differences such as these away, but we believe that workers who recognize them are more likely to act in a professionally ethical manner than those who do not. In other words, the social-work emphasis on worker self-awareness as important to sound and ethical practice is a principle we subscribe to, but we believe that it needs to be extended from an understanding of individual dynamics to an awareness of the impact on the worker of his organizational role and function and how role and function affect his interests, sometimes to the clients' benefit and other times to their detriment. For only when he cannot easily rationalize this influence on his behavior can he be open to making the client-oriented choice.

The worker who has analyzed the field of forces relative to his change goal, defined his working forces, and decided that the change is feasible also intuitively measures whether the tactics necessary to impact the working forces will be more costly to him than the attempt is worth. If the cost seems too high, he will tacitly drop the idea, however desirable or feasible he deems the change. The task, of course, is to measure those costs accurately and without too great timidity, testing the process as he engages in it while leaving open the option to advance or retreat as circumstances require.

The potential costs to practitioners as they make tactical choices are numerous, and we cite only the most significant. In campaign or contest interventions, as we have already suggested, practitioners who are perceived as overly questioning of their superordinates will enjoy little support from those in positions of formal authority; what is worse, they may be defined as brash, troublemakers, or "unprofessional." Furthermore, if they "lose" too often, they suffer a loss in reputation for influence—a highly valuable currency in the long range.

Another potential cost, even in collaborative ventures, is that the worker may put himself in another's debt as he seeks support. As Pressman and Wildavsky have pointed out, "each concession [that a colleague makes to a worker] represents a favor that may have to be returned, a claim on future resources. Following routine procedures is just doing your job; acting outside its boundaries means doing a favor." [17]

Finally, whatever the tactical choice, the worker takes the chance of feeling the personal rejection inherent in any rejection of one's ideas. Moreover, when the worker's notions are called into question with any frequency (and innovative ideas are especially likely to be subject to challenge), his practice acumen may be put in doubt as well. Thus, what the practitioner chooses to do in relation to any current change effort has relevance to what he has tried to do before and what he may do in the future.

Not only are change efforts difficult, uncertain, and requiring of a high investment in terms of time and energy, but the practitioner, in sum, takes the chance that he will be viewed as a troublemaker, ineffectual, or inadequate. In this light, one may well question how the fact of planned organizational change can be explained at all. Obviously, there are benefits too, and we believe these transcend even the worker's commitment to the content of the change.

Problem solving as a tactical intervention involves little risk and offers some significant payoffs. The conforming worker may be appreciated in

[17] Jeffrey L. Pressman and Aaron B. Wildavsky, *Implementation* (Berkeley: University of California Press, 1973), p. 130.

some settings, but in a large number of others, he will be viewed as overly passive or professionally pedestrian. Workers who generate innovative ideas, on the other hand, are often seen as creative, even when their ideas are rejected. Furthermore, when the practitioner's ideas are viewed as consonant with the organization's values (as in collaborative and success- ful campaign tactics such as persuasion and political maneuvering), his attempts to innovate reflect a commitment to the organization and its values which is likely to be recognized. Pressing for change also provides a means by which workers caught in the role conflict between their sense of responsibility to their clients and their position as agency employees can find a way out of the bind.[18]

If there is a cost to the worker in the way he is viewed by superor- dinates when he is "overly questioning," there may also be a cost if he is not questioning enough. Put positively, the worker who acts with vigor projects an image of himself as "committed," "principled," or "coura- geous." Even in defeat, he garners respect if he has pursued his goal with political acumen. The benefits of an image of principled behavior are significant in regard to both superordinates and other professional asso- ciates. That this fact is recognized is suggested by research indicating that client orientation as a determinant of decision making is increased for practitioners whose reference groups are other social workers.[19] Acting on principle or a show of courage may also stem from a worker's concern regarding his relations with his clients—or it may be a matter of the practitioner's own self-esteem. Seeking change in client interests, even at some cost or risk, is a professional responsibility, and acting on this responsibility is a source of professional gratification.

The worker in pursuit of change who is faced with goal differences be- tween himself and a target actor often has to choose between revising his goal downward to obtain the other's support or increasing his own influ- ence through campaign or contest interventions. The former constitutes a satisfactory accommodation to the realities of change practice, but if, over time and in the aggregate, it is the worker's only available accom- modation, it may breed discomfiting pessimism or apathy. Vigorous change activity has the benefit, then, of diminishing alienation and the sense of professional powerlessness. Finally, collective confrontation, as in some campaign and all contest interventions, depends in great measure on building trust and mutual support within the collectivity. The esprit de corps that is generated by these factors, along with the sharing of a common "enemy," is a further reward for the change-oriented practitioner.

[18] We noted in Chapter 1 that an excellent discussion of this role conflict is developed by Naomi Gottlieb, *The Welfare Bind* (New York: Columbia University Press, 1974).

[19] Irwin Epstein, "Organizational Careers, Professionalization, and Social Worker Radicalism," *Social Service Review* 44, no. 2 (June 1970), pp. 123–31.

The Role of Clients

The innovations with which this book is concerned are client-related, and there is perhaps no issue more significant than that of the role of clients in seeking a change. There are both ideological and tactical aspects to the question, and we identify some of them in concluding this chapter.

We start with the value assumption that, whenever possible, clients should be the partners of the practitioner in a change attempt. At the least, they have a critical contribution to make in defining a problem since the problem impinges on them, and, as we have already suggested, their perspectives provide an important element of worker accountability. At the most, they should be equally involved in the change process itself.

The practice of the institute worker and her co-leader offers an example of sensitive work in this regard:

> At the start, the patient group was withdrawn and interacted minimally with each other. I focused on the tentative alliances and friendships among them, and tried to heighten these by pointing out how they sought each other out in an extremely limited way, thus remaining unnecessarily isolated and lonely. Much negativism and denial remained, but my co-worker and I repeatedly indicated our disbelief that they could accept their biochemical illness as an overall statement of their lack of interest in getting to know one another better. My co-worker and I began to talk more to each other in the group about the difficulties of group situations and our fears of rejection in sharing parts of ourselves with other people who had the potential of hurting us. The group began to express interest. We challenged them, and used humor to mobilize them. Eventually, rapport was established.
>
> During this time we suggested that they might feel distrustful of us since we were staff, and increasingly began to focus on the ward policies they felt were oppressive, as well as their fears of staff members. They began to vent their feelings, and ultimately we confronted them with their compliance in relation to inconsiderate and inhumane treatment. We encouraged the most outspoken group member to voice his concerns about mistreatment by staff, giving sanction to complaints and asking for their ideas about ways to intervene.
>
> We mentioned the experience of some hospitals with community meetings of staff and patients, and encouraged a member to speak about such an experience he had had at another hospital and the difference in staff/patient interaction which resulted. Several times we emphasized content which engendered anger at the indignity of their treatment in the unit or by particular staff, helping members to recall from one meeting to the other the injustices they felt. We suggested that they raise these grievances and ask for community meetings to foster communication between themselves and staff, and pointed out that we would be present and support their ideas. They were fearful about bringing anything up, and we role-played how they could raise their concerns without increasing the aliena-

tion of staff members. The patients agreed on a spokesman and planned to ask for a community meeting. I said that I would be present, would back them up, clarify what was not understood, and if necessary, I would run the meeting in the event that matters did not proceed smoothly.[20]

Three aspects of the process are worth noting. First, it was possible to activate persons as severely damaged as those in the institute's metabolic unit. Secondly, the workers were personally sharing, directive, and encouraging of anger—and although they were skillful, considerable time was necessary before the patients were ready to deal with their grievances and propose a meeting. Third, the workers did not avoid responsibility themselves. They indicated their intention both to protect the clients (thus reducing the risk to them) and to advance their cause (thus increasing their clients' optimism and sense of strength). The point is an important one, for some workers may encourage client action under the guise of its psychological usefulness to the clients, when in fact it serves to shield the workers themselves from incurring difficulties. It is, of course, untoward to suggest that clients risk themselves when workers are not prepared to make a comparable investment.

Some workers hold the professional dictum that it is obligatory to interpret agency policies faithfully to clients and to avoid supporting client criticism of other staff. It precludes clients from becoming confused, they say, protects them from being "used" in the service of worker interests, and is important to maintaining professional solidarity. Although this principle is rationalized as being in the clients' interests, one consequence is to close agency ranks against the client. And indeed it is true that practitioners who form coalitions with clients risk the fury that is reserved for renegades.

Although there are pragmatic limitations to worker-client coalitions, to which we refer subsequently, neither professionalism nor morality precludes coalitions with clients. The reverse is true in our view, for the touchstone of professionalism is whether the worker is acting in his clients' interests rather than his own. In the matter of client-worker coalitions, we believe that the fear of unprofessionalism is the straw man of straw bosses.[21]

Most social workers will have little difficulty with the example of the institute worker's "use" of clients to advance her change goal because her interventions served the therapeutic needs of the patients, along with the advancement of the change effort. Meeting the psychological needs of clients and satisfying the requirements of a change process often go together, but it is not inevitable that they occur in tandem. When they do not, the worker has to make the choice of emphasizing the change over the

[20] Rubenstein, op. cit., pp. 7–8.

[21] These ideas are developed further in a different context in Brager and Specht, op. cit., pp. 246–47.

treatment plan, or the reverse. And sometimes he has to move on one to the exclusion of the other.

There are a number of criteria for making such a decision. One has to do with the primary source of the problem. If the issue is deeply rooted in agency malfunctioning, it is unfair to require that those on whom it impinges negatively carry the burden of righting the wrong. For example, a client was erroneously declared incompetent by a mental hospital. To focus on his learning through his participation in reversing the decision is to get one's priorities askew. The onus for the error—and therefore for its reversal—belongs with agency staff. Another criterion is the client's coping capacity, his ability to deal with the problem. This is particularly relevant when action on the goal, to be effective, must be immediate, since, as we have seen, time is required to develop client readiness. The client's vulnerability to retaliation by the organization is another factor to be considered. Furthermore, clients should have the option of participating or not. In our example of the patient who was unjustly declared incompetent, the decision to advocate on his own behalf, however therapeutic, may represent a strain, and he should have the choice of bearing or avoiding it. If his input is important to achieving the goal, this can be explained to him, but the final decision should be his.

A major aspect of client participation in the change process has to do with the tactical effectiveness of such participation. In some cases, it is effective for agency actors to have to face the raw upset of clients rather than having the latters' feelings filtered through the worker's one-step-removed recital. An organized, cohesive, and angry group of clients also may provide a significant resource for influencing the process positively.

But there are risks as well. As noted, a worker-client coalition encourages perception of the worker as a renegade and may reduce his ability to obtain current objectives or reduce his future effectiveness. In collaborative and campaign interventions, client participation may be tactically disadvantageous as too threatening, incurring an unnecessarily adversarial response from agency actors which endangers goal achievement. When the active participation of clients in a change effort is too challenging to the hegemony of critical actors, it "ups the ante," increasing the stakes of all parties. Unless such a challenge is necessary to win the change, it is best avoided. In such cases, less controversial forms of client input (e.g., their attendance at exploratory meetings, a survey of their attitudes about the problem and goal, etc.) may be acceptable and should be explored.

To summarize, we have suggested the range of tactics available to workers to increase or decrease working forces and have indicated some of the variables—goal commonality, resources for influencing, relationships, and parsimony—which determine their selection. Because of its controversial nature, particular attention was paid to the use of covert tactics. We concluded the chapter with two additional considerations of initial assessment: the costs and benefits to the worker and the role of clients in a change attempt.

One caution is in order before we move to an exploration of the subsequent phases of the change process. In exploring the specifics of tactic selection, we have necessarily presented a fragmented and partial view of change practice. It should be understood, however, that we view organizational change as a process that, once begun, has an integrity and momentum beyond specific tactical behaviors. For one thing, the *content* of the change—its theoretical and value underpinnings, its goal characteristics, and programmatic details—determine its nature at least as much as the tactical efforts of the practitioner and his allies. In addition, the change process has an intrinsic momentum that ultimately transcends tactics. At some point, the operations begun by the worker and his colleagues develop a pace that becomes almost self-propelling. Thus, as we turn in the following chapters to an exploration of the methodological aspects of organizational change, it is important to keep these two characteristics of change-as-process in mind: the importance of the substance of the change and the phenomenon of its semi-independent momentum.

Part III
THE CHANGE PROCESS

The process of planned organizational change can be thought of as including four action phases: preinitiation, initiation, implementation, and institutionalization. In each, there is a function or set of tasks that must be accomplished if the process is to move on to the next phase. When these tasks are not completed, the process runs down. Viewing the phases in terms of their intrinsic functions and the tasks that must be accomplished before the next phase can begin provides the practitioner with an agenda or approximate guide to issues in practice as the change process unfolds. We devote Part III to an exploration of the tasks, practice concerns, and tactics relevant to each of the four phases.

Preinitiation begins as the worker takes his first act to impact one or a number of working forces. Here, as in all social processes, one phase overlaps another, and the activities of initial assessment continue as preinitiation tasks commence. The function of preinitiation is to set the stage for the introduction of the change—that is, to create a climate of organizational receptivity. One major task is for the practitioner to enhance his own position in the organization for promoting the change. Another is to heighten the participants' awareness of and dissatisfaction with problems related to the change goal. The intent here is to induce stress with regard to the organization's current state so that when the change idea is introduced it will be welcomed as a resolution of what participants have come to experience as an increasingly vexing problem (Chapter 7).

Initiation begins when the change idea is formally introduced into the organization following a judgment by the worker that he and the system are "ready" for it. The major function of this phase is to ensure the favorable introduction, diffusion, and ultimate approval of the goal. Initiation is completed with some form of organizational commitment to the idea (or its rejection).

The critical task of the initiation phase is to bring the change goal into conformity with the influence necessary to move its adoption. Essentially, this entails winning over critical actors through the skillful conversion of resources into active influence. To achieve this, coalitions are organized, and an attempt is made to win over or neutralize opposition. The worker is involved in a series of significant decisions—to which audience the proposal ought to be addressed and in what sequence, who might most effectively introduce and advocate the idea, what kind of appeal might be most convincing to significant participants, and through what channels or forums the proposal should be transmitted.

The initiation phase is the most critical of the four subprocesses. The practitioner finds himself in the precarious circumstance of unfolding the idea—thus clearly reducing his flexibility—and for the first time actually observing its impact on significant actors. This provides information heretofore available only imprecisely. Having access to important new data which might suggest modifications in the change idea while at the same time being required to function in a field where the opportunity to alter strategy is diminishing pose a characteristic dilemma of this phase (Chapter 8).

Implementation follows the organization's adoption of the change idea. The idea must now be moved beyond its formal acceptance to actions geared to actualizing it. Here, the process typically develops a momentum beyond the direct control of the practitioner. As the change idea confronts reality, a set of unanticipated problems is likely to emerge. In moving from a general agreement to specific actions, prior understandings often break down, and the implementation process itself permits opponents who wish to sabotage the effort to do so. Increasingly, other participants are involved in ways and degrees that transcend the worker's orchestration. Holding onto the tail of this tiger is, then, a major practice concern during this phase. Maintaining the commitment of critical and facilitating actors as implementation goes forward is an important practice task. Another is to gain and hold the support of those charged with bringing the change into being and to ensure that they know what is required of them.

Institutionalization is that phase of the process when the change is "anchored" in the system so that it becomes an ongoing component of organizational life. Until this task is completed, the change has not been successfully achieved. One reason change is so difficult to accomplish is that the change proponent must "win" at each of the four action phases, whereas the defenders of the status quo need only to block the attempt at any one of them.

In assuring the permanence of his goal, the worker's task is, first, to evaluate its current status, since the change can now be fully observed in practice. Assuming a positive appraisal, his final effort requires linking the change to other ongoing organizational elements and standardizing it. The tactics and tasks of both implementation and institutionalization are discussed in the book's final chapter. With their successful accomplishment, the change process is complete.

7. Preparing the Organization for Change

IT IS IN THE PREINITIATION STAGE of the change process that the practitioner prepares the system for the introduction of his proposal. This is the most frequently overlooked aspect of change practice. Once a problem and an appropriate solution have been identified, there is a temptation to share the "bright idea" with one's colleagues and suggest that it be adopted at the next supervisory conference or staff meeting. Occasionally, if the change is modest and the system predisposed to the proposal, this kind of single-step process is sufficient. But rarely does a change occur with such ease. Typically, the field of forces impinging on the change goal is complex, and the receptivity of critical actors to the proposal cannot be counted on so readily.

Decision makers must *perceive* a problem before they will consider its solution.[1] Their awareness is dependent not on the substance of the problem alone but on the tension it generates within the organization. Decision makers evaluate the costs and benefits of proposals within the context of their organization's structure and ideology. In some measure, therefore, whether a solution will be acted on (and sometimes even whether a problem is perceived as one) depends on where in the organization's structure the problem is located and which individual or group seeks to solve it.

In Chapter 5, we suggested that change occurs as a result of an increase or decrease in forces impinging on a particular aspect of the organization. We noted how this alteration in forces accompanies an increase in system tension or stress, ultimately causing a shift in equilibrium which constitutes the desired change. In the preinitiation phase, the worker begins to alter the forces bearing on various actors so as to heighten their receptivity to the change idea, by increasing their awareness of the problem and their dissatisfaction with the status quo.

---

[1] This is probably not quite precise. There is a question, for example, of whether innovations develop as a response to a problem or whether the awareness of an innovation generates its own need. Undoubtedly, both occur. See Gerald Zaltman et al., *Innovations in Organizations* (New York: Wiley, 1973), pp. 62–63.

The worker's first task is to accumulate personal resources. According to Loomis, persons planning to initiate a change must develop "social capital"; that is, build their reputation and influence in the social system they intend to change.[2] They must, further, induce or increase system stress related to the change problem in order to increase the likelihood that critical actors will be receptive to a solution. Finally, as they move toward formally introducing their change goal within the organization, they must locate or create aspects of the agency's structure that are most likely to "hear" the problem sympathetically and to act on its solution positively. In the following sections of this chapter, we discuss each of these components of preinitiation in turn.

Practitioner Positioning: Maximizing Resources for Influencing

Practitioner positioning refers to the task of developing a "place" or reputation in the organization in order to increase the likelihood that one's subsequent change proposal will receive positive attention. Positioning often entails a long- rather than short-term effort; how the practitioner is perceived cannot be fashioned in the moment but is the consequence of interactions over time. The worker who has been inattentive to the concerns of colleagues can hardly expect that sudden attentiveness (because he wants something) will now exact the desired dividends. Positioning is thus an ongoing process, a concern of the practitioner long before he has a specific change idea in mind.

The socially desirable way of conceptualizing the task is to suggest that the practitioner must be sensitive to the needs of those in complementary relationships with him. The responsive practitioner, one who "tunes into" the feelings of his colleagues, who listens, hears, and empathizes, is more likely to elicit responsiveness in turn—in other words, to have more ability to influence them. Similarly, the ideas of workers who perform their jobs competently and with loyalty will receive more sympathetic attention from decision makers than the ideas of those who do not.

Another way of conceptualizing the task is to view the practitioner as increasing his resources for influencing or converting them for use. The worker who seeks to enhance his attractiveness to others, dispenses social rewards such as recognition and approval, or highlights shared values in interaction with others may be said to be trading appeal, social rewards, and shared values in return for the others' thinking, feeling, or acting as he might wish—in other words, converting potential resources for influencing

[2] C. P. Loomis, "Tentative Types of Directed Social Change Involving Systematic Linkage," *Rural Sociology* 24, no. 4 (December 1959).

to use. Similarly, the subordinate who demonstrates special ability or contributes more than his fair share of work expects to gain prestige, credibility with higher-ups, or other responses that are translatable into influence in return. But however one chooses to conceptualize this behavior, whether as sensitivity to the needs of role partners or as converting resources for influencing to use, it is common to much interaction and frequently escapes our conscious awareness. To the extent that a practitioner expects actor response to be affected by the uniqueness of his contribution or status, whether conscious of the process or otherwise, he is engaging in positioning.

Practitioner positioning in preinitiation may take place through increasing one's general prestige and attractiveness within the organization. A second way is to increase one's network of contacts or political debtors, particularly those relevant to the change goal. A third means is to establish one's reputation or legitimacy relative to the area of the proposed change.

Workers may attempt to increase their general prestige and attractiveness by influencing the private assumptions of others through social interaction. The impressions people form and the information on which their choices are based come, in part, from implicit assumptions they make through their observation of others. To the extent that the worker is cognizant of this process, he puts it to use in exercising influence.

Which others people allow to influence them and to what degree vary with circumstance and from individual to individual, but some generalizations about criteria can be made. The criteria include one's perceptions of the influencer's motives, the extent to which he is seen as trustworthy and respected, whether he is viewed as concerned for one's welfare, and the extent to which he shares one's interests and goals. Not only are these criteria virtually universal, but it is usually true that these judgments are assumptions based on observed behavior.

The worker familiar with these criteria is in a position to act in ways that influence private judgments. Knowing what garners another's trust or respect, the worker behaves in ways to enhance this reaction. Similarly, understanding that people are more influenced by those who are positively disposed toward them, the worker acts in ways that are appreciative of the other. Of particular importance is the issue of motivation. One is more disposed to be influenced by others if their motives are judged to be "altruistic" rather than "self-interested," and the worker's altruism is thus made evident. Of equal significance is goal commonality. Here, the worker emphasizes through conversation and deed the goals that he shares with those he is trying to impress.

Conscious efforts to affect the private assumptions of others are fraught with difficulty, however. Beyond ethical objections, unless the worker's words or deeds are real, they may be unconvincing and his credibility put at risk. Furthermore, although social approval (a smile, a compliment, an indication of agreement) acts as a social reward and reinforces positive affect toward the donor as well as the response that called it forth, it is behavior that is subject to a law of diminishing returns. Approval from a person who is always ready with approbation is less valuable—in part because less believable—than approval from someone whose support is more frugally and thoughtfully granted.[3] More importantly, if the worker has been unconcerned about the impression he has made on the other in the past, his newfound concern may arouse the suspicion that he has a hidden agenda. In such a case, the worker's reputation for guile may be enhanced more than his appeal.

As one begins to increase his network of contacts or political debtors, he begins to focus more sharply on participants related to his problem area. An important element in this regard is to establish linkages with critical actors or facilitators and others who ultimately might have an impact on his goal. In some cases, a political debt is not at issue in establishing these linkages. The work may simply be to know and be known by critical and facilitating actors. Knowing one's audience is important prior to initiating communication regarding the problem area or goal, since the information thus gained can be significant in designing later communications for clarity of meaning or intended impact. And being known may in the future serve to open otherwise closed doors.

The currency of a political debt is, of course, the sharing of favors. Sometimes the favor is simply proffered, as in the case of the Charter House worker whose change goal is discussed at length in Chapter 5. As she assessed the positions and power of agency staff, she fixed on her immediate supervisor, the director of social services, and the director of program development as potentially important links and accessible sources of support. She writes:

> I provided back-up assistance to my supervisor in her work with clients when she took time off, and in part my commitment and personal energy redounded to her credit (I came in on vacation to attend a psychiatric seminar and worked long after hours with an acting-out adolescent). With the Director of Social Services, I offered my help in giving child-care staff training sessions, supported his points at social work meetings, and made a special effort to be well-prepared and informed at the case conferences he attended. With the Director of Program Development, I simply became friends.[4]

Since the discharge policy she hoped to introduce would reduce the decision-making prerogatives of houseparents and other child-care staff who maintained close relations with top administrators, the child-care staff

[3] George Brager and Harry Specht, *Community Organizing* (New York: Columbia University Press, 1973), p. 119.

[4] Gay Fiore Shoup, "A Change at Charter House," Columbia University School of Social Work, 1976, unpublished case record.

was a potential source of significant opposition. In an attempt to neutralize resistance or even win them over, she supported their concerns at staff meetings.

> I especially supported their dissatisfactions about the amount of work they did and the lack of time they had. I did this so that when the new discharge policy was introduced, it might be interpreted as relieving them of distasteful bureaucratic duties rather than as reducing their influence within the agency.

When a favor is requested, its political utility increases. A requested favor in contrast to one which is proffered more clearly establishes an obligation of reciprocity. When favors are solicited, the practitioner can suggest their importance, although this must be done gracefully, without actually seeming to do so. One may also make a favor seem more significant than it is. An effective technique, if done credibly, is to indicate that it may be difficult to deliver on the request, thereby implying increased effort on the grantee's part.

The third form of practitioner positioning involves establishing one's legitimacy to deal with a particular problem area. When the potential innovation falls clearly within the practitioner's function or jurisdiction, his legitimacy is clear. But this may be as much the exception as the rule. In such an instance, he must create the image or reality that the problem area falls properly within his domain. One method is to attempt to enlarge one's function or jurisdiction, sometimes imperceptibly by incremental degrees. So, for example, the director of social services in an expanding medical setting hypothesized that home care was likely to become an important hospital service in three years or so. In her interest in encouraging the process and including home care under the aegis of the social service department, she began to deploy her staff to deal with home and community matters.

Another method of gaining legitimacy to influence a particular content area is to accrue knowledge and expertise in the subject matter. When practitioners are perceived as expert in a particular subject, there is a tendency for them to be called on by other staff for information and assistance. They thus become a resource to others and increase their influence in the particular area.

An example is provided by the mental health worker at the Monrad Community Mental Health Center discussed in an earlier chapter, whose goal was to develop a day hospital within the agency. He describes his participation at the community meetings held by the Department of Hospitalization Services which were attended by the hospital's inpatients, the day patients, and clinical staff.

> During the community meeting, there were several issues raised which dealt with the use of leisure time at home, attempts at job hunting, and transportation problems, all variables affecting only the ten day patients at the

meeting. I pointed out that this group of patients seemed to have several problems which are very similar to one another, and volunteered to get together with them after the meeting to continue talking if they wished.

This informal group continued after every community meeting as the day patients talked to me about the problems they were having. The meetings helped the day patients to form a mutually supportive identity on the unit, and also heightened my awareness of critical issues which these clients faced.

The next step involved sharing the information obtained above at Treatment Planning Conferences. As a result of my close contacts with the day patients, I was able to make a point of reporting the progress and difficulties facing patients who fell into this group. Staff began to look at me when some information about day patients was required, and even Dr. N., the head of Hospitalization Services [a critical actor], started to seek out my advice when the treatment plan for a day patient was being discussed.[5]

The Inducement and Management of Stress

It is essential for the practitioner to appreciate the relationship of stress to change, since change is unlikely to occur unless discomforting tension accompanies the status quo. Unfortunately for change efforts, social workers often perceive their function to be stress reduction. Although this may be an appropriate objective for some situations, it is counterproductive if the overriding goal is organizational change and the reduction of stress does not advance the goal. A case in point is the director of social services who attempted, through a series of team-building meetings, to reduce antagonisms between the social workers who staffed an outpatient psychiatric clinic and the nurses who administered it. Yet, the hospital was considering—and the director was encouraging—a transfer of the clinic's administration from the nursing to the social work department. Her tension-relieving effort, had it been successful, would have eliminated one source of pressure for the change.

Although stress is a necessary condition for successful innovation, it does not necessarily facilitate change and may act to inhibit it. Much depends on the relationship between the content of the change and the basis of the tension. Organizational stress ranges from the particularistic to the general. Particularistic stress is focused and centers around a circumscribed problem. An example is the dissatisfaction within a residential treatment center over its recidivism rate, ascribed by many to the agency's lack of an after-care program. A practitioner whose change proposal entailed the restructuring of services to devote time to clients in their own

---

[5] Alan Boyer, "A Change at the Monrad Center," unpublished paper, 1977.

communities would, under these circumstances, have the advantage of tensions already formed in his area of interest. A practitioner wishing to increase in-house treatment resources, on the other hand, would find this particularistic tension a restraining force.

The complexity of organizational life suggests that some particularistic stresses may have contradictory effects. The recidivism rate related to inadequate aftercare may be the source of tension for one group of actors, but the organizational function that the "problem" serves might make it a source of satisfaction for others. For example, when the high recidivism rate ensures that there are a sufficient number of client-customers, the problem may not be perceived as tension-producing by the agency administration. When contradictory stresses exist, the intensity with which they are felt and, most importantly, by whom, determines the use the practitioner can make of the tension and guide his intervention.

At the other polar point of the continuum is stress that is diffuse, touching a number of organizational sectors, but difficult to pinpoint and isolate. Generalized tension such as "poor morale" is an example. At Charter House, the worker found stress of this kind: unhappiness with the inconsistencies and uncertainties of top managers, the clinical staff chafing at "unprofessional" policies, the nonclinicians criticizing the "coldness" of the social workers, the child-care staff dissatisfied with wages and working conditions—all of these combined to form a state of diffuse but pervasive malaise. Generalized stress such as this can breed apathy. The tension may be too pervasive or too diffuse to encourage change behavior. Or it can, on the other hand, galvanize action, particularly if it provides the basis for the formation of alliances among numerous organizational sectors.

Thus, like other aspects of preinitiation strategy, the specifics of stress inducement are dictated by the nature of the working forces that comprise the change field. Two practice questions must then be considered. One has to do with the kinds of stresses that accompany the increase or decrease of various working forces. Sometimes the stress will have to be "created," shaped from the latent dissatisfactions to which all complex systems are subject. Sometimes the worker may need to focus generalized discontent on his own area of concern. Under other circumstances it may be necessary to magnify existent tensions that are relevant to the desired change. A second practice question relates to the ways in which stress may be induced, focused, and magnified to increase or decrease particular working forces in a prochange direction.

Our attention in this section is on heightening the awareness of problems among relevant organizational members as a major technique for stress inducement and management. Its importance stems from the fact that ignorance of problems maintains organizational equilibrium by permitting satisfaction with the way things are.

Organizations typically develop "defense systems" to avoid recognizing or acknowledging organizational problems and the tensions they generate. One might call this the "no news is good news" syndrome. For top administrators, problems that are not brought to their attention do not exist, and therefore the agency appears to be functioning effectively. Those problems about which an administrator feels he can do little, for which the price of a solution seems more costly to him than living with the problem, are most likely to be avoided. One accommodation is not to know or, if knowing, not to appreciate the full dimension of the issue.

The incentive to maintain silence is at least as great for subordinates. The onus for bearing bad news commonly falls on the messenger, and staff who bring problems to administrators court the danger of appearing to be unable to handle them or, even worse, responsible for their existence. The fact that the danger is a real one is supported by a study of fifty-two middle managers which found a high correlation (+.41) between upward work-life mobility and holding back "problem" information from the boss.[6] Empirical data on organizations consistently show that good news travels up the hierarchy more than bad news and that all news takes on a rosier hue as it reaches the organization's upper levels.[7] To make inroads into this organized "conspiracy of ignorance" is critical to setting the stage for the introduction of a change idea.

The essential element in inducing stress through problem awareness involves introducing dissonant information—that is, information that reveals the inconsistencies between how the organization actually functions (the "conspiracy of ignorance") and how the participants believe it runs or how they would like it to run. Festinger's theory of "cognitive dissonance" suggests that people will strive to reduce this inconsistency in three ways: by avoiding or minimizing the importance of the dissonant information or the bearer of it, by acquiring new information to buttress existing consonance, and by changing those attitudes and behavior involved in the dissonance.[8] To achieve the last, of course, is the purpose of pressing inconsistent data on organizational actors. As workers introduce these data, however, they must be aware of the other ways people avoid dissonance. Out of such awareness, they will attempt to prevent any downgrading of the significance of the data or of the practitioner himself. In part, this is achieved by the way material is defined and presented, who does the presenting, and with what sensitivity to the audience—matters discussed in Chapter 8.

[6] Harold Wilensky, *Organizational Intelligence* (New York: Basic Books, 1967), p. 43.

[7] For two other examples, see Leon Festinger, "Informal Social Communication," *Psychological Review* 57 (1950), pp. 271–82, and David Katz and Robert L. Kahn, *The Social Psychology of Organizations* (New York: Wiley, 1966).

[8] Leon Festinger, Henry W. Riecken, and Stanley Schacter, "When Prophecy Fails," in Eleanor E. Maccoby, Theodore M. Newcomb, and Eugene L. Hartley, eds., *Readings in Social Psychology,* 3rd ed. (New York: Henry Holt, 1958), p. 158.

In bearing bad tidings, the practitioner must understand the risk and undertake the task with sensitivity. Thus, as he is making issues visible, he must try to avoid seeming to be dissident. This requires grace and tact, since it is difficult to avoid the implication of blame in discussions with those responsible for the policies and programs that are causing a problem. Indeed, workers must find a way to appear to be raising problems out of organizational commitment and loyalty—for example, by linking the problem with predominant organizational values—rather than as a criticism of current policy. Insofar as it is possible, workers or units must minimize the possibility that a problem can be dismissed as *their* problem rather than the organization's. This happens when a problem has been identified as their particular "thing" because of their persistence in raising it. Politically astute workers carefully ration the number of issues they identify and try to get others to be problem-raisers along with (or instead of) themselves.

The exposure of organizational problems may be done either formally or informally, although informal means should usually precede an official presentation. These occur as workers discuss issues in the hallways, lounges, and coffee klatches of the agency. Ordinarily, these exchanges take place unselfconsciously and between workers of roughly similar rank or function. Effective organizational practice requires that these informal interactions be purposive and that, to the extent possible, the communications be extended to include a wider constituency.

The process is illustrated by the work of one practitioner, relatively new to a community-based mental hygiene clinic, who was discomforted to find that the screening of clients—a function of the agency's psychiatrists—was not conducted during evening hours. Thus, only mothers were present in approximately 43 percent of the two-parent families screened for treatment, and 20 percent of the people who made telephone inquiries could not be accommodated. She decided to work toward the agency's opening its doors for evening screenings at least once a week. She describes her preparatory work as follows:

> In the tension-relieving "rap" sessions that the social workers hold, the incompetence of the psychiatrists is a major topic. I both joined in decrying their lack of dedication and used these occasions to introduce the problem of screenings. I picked up the workers' complaints about cases assigned to them with inappropriate treatment recommendations and cited "horror stories" of my own. I also supported their dissatisfaction with having to elicit information from fathers in treatment that should have been obtained during a screening. Mindful that the workers might themselves resist working during the evening, I did not propose any solution, and just tried to highlight their discontent with the present process.
>
> . . . I have also pointed out to my supervisor the frustration of only having one parent available for the screening. Encouraged by her support,

I suggested that we consider together what might be done to solve the problem. We agreed that she would sound out but make no concrete suggestions to the Director of Social Services, who has considerable influence with the Administrative Director. . . . In the meantime, I directly pinpointed the problem to the Medical Director by referring to the need of one of my clients to have a medication evaluation in the evening, since he was already in jeopardy of losing his job and an afternoon appointment would have increased the risk.[9]

By the preinitiation phase workers have a change goal well in mind. In informal interaction, then, they will look for opportunities to pick up on chance remarks to identify a problem or to advance a definition of it that is congruent with their ideas regarding its solution. When issues are directly cited, the workers can provide reinforcement, as did the worker cited above, through agreement, by dramatizing the problem with examples or highlighting its adverse consequences. They may also seek a "natural" time and place for raising the problem themselves, as in the rap sessions chosen by the clinic worker. Otherwise, they may seem to be engaging in a campaign before they are ready for campaigning or may risk the appearance of harboring hidden agendas.

Communications research indicates that the transfer of ideas takes place more frequently among people who are similar in such attributes as social position, values, and education.[10] The proposition, extended to organizations, suggests that practitioners are most persuasive to others of similar rank and function. Thus, the fact that organizational interaction is most frequently horizontal, tending to take place among workers of similar organizational positions, is in one sense an advantage that change-oriented practitioners can put to use. But it is disadvantaging if it ends there. Although persons with close ties who interact frequently are more convincing to one another, they are less likely to provide one another with new information. Studies suggest that "a new idea is communicated to a larger number of individuals, and traverses a greater social distance, when passed through weak sociometric ties . . . rather than strong ones." [11] Thus, links that extend beyond rank and function are important for the diffusion of problem awareness and must be opened. To achieve the advantages of both commonality and heterogeneity, an effective network includes actors who hold different organizational statuses but who have other, nonpositional similarities such as common values, ethnicity, training, and the like. The point is important when any subgroup or faction of workers is plan-

[9] Case Record, "Evening Screenings," Columbia University School of Social Work, 1977.

[10] Everett M. Rogers with F. Floyd Shoemaker, *Communication of Innovations,* 2nd ed. (New York: Free Press, 1971), p. 14.

[11] Everett M. Rogers and Rekha Agarwala-Rogers, *Communication in Organizations* (New York: Free Press, 1976), p. 115.

ning to induce or intensify problem awareness. Who is selected to talk to whom about what becomes a critical consideration.

There are two cautions that practitioners must take into account as they interact informally to diffuse problem awareness. One has to do with the meaning of participants' griping, the other with the consequences of exaggeration.

Complaints provide pointers to organizational stress and offer a fertile soil to work in focusing and magnifying existent tensions. But griping serves other functions as well. One of the most significant is the development of group solidarity. Actors express dissatisfaction with the organization to generate the feeling that they share a common order of things; thus they may use griping more to win friends than to influence organizations. To assume, therefore, that complaints in the hallway will surface at meetings without "help" from the practitioner may be assuming too much.

Exaggerating a problem also poses risks for the practitioner's objective. Apart from endangering his credibility, if he makes the problem appear overwhelming it may appear invulnerable to change. This danger is particularly relevant to low-ranking actors who have limited resources for influencing. If a problem looms larger than one's perceived ability to affect it, action is discouraged. An actor's belief that he can influence the outcome of an event may, we believe, be as much a determinant of his willingness to act as the intensity of his commitment to the particular cause. It is suggestive, for example, that in a study of twenty-nine health organizations, Mohr found that health officers' motivation to innovate was four and a half times greater when their resources were high than when they were low.[12]

Thus, whether a practitioner will undertake a change effort relates to his optimism (or pessimism) in regard to his ability to carry it out. Wilson argues that the proponents of an innovation are not likely to perceive fully the difficulties in their way.[13] True enough—but it is also true that people do not become proponents in the first place if they overestimate obstacles. Practitioners who paint problems or the power of opponents in too lurid a color or with too heavy a brush risk encouraging apathy rather than action. In short, as the practitioner attempts to heighten awareness of a problem, he must also be sensitive to the perceptions of fellow actors regarding its amenability to their intervention.

Heightened interaction within the agency among people who agree with the practitioner's problem formulation can be fostered informally (e.g., social contacts, partisan caucuses) or, when organizational protocol per-

[12] Lawrence Mohr, "Determinents of Innovation in Organizations," *American Political Science Review* 63 (March 1969), pp. 111–26.

[13] James Q. Wilson, "Innovation in Organization: Notes Toward A Theory" in James D. Thompson, ed., *Approaches to Organizational Design* (Pittsburgh: University of Pittsburgh Press, 1966), p. 208.

mits, through more formal devices (e.g., staff meetings, seminars). This may be a necessary preinitiation maneuver for workers in organizations in which the agency's technology encourages worker isolation and an individualistic value system (see Chapter 3) and in which, therefore, there is limited staff interest in organizational functioning or the impact of policy on service. Even more effective for magnifying stress, however, is to structure the opportunity for interaction among actors known to be discontented and to encourage them to bear witness to their discontent in whatever forum is available.[14] Administrators who call as few staff meetings as possible or turn the conduct of meetings over to aides may do so because of their busy schedules, but other motivations may be operating as well, such as their awareness that interaction among dissatisfied persons increases tension and often leads to concerted action.

Formal mechanisms for locating one's problem on an organizational agenda are numerous, and our discussion of structural positioning in the next section deals with some considerations in regard to these. We have not yet noted, however, that in the early stages of the change effort the worker who first places the problem on the agency agenda holds an important advantage. It is the advantage of *definition*. The way a problem or issue is initially identified in an organization often determines the way it is conceived and experienced by others. Since the perception of the problem by key organizational actors is crucial to the ultimate appeal of a change proposal—that is, its scope, the impact on staff and clients, whose "fault" or responsibility it might be, how it embodies or assaults cherished beliefs—the opportunity of shaping the problem definition so that it is consonant with one's change ambitions constitutes a major concern during the preinitiation phase.

Skillful practitioners take advantage of the variety of formal meetings that agencies conduct as a means of diffusing awareness of a problem and heightening tension. Different aspects of an issue may be raised at different forums, depending on the nature of the issue and the type of meeting.

The mental health worker at the Monrad Community Mental Health Center who was discussed earlier skillfully orchestrated his goal of establishing a day hospital by using such gatherings. Three types of meetings were held at the center: team meetings—a regularly scheduled "feelings group" for staff to ventilate problems arising from working on the inpatient unit; a weekly administrative meeting, chaired by Dr. N., the head of hospitalization services; and inservice training sessions.

> At the team meeting, ordinarily conducted by myself and the other team leaders, I brought up how overworked and overburdened staff were. Monrad's catchment area was due to be expanded, and I "wondered" how the

[14] Devoting a portion of each meeting to encouraging members to "bear witness" to their unhappy experiences with officials is a technique used in organizing residents in regard to community issues.

new area would effect working conditions on the unit. We had a space problem as it was. With the possible increase of inpatients and "who knows how many more day patients there would be?" where would we put everyone?

The issue of the impact of an expanded catchment area on Hospitalization Services was raised at the administrative staff meeting. This naturally flowed out of the team meeting, and I encouraged Vita to raise the matter. Vita is the only female of the four team leaders, is a nurse rather than a social worker like the rest of us, and her word carries weight with both Dr. N. and the nursing staff.

The change process continued at an interesting inservice training session. Robert, another team leader and a member of our alliance, was chosen to report on the Partial Hospitalization Conference which we attended. His emphasis was on the research findings regarding the beneficial effects on patients of day hospitals. Earlier, we had assessed that Dr. N.'s primary concern would be how any projected change would affect his sphere of influence and that his favorable response was contingent on a day hospital's being administered by and located within hospitalization services rather than Monrad's outpatient department. We knew, however, that he also cared about the quality of patient care, and that discussion with him had to avoid "turf" issues and focus on patient welfare. The latter was thus Robert's main point, as he reported on the development of day hospitals within other community mental health centers. But we also hoped to heighten tension by introducing the experience of other agencies. After all, the Center had a reputation to maintain as a leader in the field.[15]

It is worth noting that at each of the three meetings, a different staff member took the "frontrunner" position—thus following our earlier injunction that politically astute workers ration their activity and try to get others to be problem-raisers along with themselves. The Monrad workers were also skillful in avoiding the premature introduction of their goal and setting the stage for its later initiation.

Formal channels may be unavailable or nonexistent, and the worker may move to convening a special meeting to address a problem. In doing so, however, he must ensure that careful preparation has been made, as was apparently the case in the example above. Unless advance work is done, there is the danger that the problem will be dismissed as unimportant or, worse, that opposition to its solution will be mobilized by the presentation.

The fact that there is some organizational action invests a problem with added significance. The same may be said when the problem is linked to an issue already under study or if a meeting, whether or not it is called at the worker's behest, concludes with some statement of concern regarding the problem. The action establishes the problem as an officially recognized one and tends to strengthen attitudes supporting its solution. In part, at

[15] Boyer, *op. cit.*

least, this is so because behavior influences attitude formation. That is, if a person can be persuaded to act in a particular way, engaging in the action itself increases the likelihood that he will develop attitudes that justify it.[16] Obtaining some official action thus serves as a preinitiation maneuver to advance participant and organizational commitment.

There is one other formal device for creating problem awareness within an organization—the introduction of outsiders. The use of third-party intervention may be as simple as the invitation of outside experts to agency meetings and conferences. Organizational circumstances sometimes make it possible for practitioners to solicit and gain the participation of third-party consultants for more sustained intervention, often under the guise of a training program. Training, it should be noted, is often employed as an avoidance tactic. That is, instead of confronting a problem area, because it is unsettling to do so, agency administrations use training so as to *appear* to be handling the problem. Training programs have a number of advantages in this regard, not the least of which is that the "cause" of the problem is implicitly defined as the staff's inadequacy rather than the system's. But trainers also sometimes provide top administrators with more than they bargained for, since the ideology of trainers, particularly if they are organizational development specialists, suggests not only the necessity of addressing organizational problems head on but the need to diffuse influence within organizational systems as well.

Interestingly, exposing dissonant information is a device often employed by consultants with organizational development backgrounds. Since they are sanctioned by the top hierarchy, their activity in this regard can be more visible and formal than the devices internal actors commonly must rely on. Ordinarily, their activity takes three forms. One is interviewing and observation, noting the dissatisfactions of participants and subunits with regard to the organization and each other, with the ultimate intent of creating an accurate and widespread perception of stressful reality.

Structured questionnaires and survey feedback are also used by organizational development specialists, often not so much to provide diagnostic data as to generate results that serve as a basis for forcing participants to address the components and causes of a problem. Information may, of course, be collected and analyzed for many purposes, but we are referring here to the feeding of information into an organizational system to be used to induce change-oriented behavior. Hornstein et al. describe the technique as follows:

> Beginning with the top family in the organizational structure, the [survey] feedback meetings descend through the hierarchy until all . . . have been involved. . . . Typically, the data include such matters as the actual and

[16] Albert Baudura, "Strategies of Attitude Change," in Gerald Zaltman, Philip Kotler, and Ira Kaufman, eds., *Creating Social Change* (New York: Holt, Rinehart & Winston, 1972), p. 57.

desired distribution of influence among different role groups, perceived and actual goals, communication adequacy, perceived norms and perceived organizational problems. The meetings are intended to become problem-solving sessions in which groups attempt to use data as a vehicle which enable them to discuss problems, determine causes, and agree upon solutions.[17]

A less time-consuming way of introducing and dealing with dissonant data, appropriate for issues requiring immediate attention, is the "confrontation meeting," developed by Beckhard. Central to this technique is the development of a structure, the confrontation meeting, in which problems are simultaneously identified and dealt with. Beckhard describes the first four steps of the technique as follows: "(1) Climate setting—establishing willingness to participate; (2) information collecting —getting attitudes and feelings out in the open; (3) information sharing— making total information available to all; (4) priority setting and group action planning."[18]

These techniques are occasionally available for practitioner use as well, but, as our earlier discussion indicates, their underlying notion— to expose dissonant information—does not require these formal means.

Structural Positioning

Structural positioning refers to the use of organizational structure to increase the likelihood that a practitioner's definition of a problem will obtain a receptive hearing. As we noted in Chapter 1, changes in organizational structure are ordinarily more far-reaching than other types of change. In regard to structural positioning, however, our reference is a more modest one. Our concern is with the "edge" one can gain for his ideas by attention to structural matters.

The "edge may entail something as simple as anticipating how rules or procedures may be used to promote or prevent attention to a problem area. The major consideration, however, is where the practitioner locates the problem on the organizational agenda (e.g., at a conference, meeting, committee or subunit), and whether new forms such as evaluation mechanisms are required to provide him with a structural advantage.

Structural positioning is as relevant to initiating a change as it is to the preinitiation phase of the process. We explore the matter here rather than in the chapter on initiation because where a practitioner first decides to locate the discussion of a problem often has significant impact on its

[17] Harvey A. Hornstein et al., eds., *Social Intervention* (New York: Free Press, 1971), p. 259.

[18] Richard Beckhard, "The Confrontation Meeting," in Hornstein et al., *op. cit.,* p. 213.

later routing and what ultimately becomes of it. Furthermore, the worker's assessment of where in the organization his change goal should be introduced takes place during preinitiation. In fact, as we have reiterated, a "real world" model of the change process is not linear; rather, it more likely reflects a series of overlapping spirals in which activities such as structural positioning first take place in phase one and are repeated in phases two and three.

Structurally locating both the problem introduction and the change goal involves a number of considerations. We discuss three of the most important ones in this section.

THE COMPOSITION OF THE GROUP

Who is likely to be included or excluded if one opts in favor of one or another structure is a primary consideration in the choice of structure. Even in a process as neutral as information gathering, the data are usually not self-evident. As Whyte claims, "Facts do not speak for themselves, but only through the people who present them." [19] Depending on their organizational positions, people have access to different information and, as noted in Chapter 4, bring different perspectives, interests, and values to their interpretations depending on how the information, or problem, impinges on their organizational roles. If one views a meeting, subunit, ad hoc committee, or evaluation procedure as an arena in which participants of different organizational characteristics vie to make one or another conception prevail, the importance of who constitutes the exploratory group becomes clear. It significantly influences whether an issue will even be defined as a problem, much less what alternative solutions can be considered.

The importance of committee composition is illustrated by the experience of the Community Service Society, the prestigious New York City agency, which radically revised its program in the 1970s following a self-study. Historically a foremost exponent of traditional social casework services, the agency eliminated these services in favor of community-based demonstration programs and research as a result of the self-study. The agency had conducted such a study every ten years, and the results of these evaluations of agency program had significantly affected policy in the past. The committee that conducted the most recent evaluation, composed of laymen and professionals and staffed by the agency's research unit, did not include a single representative of the Department of Family Services, although the department provided the major share of the agency's program. It wasn't until the results of the self-study had already been an-

---

[19] William Foote Whyte, *Organizational Behavior* (Homewood, Ill.: Irwin and Dorsey, 1969), p. 690.

nounced that the family services professionals awoke to their exclusion from the deliberations and protested; by then, the damage had been done.[20]

In recognizing the importance of who "hears" the problem, the practitioner will be mindful of starting the process with his natural allies. This suggests that by and large he will try to insure the solidity of his "home base," his own subunit, before he ventures farther afield (unless, of course, his change ideas are more compatible with the interests of other groups within the agency). He will choose to raise the problem at the meeting or subunit that is most likely to agree with his perception that the problem exists—after first sounding out some of the participants. If he has successfully located receptive allies, he may also act to increase their influence before he moves beyond problem exploration. His action may be as simple as trying to enhance the reputation for competence of like-minded participants by spreading the agency word or as complex as assisting them in expanding their organizational domains. The intervention, then, moves beyond locating the most receptive actors to strengthening their hand prior to introducing the change goal.

Receptivity to the practitioner's view at a particular meeting or within a specific committee may be enhanced by the addition of newcomers to the forum (i.e., friendly agency staff with expertise or interest in the problem area or outsiders such as consultants or guests from a related agency). The practitioner may also, as circumstances permit, suggest the formation of a committee, study group, task force, or other ad hoc arrangement, if the potential participants are likely to be more receptive to his problem definition than an ongoing group. In the latter case, he will also try to influence the choice of participants, either directly or indirectly, through the development of criteria regarding the characteristics of those who ought to serve.

LEGITIMACY

The legitimacy of a group to deal with the problem refers to the perception of relevant actors that it is appropriate or "right" for certain others to discuss and decide a particular matter. In a sense, legitimacy is something that is granted—in that a group may be considered "legitimate" for only as long as the perceiver acknowledges that it is.

The legitimacy of individuals or units to deal with a problem within an organization is ordinarily delegated by the agency's superordinates. In other words, a specific committee is the appropriate vehicle to discuss a particular subject because the boss says it is. But the matter is more complex than that. The boss will ordinarily want other participants to "under-

[20] Gertrude S. Goldberg, *New Directions for the Community Service Society: A Study of Organizational Change,* Columbia University, unpublished doctoral dissertation, 1976, esp. pp. 491–503.

stand" the basis for his designation of a particular committee or, to put it in another way, to reinforce the committee's legitimacy. Similarly, the practitioner, in selecting a vehicle for exploring his problem, must concern himself with the degree to which the decision makers and related others will define that vehicle as a legitimate forum.

By and large, the bases for the definition of legitimacy are the organizational function and expertise of the participants. That is, an issue is referred to a group when its resolution affects the members of the group, usually because the problem is related to their task or function. When there are standing committees responsible for defined areas, obtaining an "edge" by positioning may require that the practitioner redefine the content of the problem so that it "fits" the meeting that may be most receptive to his solution. Or it may entail redefining the scope of the problem so that it touches only a circumscribed area of the organization's functioning (e.g., a single subunit), thereby eliminating the need for wider and potentially less friendly exploration.

For newly created or ad hoc committees, legitimacy is most often related to "representativeness"—in other words, to whether those with a functional or expert interest in the problem are included in the group charged with exploring it (as was violated by the Community Service Society procedure). To put the matter more precisely, "representativeness" may be achieved when those who have a functional or expert interest in the problem are *perceived* to have been included. A common tactic is to form a group that apparently represents various interests but does not actually do so. An example would be a committee that draws its membership from diverse agency departments, but in which the appointed members do not reflect the positions of the department or are insufficiently assertive to maintain them. Another is to include all the various interests but to so overbalance the group with one set of interests that the others are heard only in whispers.

ONGOING ENTITIES VS. NEW STRUCTURES

A third consideration in structural "positioning" is whether to use an ongoing entity or opt for the creation of a new structure. As we have already suggested, the potential composition of one or the other group is a critical variable, but there are others as well. Ad hoc groups are in their nature more likely to bring a fresh perspective and a singleminded focus to problem solving than ongoing committees. The latter carry the burden (and in some cases the advantage) inherent in having developed procedures, precedents to follow, and a history of working together (including the trade-offs that take place between members over time).

Most important, ad hoc groups are ordinarily not decision-making entities; once formed, they must bring their deliberations to some regularly constituted sanctioning body. This requirement is advantageous when a problem is strikingly new or its solution entails a radical departure from current agency practice. The case can then be made that the matter has been thoroughly studied. Furthermore, the ad hoc group can report progress to a parent body for discussion only, thus preventing an issue that elicits negative reaction from being decided "prematurely." Finally, allowing a problem or solution to percolate without pressing for action by referral to an ad hoc (presumably legitimate and prestigious) group will make the idea seem considerably less innovative when the time for decision making nears.

On the other hand, the deliberations of an ad hoc committee might signify unnecessary postponement, a means of avoiding the problem, or at the least might create an extraneous hurdle for a new idea to overcome. Thus, the issue of timing is important in choosing an ongoing or an ad hoc structure. An operative rule of thumb is the degree of stress existent within the organization in regard to the problem and, therefore, how "ripe" the organizational circumstances are for its immediate consideration.[21]

A special case in regard to the use of existent structure versus creation of new structure has to do with the degree to which an agency has well-developed search and learning mechanisms. Some agencies collect information and evaluate imprecise data informally and on an ad hoc basis. Other agencies *program* search and learning devices either through regular annual evaluation conferences or studies or through units specifically created for the purpose (such as research and development departments).[22]

Agencies that program search and learning devices offer the practitioner an existent structure through which to diffuse problem awareness. Ordinarily, this is valuable for the innovator, since the mechanisms themselves create the *expectation* that problem areas will be placed on an agenda. When evaluation is routine, the innovator is less likely to be subject to the suspicion that those who raise problems inevitably face—namely, why they brought up the issue and what they might have up their sleeves.

---

[21] This same issue is applicable to the use of ongoing evaluation procedures. The importance of time frame is dramatically demonstrated in the Community Service Society example cited earlier. Agency policy required that an ambitious self-study be conducted every ten years. Thus, changes proposed three or four years before the evaluation was to be undertaken were postponed for self-study consideration— this in the face of the turbulent social-welfare environment of the mid and late 1960s. The result was that the society did not accommodate to its environment in modest degrees, and when change did come, it was radical and explosive.

[22] Organizations that make nonroutinized decisions, such as social-welfare agencies, and do not have programmed search and learning devices are subject to what March and Simon call Gresham's Law of planning: when organizations or individuals are faced with both highly programmed and highly unprogrammed tasks, the former take precedence over the latter. James G. March and Herbert Simon, *Organizations* (New York: Wiley, 1958), p. 185.

Search and learning mechanisms are valuable tools for promoting innovation, although the extent to which their activities actually eventuate in change is highly uncertain. For example, research and development departments that have a relatively high percentage of organizational resources are more successful in moving their proposals to adoption than are others.[23] A not far-fetched interpretation, then, is that it is the influence of the department rather than the substance of the recommendation that is the critical variable. Nevertheless, in agencies in which information is collected informally and evaluated randomly, if at all, practitioners may decide to try to create an evaluation mechanism before they "surface" with their problem area. This is a useful strategy when the very act of creating stress in regard to a problem area poses too great a risk for the practitioner or reveals his change intentions too early, thereby generating stronger resistance than he is yet able to deal with.

Practitioners may not, of course, be in a position to use or shape structure in the ways we have suggested. As we have noted, structural modifications often have wide-ranging effects, and even participants who tend not to think in structural terms are often intuitively aware of the ways in which structural modifications impinge on their interests. At the same time, however, changes that might otherwise have been accomplished with modest anticipatory structural alterations have failed because of inadequate skill in establishing the "edge."

To summarize, preinitiation interventions are designed to prepare the system for a change idea. To encourage a climate of organizational receptivity the worker has three practice foci in this phase of the process. He must first establish his own reputation and credibility in the organization relative to the change he has in mind. Secondly, he must induce, focus, or magnify stress by heightening organizational awareness of the problem he proposes to solve. Finally, he must assess and use the structural mechanisms that could give his goal an "edge" in the organizational marketplace. He is then ready to turn his attention, as do we in the following chapter, to initiating the innovative proposal and monitoring its progress until it is either adopted or rejected.

[23] Wilson, *op. cit.*, p. 208.

8. Initiating the Change

THE INTRODUCTION OF THE CHANGE GOAL into the organization signals the beginning of the initiation phase of change practice. An interactive process then ensues in which the innovation is adapted and diffused among the relevant organizational entities until it is either formally accepted or rejected.

The essential function of initiation is to make the change goal conform to the influence that can be mobilized to move its adoption. Since an influence attempt is geared to a specific target, the identity of critical actors—participants who *must* support the proposal for it to be realized—determines the worker's interventions. With those who are to be influenced as the focus, there are four practice questions to be considered: To whom should the appeal be made? Who should make it? What arguments should be used? And through what channels of forums should the message be transmitted?[1]

Human service workers often give these questions insufficient consideration. Typically, they approach the decision maker—but if he vetoes the idea, the attempt is aborted before it has gotten off the ground. The worker seeking the change is ordinarily the one to raise the issue—but without considering whether or not he is potentially the most persuasive proponent of this issue with the decision maker. The argument is frequently made in terms of professional values—but values alone are not ordinarily the prime movers of action. And the forum in which the appeal is often made is the staff meeting—a place as much for the ratification of previously agreed-on plans as for the adoption of new ones. To introduce and diffuse a change goal effectively requires greater sensitivity to the dynamics of influence than these practices suggest.

---

[1] It may be noted that these questions follow the S–M–C–R model of communications theory. A *source* (S) sends a *message* (M) via certain *channels* (C) to the *receiving* individual (R). See Everett M. Rogers with F. Floyd Shoemaker, *Communication of Innovations,* 2nd ed. (New York: Free Press, 1971), p. 11.

The Audience and the Initiator

To whom a change idea is introduced and by whom may well shape the remainder of the process. Often these decisions determine the allies who can be mobilized and the opposition that will arise. Thus these choices constitute major variables in the initiation phase of the process.

THE AUDIENCE

The practitioner's point of entry may be with administration, middle-level staff, or line workers. He may choose one or another department or program unit. Or the introduction of the change goal may be "placed" outside the agency by an appeal to a sanctioned third party, such as a consultant, or to an unsanctioned outsider, such as an interest group.

The significant element in deciding on the entry point is how it will influence the meaning to critical actors of the issue being raised. Although every situation is unique, there are a number of factors to be considered in deciding (1) whether to go directly to the critical actors, (2) whether to introduce the change ideas to facilitating actors first, or (3) whether to first seek the support or decrease the opposition of organizational participants to whom the change goal is relevant.

The worker's assessment of the driving and restraining forces that affect his change goal and his identification of the working forces that are amenable to intervention form the basis for judgment regarding his entry point. These forces indicate who may be supportive of and who opposed to his goal, on what grounds, and what respective resources for influence he, like-minded others, and opponents might be willing to commit to advance or retard his goal. Ultimately, they suggest when and how participants may be engaged or circumvented in the process (see Chapter 6). The primary aim in a change effort is to influence the critical actors to act favorably on the proposal. The decision as to the audience for introducing the goal, therefore, will be based on the practitioner's assessment of the critical actors' attitude toward the goal and the forces impinging on them that might encourage or discourage the desired behavior.

Critical actors are often upper-ranking staff with whom a practitioner has infrequent interaction. Predicting their preferences may be an uncertain enterprise. Nonetheless, the worker's assessment of their commitments must lead at least to a tentative judgment of potential support, indifference, or opposition. The entry point the worker chooses is predicated on the reaction he expects to receive.

If a practitioner is uncertain of a critical actor's stance, prudence suggests that he choose a different audience as his entry point. The risk of fully revealing his change goal "at the top" is, of course, that it will get rejected out of hand, before receiving adequate exposure or consideration.

In situations of uncertainty, it may be appropriate to talk initially to critical actors about the organizational problem, avoiding any reference to remedies.[2] Even then, caution is advisable since such discussions reveal the commitments of the participants—not only the critical actor's (which is what the worker wants to learn) but the worker's as well (which he may not want to divulge).

If this exploratory discussion reveals no common ground concerning problem definition, it might best be terminated. If commonality is found, solutions might then be sounded out, and the worker could elaborate on those suggestions of the critical actor that are compatible with his change goal. If he were then to introduce his idea, it would be with the assurance of the critical actor's positive reaction, if not active support.

Short of engaging in the exploration suggested above, inaugurating a change idea at the critical-actor level is appropriate in relatively few situations when the critical actor's reactions cannot be estimated. One occasion is when the worker's own commitments are not commensurate with his engaging the kind of extended process that might be necessary. He thus "goes for broke" because otherwise he would not go at all. The worker at the Monrad Community Mental Health Center, for example, would not have invested the time or possible risk in the preparatory efforts described in Chapter 7 if he had not had a strong commitment to the organization of a day hospital. If his commitment had been less, he might have gone directly to the head of hospitalization services and taken his chances on a quick yes or no.

Another occasion calling for an introduction of the change goal to a critical actor whose potential reaction has not been determined is during a crisis in the organization, when immediate action is a requirement of success. Finally, the practitioner may broach his idea to the critical actor when taking this step constitutes an organizationally unusual act and he sees advantage in thus dramatizing his proposal.

On the face of it, the support of critical actors appears to be all that is necessary to attain the adoption of an innovation. If the decision maker is expected to agree with the change, he becomes the audience for the appeal, and the process is completed with his assent. Although this does occur, it probably happens less frequently than workers expect. Even when the critical actor supports the substance of the proposal he will act on it only insofar as its advantages to him are balanced against its liabilities (e.g., the negative reaction of other participants may be a major organizational cost). A decision maker may thus desire the change but not move to secure its adoption if he believes that it will be more generally upsetting to other participants than it is worth to him.

Research conducted by Hage and Dewar indicates the importance of

---

[2] These represent acts that commonly take place in the preinitiation phase of the process, discussed in Chapter 7.

the attitudes of those close to a decision maker in effecting organizational change. The study found a correlation between program innovation in a number of health and welfare agencies, on the one hand, and values favoring change on the part of the agencies' executive directors, on the other. This is an expected finding. More interesting is the finding that when the executives' lieutenants share change-oriented values, the likelihood of innovation is considerably increased. The attitudes of an agency's inner circle are thus a more accurate predictor of change than the attitudes of its top leaders.[3]

The practice implication of this finding is clear. If the practitioner anticipates the critical actor's support but also organizational opposition, his entry point might be the critical actor alone. In this way, he can either obtain an "undiluted" reaction to the proposal or sound out what steps might need to be taken to assure the critical actor's endorsement. There are occasions in this interaction where the two "use" each other. An implicit coalition is developed whereby the practitioner is expected to help line up organizational support in return for the critical actor's endorsement.

This might be termed a "top-down" strategy: the worker seeks the support of the decision maker to make it easier to gain the support of others who otherwise might not go along. It contrasts with a "bottom-up" approach, in which lower-ranking members are mobilized first as a source of direct or indirect pressure on the critical actor. The tactics described in this book deal largely with the latter approach, but it is obvious that whether workers first try to gain the support of the decision maker in order to influence his subordinates or the other way around depends on the forces at work.

Apart from the strategic question, introducing a change idea directly to a potentially supportive critical actor has the advantage that the proposal will have a shorter distance to travel in reaching its decision point and will be less subject to the information loss and distortion typical of organizational communication. This will also reduce the delay in moving the proposal to adoption.[4]

If the critical actor's commitment is less than expected (i.e., ranges in the direction of indifference), his stake in the proposal will often depend on his assessment of how other affected persons or units might react toward the proposal. The practitioner will then either have to activate other adherents, make their advocacy more visible, and/or neutralize opposition before the critical actor can be expected to endorse the change. Since, in this instance, the critical actor will not resist the change, intro-

[3] Gerald Hage and Robert Dewar, "Elite Values Versus Organizational Structure in Predicting Innovation," *Administrative Science Quarterly* 18 (Sept. 1973), p. 296.

[4] Issues relating to organizational distance are discussed by Rino J. Patti, "Organizational Resistance and Change: The View From Below," *Social Service Review* 45 (September 1974), pp. 376–78.

ducing the proposal to him (or avoiding him as the entry point) is less important than increasing the driving forces and decreasing the restraining forces in his field of vision.

If, however, the critical actor is opposed to the change goal and has expressed his position to others (even if only to the worker), it becomes more difficult to convince him to revise his judgment. Studies have shown that public avowal of a position increases one's adherence to the position, thereby immunizing the person against counterargument. People become more committed to their opinions when they have given public witness.[5] Greater resources for influencing will thus be required to obtain a decision maker's turnaround than if his opposition had remained latent. In short, if a practitioner anticipates opposition from the critical actors, he needs to maximize whatever countervailing forces he can muster before he faces the potential negative reaction.

These issues in regard to the introduction of a proposal to critical actors apply as well to its introduction to facilitating and related actors. The general principle is that the more important an actor's influence is in regard to a particular change goal, the more sure of the actor's support (or of his own resources for influencing) the practitioner must be, or the more important it is to seek the aid of other potential proponents before introducing the proposal to that actor. On the other hand, the more reason the practitioner has to expect support, the closer to the point of impact his entry point should be. In short, as we noted in our discussion of pre-initiation, sequencing which moves from natural allies to probable proponents to uncertain but increasingly influential actors is generally the prudent procedure. It allows the practitioner to increase his resources as he moves through the process with less risk of either a premature veto or activating the opposition.

ALLIANCES

As is suggested above, the successful initiation of a change proposal ordinarily requires that the practitioner seek to organize support from his natural allies and other potential proponents. Wax notes that there are two types of alliance in organizations, standing and ad hoc.[6] The standing alliance is one that persists over time and covers a broad range of issues. It is formed of three types of participants: those with basically similar organizational interests, ideologically compatible partners, or people who have developed friendships on other grounds. Standing alliances may be so informal that they are barely recognizable as coalitions. Their mani-

[5] Marvin Karlins and Herbert I. Abelson, *Persuasion,* 2nd ed. (New York: Springer, 1970), pp. 59–61.

[6] John Wax, "Power Theory and Institutional Change," *Social Service Review* 45 (September1971), pp. 279–80.

festation may be no more than a predisposition of members to agree on organizational positions or an implicit understanding that they will avoid public disagreement. "A standing alliance," according to Wax, "is something like a credit card," in that the practitioner can "borrow" the influence of the coalition in the service of his change goal.

The ad hoc alliance is organized around a particular issue and persists only until the change goal is attained or abandoned. The coalitions or factions that compose a large organization are more fluid than is generally credited. Individuals group and regroup into ad hoc combinations so that "each coalition . . . include[s] people who are diverse with respect to other latent or active conflicts." [7] Thus, ad hoc coalitions are not necessarily composed of like-minded people (a point often not appreciated by practitioners who attempt to seek support only from those with whom they can develop positive affective relations). All that is necessary are participants who are like-minded in respect to the question at issue.

Standing alliances are likely to have started with or to have developed affective relations among their members. This factor, combined with the experience of working together, suggests that standing alliances will maintain a common front in pursuing common goals. The weakness of an ad hoc alliance is that schisms among its members are more easily exposed, thus weakening its image of determination and strength. Effective collective action requires that while differences may be aired in private, they will be minimized in public. The worker must keep this fact in mind as an ad hoc coalition acts to move a change.

The practitioner who has effectively stimulated problem awareness during preinitiation will know which participants to try to attract or avoid in forming a coalition. Indeed, the very act of generating interest in an issue is the first step in forming an alliance. When sufficient interest has been elicited, it is well to "up the ante." One way is to fix the position by ensuring that the actor's stance is made public, if only within the confines of the budding coalition. The support of one actor, depending on who he is, may activate the support of others. Another way, once the position is fixed, is to make the requested assistance concrete—that is, to find something specific for the potential proponent to *do*. A commonly observed phenomenon is the increase in commitment that stems from the very act of engaging in a change process. This is of course as true—or more so—for the practitioner as it is for other supporters.

What makes for an effective alliance? [8] Obviously, potential members

---

[7] Cyril Sofer, *Organizations in Theory and Practice* (New York: Basic Books, 1972), p. 367.

[8] Typically, alliances are formed of persons and groups who are available and will join, and practitioners have limited options in their choice of partners. But the time spent in random recruitment often constitutes a high cost, which might be more profitably expended in pinpointing and recruiting those with the most to contribute.

who have influence with critical actors are primary candidates for a coalition. Sometimes, too, participants or units have to be drawn into a coalition because they have a special interest in the change issue and their absence would challenge the legitimacy of the effort. Another significant consideration is the heterogeneity of the alliance. The more heterogeneous, the more powerful it is likely to be in effecting change.

Most important in regard to heterogeneity is the diverse resources for influencing that coalition members bring to the alliance. Participants with differing sources of information, a variety of types of expertise, and links to different standing alliances, for example, make a more potent combination than coalitions in which the members' information channels, expertise, or informal relations are merely additive. Actors with different talents also contribute differentially and may fill distinctive process roles in the change effort—for example, as spokesman, symbolic leader, expressive leader, analyst, mediator, negotiator, etc.[9]

Another source of heterogeneity has to do with difference of interests and ideology. Indeed, the more unexpected the combination of these differences among members in an alliance, the greater its strength. When persons with potentially conflicting interests or known ideological differences join together, they gain attention that is not otherwise available. It is often assumed that, in light of their wide divergencies, they must be "right" on an issue about which they agree. Furthermore, such a coalition cannot be neatly pigeonholed and is therefore more difficult to dismiss. The extent to which persons or groups (and their values or opinions) are subject to stereotyping affects the likelihood that they will be ignored or that their positions will be unconvincing.

A change process undertaken by a middle-level staff member at Somerville Hospital illustrates, among other things, the advantage of diversity within an alliance. The worker was team leader of a dayroom program which, with a counseling clinic, was part of a comprehensive treatment program for alcoholics at the hospital. His goal was to add an occupational-therapy and vocational service to the day program or, failing that, to gain the assignment of additional staff to the day program's inadequate complement of three workers.

The critical actor was the program's administrative director, who had worked previously with a large number of college-trained counselors in an innovative and cohesive drug program. The professional counselors (MSWs) had originally proposed the day program to get "unreliable" and "unmotivated" clients "out of the clinic's hair," but the day program was now attracting the bulk of their clientele.

In the preinitiation phase, a major force for change—the inundation

[9] For a further discussion of process roles, see Richard S. Bolan, "Community Decision Behavior: The Culture of Planning," *Journal of the American Institute of Planners* 35 (September 1969), p. 304.

of patients coming to the day program as compared to the other services— had been effectively increased. The team leader heightened the visibility of the force by distributing activity lists that indicated what the patients were doing in the program (and, incidentally, the large number of the clinic's clients who were active there). The payoff came at a staff meeting when the administrative director made unexpected reference to the "problem" of large numbers of clients in the day program. For the first time outside the confines of the day program, the team leader introduced the idea of vocational training. He stressed the appropriateness of an informal activities-oriented approach "to start where the clients are," and suggested that the day program offered the key to the alcoholism service, since it was a modality to which their clients responded.[10] The response was unenthusiastic interest expressed by the administrator and covert resistance from the rest of the staff.

Although the team leader's initiation of the change goal was precipitous, it pointed to his need to devote attention to the facilitating and related actors, and so he began to organize his support. The BA counselors, although low in formal power, were influential with the critical actor. Since one of the dayroom team members was a highly respected former member of that group, he was recruited to assist in neutralizing the opposition. Two of the MSW counselors had positive informal relations with the team leader as well as with the other trained professionals, and the worker saw them as a source of information and a communication link with the professionals in the clinic. This was a channel that had hitherto gone unused. Members of the patient government had a significant contribution to make to the informal alliance as well, since the hospital was concerned about the local community's distrust of it. It is clear that the participation of these varied groups made a greater impact on the worker's goal to develop a vocational service than would have been the case if the same number of participants had brought similar rather than diverse resources and interests to the effort.

In concluding this section, it is worth calling attention to a point made in Chapter 4. Generating support from others often involves practitioners in a further trade—with payment to be required at some later time. As such, coalition building can be conceptualized as entailing a future cost, which the practitioner must be willing to pay. It has been suggested that the larger the number of resources necessary to influence an action, the more complex the system of exchanges.[11] It is advisable, therefore, to keep the use of resources to the minimum necessary to accomplish the change.

---

[10] It may be noted that the team leader *implicitly* answered the four questions that were posed in introducing this chapter. The idea was introduced by him directly to the critical actor in the formal setting of a large staff meeting and his argument highlighted a professional tenet.

[11] Terry Clark, *Community Structure and Decision Making* (San Francisco: Chandler, 1966), p. 53.

Assuming that one can make an informed judgment about when to limit the size of a coalition, it is advisable to do so for another reason. In recruiting support, bargaining inevitably takes place (although it is often implicit), and the practitioner may well have to concede some part of his objectives to attain consensus. The more divergent the views of its members, the more pressure for the coalition's position to represent a least common denominator. The question for the practitioner, then, is whether the price he must pay is worth the benefits he expects to receive.

OPPOSITION

By implication, a discussion of who should be the audience for an appeal in initiating a change and where support may be garnered implies the reverse, namely, the issue of where opposition may be anticipated and how it may be avoided. In this section, we discuss resistance: its sources, how it is manifested, and some of the means by which opposition is averted or reduced.

As has been pointed out earlier, the locus of opposition may be inferred from the way in which the change goal impinges on the interests and values of affected participants. But resistance to change may stem from other factors as well, and these are ordinarily more amenable to worker intervention. Opposition may come from little more than lack of knowledge on the part of actors regarding the negative consequences of current program and policy. (This is, as a matter of fact, the implicit assumption of those who espouse improved communication as the solution for interpersonal and social problems.) If lack of knowledge is the barrier to change, we may assume that the skilled worker will have dissipated most or all of it during the preinitiation phase of the process.

Sometimes, in the initiation of change, lack of understanding of what is intended operates as a basis for resistance. This is often due to differences in vocabulary among various professional groups or program units. It might be called "jargon at the interfaces." Although one's shorthand language may be efficiently decoded within a profession or department, it can cause misunderstanding among outsiders. In complex settings particularly, the change-oriented practitioner must take care to translate his proposal into the language of his listeners.

Other sources of resistance during the initiation phase of the process are inertia and apathy, fear or uncertainty regarding the outcome of the proposed change, and psychological investments in things as they are. Inertia often stems from the perception that the proposed change cannot be accomplished or that its accomplishment is not worth the effort. Under these circumstances the extra energy required to get a static body moving will have to be supplied by the practitioner; he will have to show that it *can* be done and is worth the doing. When inertia is the only obstacle, supervisors may let practitioners devise new procedures or undertake new programs on their own provided that additional funds are not entailed and that the cost in time is solely the worker's. In his turn, the practitioner moves ahead singly in the hope that he can demonstrate the effectiveness of the new program or procedure and thus ultimately encourage its wider acceptance within the organization.

Fear of the future or uncertainty about the outcome of change may reflect either the conservatism of particular actors or an organizational ambience. It can be considered resistance only when it is not objectively based—that is, when the fear is exaggerated or the organization's desire for predictability regularly supersedes its need for adaptability. Practitioners must also take into account that actors have long- or short-range perspectives on change depending on their position and tenure in an agency. Upper-ranking members and those who have served for long periods tend to have a longer time perspective about change than lower-ranking and more recently hired staff—in which case the former's resistance may not be to a change itself but to the pace at which its proponents hope to bring it about. When participants' resistance is due to a long-range perspective or even to natural caution, attributing the resistance to the specific change itself can lead to ineffective counteractions. Fear or uncertainty about the outcome of a change may require no more than the assurance of time. Thus, the leaders of organizations in which vote taking is required sometimes use the introduction of agenda items for discussion only as a political maneuver. After a number of such discussions, the item is presented for a decision. If the participants are not already talked out, at least they cannot maintain that their views did not receive a hearing, and they are more likely to accept the inevitably of the item's adoption. The item has, in short, ceased to be a new idea and has become a position to be formally ratified.

Finally, psychological investments in things as they are may be the basis for opposition. This form of resistance sometimes stems from the time, energy, or personal commitments that organization members have devoted to developing and sustaining current procedures or programs.[12] Or it may reflect a perceived threat to existent social relationships. Unless the goal can be shaped to skirt the *visible* threat to "sunk costs" or old ties, or sufficient rewards can be offered for loosening patterns of social relations, the practitioner may have to make an effort to avoid involving participants who have these psychological investments.

How may opposition to change be revealed in the initiation phase of the process? The question may seem a curious one to practitioners who have experienced an unequivocal no from either critical or facilitating actors. There are, however, many no's that are masked as assent, and they must be recognized.

---

[12] Patti reviews these "sunk costs" as a source of resistance. *Op. cit.*, pp. 378–79.

Some manifestations of opposition are difficult to identify because they represent the very tactics that are employed in promoting a change. For example, a critical or facilitating actor may respond ambiguously to a proposal; he may postpone attention to it for a future agenda or exploration by a committee; or he may reduce its scope to what seems tokenism. These actions often represent the behavior of an actor who is opposed to an idea but wants to appear to be open to it. But they may also signal that he favors the goal and is buying time for its broader acceptance. An ambiguous response or a delay needs supporting data before one can define it as an opposition tactic.

Another means of opposing a change without appearing to do so is to embrace a proposal, particularly its "essence," and then suggest revisions in structure and substance that effectively cripple it. The less obvious the revision's effect on the integrity of the proposal, of course, the more effective the tactic since it becomes more difficult to identify or expose. This is a particularly useful technique when the proposal is a popular one and the opponent (*qua* supporter) needs to make inroads into the contingent of its supporters.

Sometimes, too, critical actors may obscure their responsibility for the decision—suddenly transforming themselves into facilitators or powerless "supporters." [13] Another maneuver is to attempt to separate a proponent from his allies or cause tension among members of an ad hoc coalition. Especially for top-ranking participants who have sanctions to dispense, the opportunities to do so are numerous. (There are a number of other techniques that mask opposition, but these tend to be used during the implementation of change and are discussed in the next chapter.)

How one counters opposition depends on several factors. As suggested in Chapter 6, it is the configuration of working forces that determines where on the continuum from collaboration to contest the practitioner's tactics will fall. In collaborative efforts, opposition is minimal and is not a significant issue; in contest tactics, a major aim is to display "muscle," and opposition is provoked or met head-on. The handling of opposition between these polar points has been largely neglected in the literature, although for the low-ranking practitioner within an organization it assumes special importance. Particularly in the initiation phase of the process, proponents often need to maintain a low profile and behave in ways that will not stimulate opposition. Thus workers sometimes attempt to highlight the existence of a problem by dramatic or impassioned action in order to get the problem placed on the organization's agenda or to

---

[13] Alinsky, writing about conflict tactics, advises that when a target denies responsibility, a contending protest group's focus should remain fixed on him nevertheless. If he is in fact not responsible, his friends—who undoubtedly *are* responsible—will soon emerge. Saul Alinsky, *Rules for Radicals* (New York: Random House, 1971), pp. 130–31.

generate support for its solution. Although activism of this sort is sometimes effective, it also risks arousing opponents as much as supporters. The point may be missed that latent opposition that can be kept quiescent or unorganized hardly constitutes an opposition at all.

Co-optation is a classic means of averting opposition. It refers to the absorption of potentially antagonistic elements into a system so as to neutralize their dissidence. Potential opponents may be muted or their positions transformed by including them in the change effort—assuming, of course, that the price of accommodating their interests is not too high. A device similar to co-optation commonly used by human service workers entails incorporating the beliefs or values of potential opponents into one's idea system, if these beliefs do not conflict too strongly with those of the practitioner and his allies. For example, in the "sounding out" process regarding organizational problems, the worker may include the ideas of others in his goal insofar as it is possible. Practitioners who are more committed to their objectives than to their images may go even further and share or forgo credit for the innovation. Conceding the approbation that comes from initiating a good idea to a potential adversary turned sympathetic supporter is a psychologically difficult but tactically effective act.

Another means of averting opposition is to implicate the potential adversary in the process. We have noted that formal commitment is a powerful influence on subsequent behavior. If the worker is able to elicit a promise from an actor for a particular deed in the future, the chances of his fulfilling that commitment are substantial. One way of doing this is to introduce his change goal to the actor in isolation, before it has been widely discussed in the agency. Without apparent opposition to the idea— and the fact that feedback more often than not tends to be approving and positive—the likelihood of agreement is enhanced. Another and somewhat more effective way of engaging a potential adversary in a change is to transmit the idea in a setting in which disagreement is psychologically difficult because of group pressure or other social aspects of the situation. Forcing a commitment from the actor at such a time makes it more difficult for him to retract the commitment at a later date.

Bypassing a potential opponent is another mechanism to avoid opposition. When an actor cannot be co-opted or implicated, he may have to be circumvented. This is particularly true if he is a facilitating actor who is perceived as a nay-sayer while the critical actor's support might otherwise be obtainable. Unless there are organizationally appropriate means to accomplish this—for example, locating the consideration of the change in a component of the organization outside the opponent's legitimate authority—the question for the practitioner is how to evade the opponent without violating organizational protocol. This is an important consideration, for unless organizational protocol is observed, the worker risks creating or increasing opposition rather than neutralizing or transforming it.

Ignoring channels is usually a serious violation of organizational manners and must be done with care. Informal and seemingly fortuitous meetings with upper-ranking members sometimes work. The test is whether they are perceived as fortuitous or premeditated by those concerned. Sometimes, too, agency procedures allow communication with high-ranking members without requiring the permission of intermediate actors who might be predisposed to prevent the contact, either because they are opposed to the innovation, because their status has been compromised, or for other reasons. If sending a memorandum is standard procedure, for example, the practitioner can communicate with upper-ranking members by including them in the distribution.

Depending on agency norms, there is a fine line that separates a practitioner's decision to act on his own and the requirement that he obtain supervisory sanction for an action. Often permission is refused for an act which, had it been a *fait accompli,* would have caused little upset. It is the skillful practitioner who can define that line and knows when to inform his supervisor of his intentions rather than request his consent. Minimally, however, the practitioner must inform those organizational participants who have a right to expect to be kept apprised of what he is doing. Many change efforts founder because the practitioner neglects to touch base with appropriate and interested parties.

THE INITIATOR

Sometimes the initiation of a proposal emerges spontaneously from what has gone before, and the choice of the actor who introduces the change stems "naturally" from the preinitiation process. If preinitiation activities were conducted sensitively, the initiator may turn out to be the critical actor himself.

Such was the case in regard to the establishment of the day hospital at the Monrad Community Mental Health Center cited earlier. It will be recalled that the worker had informally organized a group of day patients. This was intended both to highlight the special needs of these clients and to gain legitimacy and expertise for himself in the area. Then, in a series of meetings, problems associated with the goal of a day hospital were carefully orchestrated by different staff. One of them reported on a conference he had attended at which other mental health centers described successful experiences with day hospital programs. The worker noted:

> Over lunch soon after, Dr. N. asked me how things were going with my informal meetings with the day patients. I said they were going very well, that all of the day patients appreciated the opportunity to meet as a group and discuss their problems together. They had indicated how helpful it was to do this.

> Dr. N. said that *he* was thinking about the idea of setting up a day hospital program and was going to discuss it with the team leaders. I said that from Robert's presentation it made a lot of sense. I had previously worked in a day hospital as a college volunteer, I told him, and it seemed to be effective in reducing the number of twenty-four-hour admissions while improving the continuity of patient care.

The worker understood the risks in letting the matter rest with the critical actor's "thinking about the idea." For one thing, Dr. N.'s support was not yet firmly established and would have to be reinforced. For another, there was the danger that the innovation would move beyond the worker's control, thus hindering his ability to influence its development. Thus he followed up the earlier conversation.

> The next week I made it my business to meet with Dr. N. again. I told him that I had thought about his suggestion for a day hospital and that I would like to work on it. Would he want me to develop some notes for a proposal? He agreed.[14]

Often, however, the selection of an initiator requires conscious determination, depending in large part on the audience to whom the change message is directed. Tactical considerations play a role as well. As the practitioner reviews his working forces, he finds that collaborative interventions are appropriate with some organizational participants, other interventions require maneuvering, and some forces may be subject to modification only by confrontation or conflict. The message may thus be directed to a number of different audiences and require a number of different initiators. Where contest is the mode of intervention, the appropriate vehicle for introducing a change may be a group composed of persons who are most threatening to the critical actor or actors. By and large, however, the aim during the initiation phase is to educate or persuade rather than to threaten. Initiators, then, are selected for their ability to persuade the audience in question.

The initiator of the change and the one who is publicly seen as its advocate may or may not be the practitioner who has conceived the effort. Rogers and Shoemaker indicate, as a matter of fact, that studies of the diffusion of innovations reveal that the stimulator of an idea and its initiator typically have different characteristics.[15] Although their reference is not to an internal organizational process, the characteristics they describe are suggestive. Stimulators are people who are message-oriented, know the innovation, and tend to have far-ranging contacts and a cosmopolitan outlook. In contrast, the forte of the initiator is his knowledge of the system, the security of his place in it, and his predominantly local orientation.

---

[14] Alan Boyer, "A Change at the Monrad Community Mental Health Center," unpublished paper, 1977.

[15] Rogers and Shoemaker, *op. cit.*, p. 278.

One need not accept these descriptions as valid to note that there are often participants in organizations who are peripheral to the mainstream of the agency, act as critics or intellectual gadflies, often play havoc with agency norms, and for these very reasons are unable to obtain widespread support for their ideas. An effective initiator, on the other hand, is well established in the agency and "maintains contact ideologically with the basic values of significant others"—an essential prerequisite for effective social influence.[16]

Two salient factors in attempts to persuade are the prestige and attractiveness of the communicator *to the audience* to be inflenced. If the practitioner has prestige and attractiveness with the relevant audience(s), he will be the most effective initiator—for when he makes the case, he knows that it will be made as he intended. Frequently, however, he will have to borrow from the social capital of others. It might be noted in this regard that the prestige that flows from perceived expertise is more convincing when technical issues are under consideration (which is one reason why, in preinitiation, the worker must develop a reputation for command of his subject matter), whereas the attractiveness emanating from peer status and a convergence of values is more convincing in value-oriented matters. The initiator who combines expertise *and* commonality with his audience is doubly effective in persuading.

The credibility of the communicator to his audience is another highly salient factor in deciding who should introduce and advocate a change.[17] In a classic experiment, Hovland and Weiss demonstrated that more attitude change takes place when a message is attributed to a high-credibility source than to a low-credibility one.[18] Some determinants of credibility transcend the person or group identity and include the content of the argument and the mind set of the audience. But there are also factors relating to the communicator himself.

One is the ascription of self-interest that may be made. Credibility decreases when a worker is perceived to be arguing in his own interest, or in the interests of his subunit. When he is so perceived, the audience is more likely to expect selective interpretations and less than complete candor. Unless the practitioner or the group to which he belongs has built up a store of trust, his arguments will be taken with a grain of salt.

Sensitivity to the ascription of self-interest can sometimes help to close the credibility gap. If the worker's argument includes advantages to himself or the group with which he is identified but there are other cogent reasons for making it, he might just say this. When there is no choice but

[16] Wax, *op. cit.*, p. 277.

[17] This paragraph and the three immediately following it are summarized and revised from George Brager and Harry Specht, *Community Organizing* (New York: Columbia University Press, 1973), pp. 306–8.

[18] C. I. Hovland and W. Weiss, "The Influence of Source Credibility on Communication Effectiveness," *Public Opinion Quarterly* 15 (1951), pp. 635–50.

complete candor, candor may help and can't hurt. Less cynically, when one's audience is either unsympathetic or is knowledgeable about the issue under discussion, the practitioner must carefully transmit self-evidently unbiased messages. If, on the other hand, the worker's argument appears to be in his or his unit's interest but is not, that point should be clarified. Finally, if a position is *against* his interest, much should be made of the fact, since credibility is increased if he is arguing against his own interest.

Another factor that enhances credibility is the "soft sell." The most convincing communicator does not appear to be trying to convince at all. Apparently his presumed lack of stake in the outcome increases his trustworthiness. Furthermore, the audience is disarmed. Not having to resist an assault on its beliefs, it is more open to hearing the message. Perhaps better than the "soft sell' is no sell at all. A worker might exhort in order to mobilize the already committed, frighten the opposition, or for other reasons, but not to add credibility to the message.

Once again, of course, the practitioner may line up someone who is more credible than himself in regard to the particular change—a less obviously interested party, a participant whose position on the issue may be less expected or stereotypical, or someone whose past history of interaction with the audience has engendered trust. A number of other participants from his own or other subunits may be brought in to add credibility or prestige—and thus pressure as well—by supporting the practitioner when he introduces the change.

If he uses another's prestige, social appeal, or credibility, the practitioner must be sensitive to the other's interests. Allies should not be beguiled into doing something they did not intend or something that will result in negative consequences they might not have foreseen. If, for example, the practitioner is aware that there is risk for the other in his relations with powerful organizational participants, the risk should be shared with and understood by the potential initiator before he acts. Indeed, there ought to be rewards for those who are asked to introduce or advocate the change and, if possible, a reinforcement of these rewards, if only by social approbation.

But prestige and credibility aside, the most important characteristic of an initiator is his power in relation to the audience—the extent to which the audience is dependent on him and his ability, if only implicitly, to apply sanctions (see Chapter 4). The higher the initiator is in the organizational hierarchy, the more widespread the support he can generally mobilize and the more valuable he is as an advocate. But it is a mistake to assume a one-to-one correlation between rank and effective advocacy. Occasionally, a low-ranking member is the preferable choice as initiator. One such occasion is when the change is a radical one and needs an "innocent" or nonthreatening introduction. Another is when critical or facilitating actors are prone to identify with the underdog, and a request from a "lowly" source receives more sympathetic attention. Social work students have found, for example, that they sometimes get a more receptive response from supervisors because they are "learners" and vulnerable than they would if their status were more secure. The choice between a low- or high-ranking member need not always be mutually exclusive, however. Sometimes, both can be called on—one to initiate the proposal and the other to follow up with support. But other things being equal, it is common wisdom that the power of a proponent counts the most in convincing others to act.

The Message and the Medium

The substance of any change goal is the critical variable in molding the change process. As the worker analyzes his field of forces, determines potential interventions, and engages in such preinitiation activities as heightening awareness of the problem within the organization, he has simultaneously molded and reshaped his "final" goal. The more interests are perceived to be threatened by the goal, the more opposition it will generate—and conversely, the more interests are perceived as consonant with the goal, the more support will accrue. Whatever the reality, it is how the parties define the situation—their *perception* of reality—that is crucial to their response.

Definitions are malleable, affected, as we have said, by the particular audience and their reaction to the initiator. In addition, how an innovation is designed, defined, and transmitted governs its meaning to relevant organizational actors. The definition of the change goal (i.e., the practitioner's message) and the choice of the medium or forum in which to transmit the message are significant in the initiation phase of the process.

DEFINING THE GOAL

In Chapter 5, we indicated some of the characteristics of goals that make them more or less likely to be perceived positively. Thus, a goal that can be designed and defined to be compatible with current practice, requires a minimum number of clearances, and can be reversed if found wanting is more likely to be adopted. The practitioner must shape his goal and its presentation so that the content of the change idea, its format, and the arguments favoring it maximize its potential for acceptance.

There are a number of ways in which this may be done, but we shall discuss only three of the most important here. One has to do with whether or not to present the full goal and another with how the goal is interpreted. The third relates to the bargaining components inherent in the goal—that is, the degree of maneuverability its presentation permits either the practitioner or the agency.

Partializing the Goal.   We noted in Chapter 5 that partializing a goal is often an effective and sometimes the only means by which practitioners with limited influence can achieve their ends. Limiting the scope of a goal may take a number of forms. The goal may lend itself to a sequence of steps; that is, point A must be effected before moving to point B, and completing point B is a requirement of C. If the worker believes that B and C are likely to be rejected, or if they have already been rejected, his tactic is relatively simple. He introduces only A as his change goal, or he retreats to it if he has already put forth the entire goal. He thus hedges the risk to the organization of a broad-scale change. Possibly B and C will be perceived as acceptable later, after A has been experienced. Furthermore, actions taken in the early stages of a process (e.g., step A) can subsequently be invested with meaning that was not fully understood or explicit in the initial action. A first step can thus be defined retrospectively as a moral commitment to a fuller action—in this case, a commitment to B and C.

Change goals may not be so obviously sequenced, however. In that event, the choice of one specific aspect of a goal to focus on from the total universe of its content is not so readily apparent, and criteria must be developed for determining choices in partializing goals. We suggest a balance or trade-off from among three criteria: the likelihood that the organization will accept the partial goal, the contribution of the partial goal to reaching the worker's full objective, and the intrinsic validity of the partial goal in its own right—all evaluated with reference to other possible choices.

Another means of partializing a goal is to ignore the goal directly and concentrate on establishing a precedent in a related area. Thus, if a worker hoped to move his treatment agency to serving adolescent clients without also serving their families, he might try to establish a precedent by suggesting only that adolescents in crisis be seen in intake prior to attempting to gain family involvement which is a much less loaded proposal. Establishing a precedent in a benign and noncontroversial area is often a stepping-stone to similar action later in regard to more controversial matters. Similarly, if a change goal appears to necessitate a change in policy, the practitioner might instead request that exceptions to the policy be made in given instances and encourage other staff to do likewise. When enough exceptions have been granted, a policy becomes inoperative. At the least, the exceptions might conceivably soften resistance to the policy change or, better still, demonstrate the wisdom of making the change.

Practitioners must be mindful of the risk that the partialization tactic may lend itself to worker misperception—namely, that they will define as a victory what has essentially been a defeat. Administrators often make concessions or grant exemptions to policies as a device to reduce demand for more significant innovation or to alleviate pressure on them to modify a policy. In such cases, they may be able to purchase worker satisfaction too cheaply.

Although limiting the scope of a goal through partializing ordinarily increases its chances of adoption, there are occasions when the reverse is the tactical choice. An increase in the scope of a goal can serve to include content that is meaningful to other actors and thus increase their incentives to join an alliance. Sometimes, too, a change design is broadened in order to encompass an area in which the worker's intervention would be defined as legitimate whereas a narrower focus might exclude it. Primarily, however, increasing the scope of an innovation usually takes place when contest is the mode of intervention. The contending actors either wish to make the action more visible or up the issue-ante to mobilize additional or more zealous support.

Interpreting the Goal. Some of the same issues apply with regard to how the worker interprets a change as apply to partializing a goal. Some change ideas lend themselves to a definition of limited scope, and indeed all changes, even the basic ones, can be presented as less far-reaching than they in fact are. One technique is to minimize the threat or uncertainty inherent in any change by presenting the proposal as involving little or no change on the ground that it is related to the traditional values of the organization or more closely conforms to current programmatic directions than the procedure or policy it is intended to replace. Haley speaks of the talent of Jesus in this regard. Although Jesus managed to call attention to himself as someone presenting new ideas, at the same time he defined what he said as the proper orthodoxy.[19]

If appeals to tradition or current directions cannot be made, the experience of other agencies may be highlighted to reduce the unpredictability of the measure under consideration (and, incidentally, to reap the benefits of agency competitiveness as well). These, of course, were the purposes served by the Monrad worker's description of successful day hospital programs conducted by other community mental health centers.

Sometimes workers may define their goal as a procedural rather than a policy change, for procedural modifications are less threatening than policy changes and are typically decided at a lower level of the hierarchy. They are thus more directly accessible to practitioner influence. Another technique, suggested earlier, is to allow a new idea time to percolate until it does not seem new at all.

A major issue in choosing the little-or-no-change approach has to do, as does any persuasive effort, with the audience to whom the message is beamed. There are some critical actors who respond to novel approaches

[19] Jay Haley, *The Power Tactics of Jesus Christ* (New York: Grossman, 1969), p. 23.

and some agencies with change-oriented values; in such cases downplaying the novelty of an idea would obviously be an error. Practitioners must distinguish between those who speak of their openness to novelty and those who mean it. This, of course, is no simple matter, although previous history often offers a significant clue.

Since most change efforts entail intervention in a number of working forces that affect different actors, workers are commonly involved with a number of different audiences, requiring that they raise or lower the change decibel in their message depending on the predilections of the particular group. Yet they would do well to exercise caution. Objective reality critically shapes perceptions. It should not be underestimated, nor should the practitioner underestimate those he wishes to influence. People generally understand where their short-term interests lie even if their long-term interests are sometimes more elusive. "Creative" definitions of a change goal are unlikely to influence perceptions unless there is a reasonable basis for the worker's interpretations and some ambiguity or ambivalence in the position of the audience.

Bargaining. Bargaining takes place in most collaborative undertakings and in all campaign and contest interventions. Positions are put forward, reactions to them assessed, and an agreement reached that entails some exchange of benefit or reward (if only out of gratitude, for the sake of friendship, or "keeping the peace"). The bargaining is often implicit and may not be perceived or experienced by the parties as such at all.

Nevertheless, as the worker moves through the initiation phase of a change effort, he engages in a series of bargaining processes of varying types. Indeed, with allies, the shape of the change goal as it is finally proposed often constitutes the resolution of a collaborative exchange process. For bargaining to take place between opponents, parity in power is necessary. The process entails seeking out clues to determine which positions are fixed and which have "give" in order to locate the maximally beneficial deal. Thus, to the extent that one can demonstrate commitment to a position, a commitment that is credible to the other as irrevocable, he is more likely to win his point in the settlement.[20]

Our primary interest here, however, is the potential for bargaining with critical and facilitating actors. They tend to fall somewhere between allies and opponents, and there is ordinarily an imbalance in resources for influencing, with the practitioner in a disadvantaged power position. In light of these circumstances, how can the practitioner's message—his presentation of the change goal—help him to strike the best bargain available?

The content of the argument and how it is framed will influence an

[20]Schelling refers to the ability to "bind oneself;" that is, to make so firm a commitment that retraction is virtually impossible. He explores a number of techniques by which this is done. Thomas C. Shelling, *The Strategy of Conflict* (Cambridge, Mass.: Harvard University Press, 1963), pp. 22–28.

actor's predisposition to accept the practitioner's goal. It is perhaps obvious that the goal must be justified by reference to the target actor's interests and values and that a congruence of interests and values with the practitioner on one topic promotes agreement with the worker's other positions. That these points are so frequently ignored in practice may be due to the partisan bias of practitioners and their conviction of moral or intellectual rightness. The case of the Somerville team leader, to which we referred earlier in this chapter, exemplifies this common practice. His argument in favor of the expansion of his program emphasized that a dayroom structure formed the *core* of treatment for skid-row alcoholics, thereby challenging the interests of the clinicians in his audience and increasing their resistance. It was only later, when the team leader redefined the change as aiding and extending the role of the counselor, that he gained a receptive hearing.

In explicit negotiations, the way in which demands are formulated often determines the outcome of the exchange. In internal organizational change practice, however, the bargaining is most often implicit, and "demands" are not often in order. But how the change goal is structured and presented may be as critical to the result, and there are a number of advantages to the worker's offering a range of alternatives in presenting his proposal. For one thing, it is a useful device for obtaining expressions of interest and assessing the commitments of critical actors, adding clarity to the practitioner's ultimate negotiating position. For another, it gives the appearance of moderation, and in collaborative and campaign interventions this is ordinarily an important bargaining stance. Studies of attitude change suggest that moderate presentations are most effective with educated audiences, those who are suspicious of the speaker's "angle," or when the speaker has limited credibility and the issue is one of high salience for the audience.[21] These are characteristics that often apply to critical actors and their relations with low-ranking staff who are seeking change.

Furthermore, presenting a series of alternatives gives the actor some feeling of choice, and greater "ownership" of the change is likely to be engendered. Most important, it limits the likelihood of a flat no. That is, in an uncertain field, a range of alternatives increases the chance that one of the options will be accepted, thus keeping the process alive for future and further advances.[22]

Better still, when the practitioner can offer a range of alternatives, he enhances his cause by giving prominence to his desired outcome. There

[21] E. Aronson, J. Turner, and J. Carlsmith, "Communicator Credibility and Communication Discrepancy as Determinants of Opinion Change," *Journal of Abnormal and Social Psychology* 67 (July 1963), pp. 31–36; J. Whittaker, "Attitude Change and Communication-Attitude Discrepancy," *Journal of Social Psychology* 65 (February 1965), pp. 141–47.

[22] There are dangers in excess flexibility as well. The major risk has already been identified—namely, that the practitioner might settle for less than he might otherwise have obtained had his commitment been a fixed one.

are a number of mechanisms by which this may be done: implying a "natural" compromise, offering a least objectionable alternative, and drawing critical fire away from his preferred solution.

The critical actor may be channeled to choose the worker's preference if there is a focal point in the alternatives—a place to which attention is directed.[23] One such focal point is the "natural" compromise. An example is provided by the decision of an administrator faced with conflicting demands for scheduling evening intakes. The agency's psychiatric staff resisted all evening appointments, while the workers who were pressing for change proposed a weekly evening intake session. The administrator's decision was to develop biweekly evening appointments, which represented a natural compromise. In the same vein, a practitioner may propose a number of alternatives to deal with a problem, his preferred alternative falling "naturally" between an alternative that does too little to affect the problem and an alternative that risks too much in solving it.

A different focal point to which critical actors may be channeled is the least objectionable alternative. In this instance, the practitioner offers a series of alternatives representing gradations of scope, divergence from current practice, or some other characteristic of a change goal. Assuming that the administration has an incentive to deal with the problem represented by the alternatives, attention will be drawn to the least far-reaching or risk-inducing alternative. But the least objectionable alternative may go a long way toward the worker's goal. And it may not be "least objectionable" in fact but only in presentation.

An example is provided by the practice of a planner employed by the urban-affairs department of a large city bank. Following pressure from the news media and the threat of regulatory action by the state legislature regarding ethically questionable mortgage-lending practices in predominantly black neighborhoods, the worker was assigned to investigate the possibility of the bank's experimenting with lending to low-income markets. The bank, she determined, would want to make some public-relations gesture to demonstrate concern for the less financially advantaged. Following exploration of the low-income lending practices of other banks and the risks to profit inherent in various plans, she wrote a proposal that structured the alternatives and arguments in such a way as to channel the choices of the critical actors. There were two alternatives—one proposed a citywide program with lending authority in the various branches, and the other centralized the authority within a small unit that would review loan applications from a limited number of low income neighborhood branches. The latter, clearly the "least objectionable" to the bank's administrators, represented more than the tokenism the worker initially feared.

Another bargaining strategem is to draw attention *away* from the core of the goal by including some elements that are likely to attract critical

[23] Schelling, *op. cit.*, p. 68.

fire. For example, in the Charter House case cited earlier, the worker included a provision in her proposed client-discharge procedure that gave the adolescent clients a right to attend the discharge proceeding and to submit oral or written arguments on their own behalf. She believed the provision to be a sound one which had little chance of adoption. It was included to reduce the radical-seeming nature of her central goal (i.e., the involvement of clinical staff in discharge proceedings). She was also sensitive to the fact that it would provide a focal point for the resistance of potential opponents of the proposal, drawing attention away from its central component. More important, it gave her an item that could be surrendered in the face of opposition, thus demonstrating her own reasonableness and giving the opposition a face-saving victory as well.

DETERMINING THE MEDIUM

How a change idea travels from a worker to his audience influences how it will be heard. In the study of the diffusion of innovations, two major channels have been identified, the mass media and interpersonal communications. The evidence suggests that the former serves primarily to create knowledge and transfer information whereas face-to-face contact is more effective in persuading others to change their attitudes.[24] Unfortunately, there are no comparable studies of the impact on change of the use of various channels within organizations.

There are two sets of variables that might profitably be considered in exploring organizational channels. The first, following the diffusion studies, distinguishes between the written and the spoken word.[25] The second refers to the formality-informality dimension of the channel. If extending the diffusion studies to organizations is valid, one might hypothesize that the written word and the more formal mechanism are useful in transferring information whereas interaction and informality are preferred if persuasion is the purpose. We focus here on the formal mechanisms, since much of what has already been suggested in this book implicitly relates to the use of informal channels.

The Written Message. Memoranda, minutes, manuals, position papers, and program proposals are ubiquitous in organizational life. Yet their use (or misuse) in organizational change has not to our knowledge ever been considered. Two questions in particular are relevant for practice purposes. What are the factors to be considered in choosing the written over the spoken word? What are the conditions under which one would decide upon one or the other as he engages the initiation process?

[24] Rogers and Shoemaker, *op. cit.,* p. 252.

[25] Although this is not quite precise, since the media may include the spoken as well as the written word, it does represent an essential difference between the media and interpersonal communication; that is, the media and the written word do not permit direct feedback.

Differences between the written and spoken word are often matters of degree. The style and content of the message determine its influence upon a receiver as much as or more than the channel through which it is transmitted. Once that is said, however, whether one uses one or the other medium depends, in some measure at least, on the intrinsic properties of the medium. Written messages do not lend themselves to immediate feedback, for example. They entail little of the back-and-forth communication, the clarifying, elaborating, and modifying, that take place in face-to-face contact. The written word is generally efficient as regards the receiver's time, since he can absorb the message more quickly than he could by discussing it. But it is less receiver-oriented in that the communicator is not present to assay the receiver's reaction. This may be why unassertive persons are often more effective in writing than in speaking, since they avoid experiencing the emotional overtones of the recipient's reactions.

Memoranda and other written messages also constitute a permanent record. They tend to be more explicit and committing and cannot be "taken back" or defined as a misunderstanding as easily as spoken interchanges. They are also less subject to the practitioner's control in that their distribution is partly in the hands of the receiver.

Furthermore, written messages can be more deliberate; they encourage careful thought. As such, they can make their points more precisely or impressively, and with better documentation. More than verbal presentations, they lend themselves to the display of knowledge. This may be one of the reasons why, in upwardly striving professions, emphasis is placed on the written record, and somehow a message that is not down in black and white is perceived as less "professional."

It is these properties of the written word that practitioners must weigh in choosing to send a memorandum or deciding whether to document their proposal. Sometimes organizational structure or protocol allows little leeway; sometimes, however, the worker has an option. In such a case, he frequently must trade off the advantages of a written message against its disadvantages. For example, a critical actor might appreciate a summary of a proposal before he decides whether to invest his time in pursuing it, and the practitioner gains credit for himself and his idea if he is sensitive to this fact. On the other hand, the practitioner may feel that he can be more persuasive if he has not forewarned the actor in writing. He will then have to decide whether or not to forgo the credit he might gain in favor of increased persuasiveness. As with any social process, there are no immutable principles separate from the actors, the context, and the worker's intentions. What is required of the effective change-oriented practitioner is that he understand and consciously weigh the properties of the channels as they affect his immediate objectives.

In choosing to use the written or spoken word the practitioner must consider the response he wishes to elicit, the character of the message to be transmitted, its distribution (that is, what participants might best receive or not receive the message), and, finally, issues relating to verification and accountability.

As we have suggested, in face-to-face contact feedback is immediate and potentially full. In contrast, the use of writing as the channel leads to a more considered but more partial response. But this may be exactly what the practitioner wants during the early stages of the change process. In that event, although communication theorists equate feedback with effectiveness, a written message constitutes the more "effective" communication medium for him. For example, if protocol demands that the practitioner inform a participant of his activity but he hopes to avoid making a full explanation, writing may be the preferred choice. Or it may simply be more efficient of time because, in the particular circumstance, a full explanation is unnecessary. The practitioner may also wish to make reaction more costly by putting the burden of response on the other. Thus, he may indicate that he intends to proceed on a matter unless there is a reply mandating the contrary. When this device is used to obtain "permission," the memorandum would of course be composed so that the message is as unobtrusive as possible.

On the other hand, when the worker feels he needs an actor's response to explore, clarify, or modify the design of his proposal, he will opt for an interactional process. Similarly, when it is important for an actor to get a feeling of participation in the process, his immediate and full feedback will ordinarily be elicited.

A second factor has to do with the content of the message. High-intensity messages—those carrying a high emotional or value load—are generally better spoken, since tonal qualities and other nonverbal cues elaborate their meaning and add intensity to the communication. Facing the recipient directly also makes neutral handling more difficult. Similarly, complex messages, those which might not be readily understood or are subject to varying interpretations, may require the feedback of personal interchange. Finally, selective perception or "tuning out" is less likely in a direct contact, so that when particular arguments must be featured or dramatized, the worker can reduce the "noise" level of the exchange with more assurance if the channel is an interactional one.

The converse is obviously true as well. Matter-of-fact and routine messages lose little by written transmission. Or when a well-reasoned and well-documented argument is required to impress decision makers, the case may best be put on paper. However, practitioners must guard against information overload. The number of documented arguments that go unread in organizations is undoubtedly enormous. Succinct prose is appreciated by busy administrators, and indeed a tactic for *appearing* to communicate without actually doing so is to encumber the information with voluminous verbiage.

Another factor affecting the choice of channel has to do with who is to receive the message. As noted earlier, part of the art in a change process relates to the routing of the change idea. In some measure, this is accomplished by shaping the content of a proposal so that the content itself determines the audience (that is, the substance of the idea is defined so that it requires that X Unit receive or not receive it, or that it go to X Unit in addition to or instead of Y Unit). But routing is also accomplished by one's choice of channel.

We suggested earlier in this chapter that one way to circumvent a facilitator in order to reach critical actors directly is by memoranda. A written message may also be directed to one party in the expectation that it will be shared with another when the practitioner himself cannot transmit it directly without impeding its effectiveness. For example, a compliment is more credible when it is passed indirectly through a third party. Sometimes, too, threats are more effective when they reach an actor indirectly. It should be underscored, however, that the distribution of written messages may be wider than the worker intended. In taking this risk, there are two significant determinants: with whom might the recipient share the message, and what consequences might follow if he were to do so.

Since the senders and receivers of memoranda are identifiable, the message carries a record of its route. This fact has political uses not ordinarily available in using verbal channels. For one thing, the worker's superordinate, knowing that *his* boss or relevant others are reading the same material, may be more disposed to pay attention to it. For another, the worker's boss may be more willing to raise the matter with his boss when his responsibility is circumscribed by the practitioner's having initially raised the issue. Indeed, the practitioner may himself solicit a memorandum from subordinates or colleagues to diffuse responsibility or to create the image of clamor from below. Furthermore, the solicited memorandum may provide an opportunity for a practitioner to respond favorably, committing himself on paper to a course of action and thus raising the cost of reversing the action for higher-level participants.

There are, finally, two other elements to which we wish to call attention in choosing a channel: verification and accountability. Both are related to the fact that the written word is more explicit and permanent than an oral interchange.

The practitioner who has discussed a value-laden or complex idea (or even a factual or simple idea, if it is controversial) with critical or facilitating actors needs to consider the means by which their understanding may be verified or their agreement fixed. One way is for the worker to suggest that he will himself confirm the discussion in writing. Care must be taken that the critical actor does not perceive this gambit as indicating distrust of him, and publically acceptable grounds must thus be found for making the suggestion.

There are times when such explicit behavior is contraindicated, particularly when a superordinate is willing to go along with an action that he simultaneously knows about and does not know about—that is, when he will not be held directly accountable if it becomes visible. For example, the executive director of a neighborhood council with a conservative board of directors was willing to let his assistant plan and execute a community conference with militant overtones until the moment the assistant committed the plan to paper, at which point the executive backed away. Either the nature of an issue or the juxtaposition of roles may require that an actor not explicitly commit himself, as in the instance of the executive mentioned above. But he may suggest—again implicitly—that there is no risk to a worker in pursuing their common unspoken compact. If the worker does not "hear" the compact or trust it, he may put their agreement in writing. Such an act would constitute an alteration of the nature of their "contract," in the other's view. It would imply to him that the writer was being self-protective and thus might lead him to become wary and back off.

The Formal Meeting.   It has been said that the function of meetings is generally to ratify decisions previously arranged. If so, it is fitting that we conclude this chapter with a brief reference to the formal meeting, since the ratification (or rejection) of the change goal represents the completion of the initiation phase of the process. There are, it is true, any number of spoken exchanges among individuals and groups, formal and informal, during which a goal may be adopted or discarded. But most of the issues germane to initiation discussed in this chapter culminate at a formal meeting.

It may be an overstatement to suggest that the function of agency meetings is to ratify rather than to decide. Even as a partial truth, however, this offers a significant practice guideline. If the stage has been set in advance for ratification and the meeting is well orchestrated, it is likely that the goal will survive to be implemented.

Not all meetings, of course, call for advance preparation. If the benefit of the change to the worker is not worth the cost of time, energy, or future debts that might be incurred, he may introduce the change offhandedly and reserve his resources for a future investment. If the content of the change is relatively noncontroversial, little may need to be done. Or if, on the other hand, the change *is* controversial but there are common linkages among the several factions (and therefore the risk that early maneuverings will be "leaked"), advance preparation may generate more opposition than support.

Nevertheless, as exemplified by the Somerville worker who introduced his goal without forethought at his agency's staff meeting, practitioners too often take the step blindly. There are at least two reasons why failure to prepare for such meetings is unwise. For one, staff meetings often represent a "gathering of the clan." Critical and facilitating actors, as well as potential supporters and others whose interests may be challenged by the change, may all be present, and the arguments that are effective with one person or grouping may be ineffective with another. Thus, the practitioner either risks the disaffection of some for the favor of others, or else he may have to couch his statement so generally that it is convincing to none. Pre-meeting activity allows him to segregate his audiences, so that participants are convinced or not before the meeting, and the statements at the meeting can be largely ritualistic rather than designed to persuade.

Further, unless the practitioner has done some preliminary exploration, he has little basis for predicting the process of the meeting or its outcome. He may thus be unprepared to counter opposition or make full use of potential support; worse, he faces the prospect of his proposal's demise before its birth.

The process undertaken by a second-year social work student with the aid of his supervisor illustrates the value of careful pre-meeting activity. The student's goal was to institutionalize a group service on his ward of a mental hospital to prepare patients for reentry into the community, and he intended to demonstrate its efficacy by organizing and staffing the first group himself. Since decision making on the ward was participatory, requiring consensus, the full staff constituted his critical actors.

Prior to the ward's formal meeting, he initiated his idea with the staff psychiatrist, who was dissatisfied with the ward program (as was much of the rest of the staff) but apathetic about modifying it. The student defined his program idea as task-oriented, offered a concrete (i.e., nonpsychiatric) service. When the psychiatrist suggested that records of group meetings be kept, the student concurred and thus secured the psychiatrist's support. He next explored the reaction of friendly professionals. With those who appeared receptive, he discussed which patients might benefit most from the experience. To an opinion leader among the aides, a low-ranking but influential group, he noted that his staffing a group was a requirement of his school of social work but also argued that it might be helpful to the aides as well, since they would be relieved of the burden of caring for patients when the group was in session. These were arguments that would have seemed untoward to the professionals but helped to obtain the aide's agreement to endorse the proposal.

At the formal team meeting, his argument fixed on the recidivism rate of the patients and their need to be prepared to deal with the outside world. He avoided all reference to "therapy" or the group's therapeutic advantages, since the aides might associate it with professionals, with whom they were at odds, and the professionals might view it as an incursion on their turf or as entailing an additional task they might be called on to do at some future time. The student's proposal generated some heated discussion at the meeting, but with the active help of the psychiatrist and the aide, he was able to defend it successfully. Had he not lined up the varying factions, the outcome of the meeting might have been quite different.

This process constitutes in microcosm a summary of this chapter. The questions with which we began the chapter were each considered: to whom should the appeal be made, by whom, with what arguments, and through which channels?

In regard to the initial appeal, the student chose to begin with the psychiatrist, a passive but high-ranking member of the team who was likely to support a private appeal. He gauged which professionals might be allies and successfully enlisted their support. He identified the aides as a source of potential opposition and effectively neutralized them by winning over one of their opinion leaders.

Once he had assured himself of backup support, the student served as his own initiator and advocate at the formal meeting. In this particular setting, the student was an appropriate choice to introduce the change since he was not identified as a member of either the professional or the nonprofessional factions of the clique-ridden ward.

His goal was partialized, a first step in a planned sequence of moves. His definitions were formulated with a sharp eye on his audience; for example, with the psychiatrist he was careful to avoid what might be seen as presumption in his suggesting a new psychiatric modality. Rather, as a low-status participant, he proposed to perform a low-status task (i.e., a concrete service). His arguments were designed in the context of the interests and ideology of each of his segregated audiences, were honed to be nonthreatening, and capitalized on his personal equity and student status.

The process did not require consideration of which channels to use. Informal channels were the only appropriate ones, readily available in this small interacting group. If the student's goal had required approval beyond the ward, by the next hierarchical level, the channel to use might have become a concern. Indeed, if the change had required higher-ranking approval, the process outlined here would be descriptive only of one step in the initiation process rather than its completion. If there had been a need for further approval following the ward meeting, the questions of to whom to appeal, who should initiate the appeal, with what arguments, and through what channels would have had to have been repeated for the next higher level. The initiation process would thus have spiraled on.

In any case, the adoption of a change proposal completes only the initiation phase of the process. It does not insure its implementation and institutionalization. Practitioners with a skeptical bent will temper any self-congratulatory feelings they may have until an innovation is firmly in place. They know that all too frequently no good idea goes unpunished.

9.   Implementation and Institutionalization

IMPLEMENTATION MARKS the period between the adoption of an innovation and its realization. A formal decision has been made, but a series of actions are now required to bring it into being. Once the change has been operationalized and a period of trial and error passed, its stabilization is the last step in the process. It can then be said that the change has been institutionalized.

We assume, in discussing implementation and institutionalization here, that the change that has been adopted will meet its intended purposes. This may not, of course, be the case; as a change is implemented or institutionalized, inadequacies in its conception are revealed. Although we discuss the matter of evaluation later in this chapter, one caveat is necessary at the start: practitioners have to be ready to revise a change or abandon it if irremediable flaws are revealed as the process goes forward.

Barriers to Implementation

Implementation is a complex subprocess of a change effort. Even powerful decision makers are frequently unable to obtain the organizational action necessary to implement an idea successfully, and many formally adopted procedures, policies, and programs are never in fact operationalized. Or if they are, their aims have been so distorted that the original shape cannot be recognized. Thus, the practitioner who has seen his change idea through to adoption is by no means assured that it will be implemented as intended.[1] The obstacles are formidable, and we begin this chapter with an exploration of these barriers in the assumption that pitfalls are more likely to be

---

[1] Pressman and Wildavsky compute the probabilities of program implementation in situations requiring high interdependency among units. When there are thirty decision points (or required clearances) and the probability of favorable action at each point is 95 percent, the probability of overall program success is only .215! Jeffrey L. Pressman and Aaron B. Wildavsky, *Implementation* (Berkeley, Calif.: University of California Press, 1973), p. 108.

avoided when workers are aware of them. We proceed in the following section of the chapter to identify the practice alternatives available to the worker in confronting these obstacles.

As has been emphasized throughout this book, each phase of the process is shaped by the content of the goal and how the goal energizes forces which move toward or away from the desired change. Implementation is no exception, and the barriers to implementation thus vary with the content of the change. Some changes require only one or a limited number of steps to be implemented (e.g., the agency changes its policy to serve clients drawn from a new population group). Other changes require a series of steps over an extended period of time (e.g., a new program is phased in, staff hired, activities organized). Obviously, the requirements of the former are less complex than those of the latter. Thus, the barriers discussed below are applicable to particular change goals, depending on their content and structure.

The obstacles to implementation may be grouped in four interdependent categories. The first has to do with the interests and commitments of the participants, forces that are potent in all phases of a change process. Another set of obstacles has to do with the extent to which the change is general or specific; that is, whether it has been well defined in the initiation phase or a "fleshing out" of details is required as it is being implemented. A third potential barrier relates to the innovation's need for organizational resources and supports in order for it to be successfully tested. Finally, there are obstacles stemming from the way in which the change is implemented—the pitfalls, inherent or unintentional, that grow out of the methods used by proponents to actualize the change.

The Interests of Participants

However effectively the practitioner has taken into account the interests of participants in moving a change to adoption, the issue is likely to be reopened as the change is being implemented. For one thing, if there was prior resistance to the idea, operationalizing it allows new outlets for the opposition. Both proponents and opponents tend to be better armed for conflict at this time. Change proponents have a new and significant resource for influencing—the sanction of official endorsement and the approval of critical actors. Opponents, on the other hand, have something more concrete than an idea or proposal to deal with and can fight a rearguard action on the specific acts necessary to implement the idea. Evidence suggests that lower-ranking participants are considerably more able to prevent a change through such rearguard methods as inaction and subversion than they are to create change.[2]

[2] For example, the cases cited by David Mechanic in "Sources of Power of Lower Participants" all refer to situations in which the lower participants acted to

Even those who were not opposed to a proposal may find during implementation that the adopted change is a challenge to their interests. The new perception arises because actors often do not anticipate the impact of a change proposal until they have actually experienced the change. Finally, implementation introduces new interests as new actors are introduced into the process. The participants who decide to make a change and those who implement it are often different. In change that occurs from the top down, one group ordinarily makes the decision while another implements it. This also occurs in practitioner-initiated changes, even when there is considerable overlap among adopters and implementers. The interests of the newcomers may modify the initial field of forces in ways detrimental to effective implementation.

THE GENERALITY DIMENSION OF THE CHANGE

The more general the innovation, the more likely the outcome will reflect the views of the implementers rather than the adopters. In other words, when change goals are open to various interpretations, or operations readily permit alternate actions, the original intent can be distorted as the change is being phased in. So, for example, a change as specific as a shift in the location of a service from an agency's central facility to a neighborhood center provides little latitude for affecting the character of the change. In contrast, a change as broad-gauged as the development of a new set of services for a different population group within the agency's catchment area offers substantial latitude to implementers.

There is a paradoxical aspect to this point, demonstrating that practice that is appropriate in one phase of a change process can create obstacles in another phase. In initiating an innovation, it is often necessary to keep one's proposal broadly defined or aspects of it vague in order to ensure its adoption. For the proponents, neglecting to cross the t's and dot the i's represents a judgment that taking one step at a time is their best means of gaining the idea's acceptance. Opponents, on the other hand, may make the assessment that they must give in to the pressure of the proposal, but that its vagaries will allow them to impede its implementation later.

An example is provided by a school of social work that developed an innovative pattern of training for generic practice, one that would prove highly attractive to incoming students. The program went strongly counter to the value positions of some of the clinical faculty and posed "turf" problems as well. At the faculty meeting to decide the proposal, following its rocky course in gaining approval from the relevant committees, the

---

veto a change. In William W. Cooper, Harold J. Leavitt, and Maynard W. Shelly II, eds., *New Perspectives in Organizational Research* (New York: Wiley, 1964), pp. 136–49.

argument did not center on training arrangements at all but on whether the program was designed for students with or without social work experience. Opponents maintained that only experienced students could benefit (the effect of which would have been to drastically limit intake and make the program peripheral to the school's mainstream). Although the proposal was adopted, no decision was reached on admission requirements by common consent, and each side left the meeting with the impression that its view would prevail. In effect, both had implicitly agreed that it was in their interests to postpone the conflict to the implementation stage.

Even when political considerations are not at issue, innovative proposals are often necessarily general. As an idea moves from initial planning to adoption and implementation, its contours become clearer, and new and unanticipated problems inevitably arise. Particularly when a change goal is complex or experimental, its details cannot be sufficiently worked out to constitute a prescription for implementers. Forging new directions, by definition, suggests taking steps along an uncertain path, and the new behavior required may be unclear.

An example is provided by an agency that adopted a family advocacy program, hiring a new worker to implement it. The program's mission was relatively clear, as its name connotes: to provide families with a partisan advocate in their engagements with service systems, much as lawyers provide a partisan service to clients. But the actual tasks of the family advocate could not be specified in advance, and since the role was a relatively new one for social workers, its behavioral requirements were vague. In the absence of a precise job description, the worker who was hired brought older professional imprints to her work: "objectivity," social distance, and an identification with the service-providing system. She developed the role out of these concepts, so that over time, "family advocate" became a new title for a traditional service function, a change in nomenclature rather than a change in practice.

ORGANIZATIONAL SUPPORTS

Organizational decision makers adopt proposals with varying commitments to them. Sometimes critical actors are not fully aware of what is required to make the innovation work. Or they accept the proposal as a concession to the practitioner and his allies. Practitioners, on the other hand, settle for the partial commitment, believing it to be the most they can obtain at the time. This may be a politically correct judgment, since initial commitments generate momentum and can also strengthen future negotiation. But it does pose a problem in implementation and is sometimes unwise. The latter is the case when there is a high risk of failure unless the innovation has significant organizational support. The danger is that although the innovation may never actually be implemented, if it appears as if it had, the underlying idea that propelled it can be effectively discredited. An example on a much larger scale than a single organization is provided by the poverty program in the 1960s. "Maximum feasible participation" of the poor, a central feature of the program, was deemed a failure, although a convincing case has been made that this feature was never in fact implemented.[3]

Three aspects of organizational functioning constitute major potential barriers to effective implementation. Most obvious is the lack of necessary resources—staff, materials, time, and the like. The agency agrees to the program but is unwilling or unable to grant it the wherewithal to provide a fair test of its effectiveness. Unless the new program can demonstrate at least minimal results without additional resources or can make a case for further resources over time, change proponents are well advised to accept defeat in the initiation phase and cut their losses before implementation.

A frequently unanticipated barrier to effective implementation occurs when the new policy or program runs afoul of other, contradictory organizational policies. Sometimes this occurs innocently. A rule legitimately serves an organizational purpose, and its negative impact on the innovation is fortuitous. At other times, contradictory policies are used as weapons by the opponents of an innovation to prevent its implementation. Although rules are developed to limit discretion, they are subject to varying interpretations—as every practitioner knows who has ever bent a rule in his clients' interests. Thus, when upper-ranking members, in concert with lower-ranking ones, adopt a policy, it can readily be sabotaged by middle-ranking staff who wish to invoke its contradictory counterpart or interpret some existing rule as contradictory. The dean and faculty of one school of social work, for example, agreed to a formal revision of school policy to permit field instruction by non-social workers who had advanced degrees in related professions. However, the actual choice of field instructors rested with the field-work department, a group that had opposed the change. During implementation, other school policies were called upon which had the effect of disqualifying potential non-social workers in almost every instance.

A third difficulty of implementation stems from the interdependent nature of organizational systems. For many changes to be effectively operationalized, alterations in other parts of the system must accompany them. But other subsystems may not have been party to, or interested in, the innovation. For example, a social service department in a hospital may decide to revise its case-finding procedures, a decision within its own jurisdiction, but if the change impinges on the relations of medical to

[3] *A Relevant War Against Poverty: A Study of Community Action Programs and Observable Social Change* (New York: Metropolitan Applied Research Center, 1968).

social service staff, the decision may be difficult to engineer. Furthermore, systems theory suggests that to change behavior on one level of a hierarchical organization requires complementary and reinforcing changes in organizational levels above and below that level. The point may not always apply, but it does often enough to suggest the complexities of implementation as a consequence of structure. In brief, implementation often requires a coordination of effort—among different hierarchical levels, professional groups, and departments—and such coordination is difficult to obtain.

THE IMPLEMENTATION PROCESS

Obstacles are also created during implementation by the ways in which the implementers conduct the process. Gross and his colleagues, in their study of the failure to implement a change in a public school, argue that attention in the literature has focused disproportionately on initial resistance to a change and insufficiently on opposition resulting from the ways in which changes are operationalized. Their resesarch suggests, for example, that a significant number of teachers who had originally supported a move to open classrooms in the school became opponents of the change as a consequence of the disincentives that occurred during the implementation process.[4]

The problems of staff in implementing a change are often ignored. Change proponents, because they are partisan or their stakes are high, may be impatient with difficulties cited by implementers or may dismiss their complaints as "resistance" without examining the bases for the complaints. The teachers in the public-school change, for example, moved to opposing open classrooms in part because of what Gross and his colleagues describe as "role overload." The change added new elements to their job, yet there was no attempt to reallocate tasks nor even recognition of the increased load by the proponents of the change.[5] Unfortunately, too, the teachers felt that the burden of the change fell singularly on them—a reaction that is not atypical, in our judgment.

The sanction of authority is required to move from formal decision to agency reality. Unless implementers perceive decision makers to be actively committed, their incentive to effect a change is correspondingly reduced. But, paradoxically perhaps, they may also need the sense of carrying responsibility for bringing the change into being themselves. While there is no inherent conflict between these two needs, there is tension between them, and the implementation process must hew to the fine line that encourages both to occur. On the one hand, the support of upper-

---

[4] Neal Gross et al., *Implementing Organizational Innovations* (New York: Basic Books, 1971), pp. 142–47.

[5] *Ibid.,* p. 180.

ranking members must be certain. On the other, implementers must be accorded respect as they translate ideas into actions. Their contributions must be heard and credited, and appropriate behavior must be rewarded. Too often, however, the support of decision makers is ambiguous, and implementers feel unappreciated or imposed upon. The consequence is sabotage of the change.

What we have called "barriers to implementation" in this chapter might also be thought of as emergent restraining forces. Essentially, we have reiterated the force-field concepts developed earlier. During the initial phases of planning, the practitioner attempts to identify the relevant set of restraining and driving forces for change in order to develop a strategy of action. Sometimes, however, the full range of restraining forces is not accurately identified until implementation begins. Because of the dynamic nature of a change attempt, it is also true that assessment made at any one point in time can only be an approximation of the constellation of forces that exists at that point. As the practitioner begins the implementation effort, he will find it necessary to refine his original view of the force field, adjusting his strategy accordingly.

Practice Concerns in Implementing a Change

Practice issues in implementing a change are implicit in the obstacles that have been cited. A primary concern is maintaining the commitment of critical and other important actors. Another is gaining or holding the support of workers actually involved in implementing the change, as well as handling old or emergent resistances. And although the attitudes of participants may favor the change, a transfer of meanings from those who designed it to those who are to carry it out is necessary. Ensuring that the implementers understand what is expected of them is thus a third practice concern. We discuss each of these below. First, however, we consider the role of the worker, since it overarches all other concerns. What a worker can or cannot do and how he goes about doing it depend in good measure on the authority he has to see the change through.

WORKER ROLE

As a change moves from adoption to implementation, the worker who has conceived the change increasingly loses control of its direction. His responsibility for it, of course, varies markedly depending on the agency's authority structure and the politics of the process. Sometimes the worker brings the change into being and provides a model for how it should work. On other occasions, he may be put in charge of its implementation. Even line workers are often designated to develop a new program and assigned team members or paraprofessionals to work with them. Or an innovator may have to work indirectly—either because the authority more properly belongs elsewhere or because he has assessed that others would be more effective in the "up front" position. Obviously, the means to guide the process varies in each instance.

The Worker as Manager.   Although the arrangement may be ad hoc, the worker who is in charge of an operation must by and large deal with the same set of conditions that faces any manager. He is, in short, a mini-administrator in regard to the particular change and thus has all of the advantages of delegated responsibility. He not only represents the authority of the decision maker, but his legitimacy to act in regard to the change is clear. He is therefore more able than otherwise to obtain the resources necessary to effect the change (e.g., additional training, reassignment of personnel, acquiring program materials, devising complementary policies, and the like). He is also more directly able to influence subordinates and peers as well.

Compliance is motivated when organizational rewards for supporting a change are consistent and valuable, or the reverse, when negative sanctions for opposition are certain and severe. Practitioners in the managerial role have only limited access to these sanctions, of course. All too frequently, as a matter of fact, organizations do not sufficiently reward organizationally "proper" behavior and sometimes even penalize workers for it.[6] Furthermore, incentives exist both inside and outside an organization over which top administrators—much less lower-ranking members—can exert little influence.[7]

Nevertheless, social rewards such as support, encouragement, and recognition take on added value when they come from a person in charge. An empathetic appreciation of how the change affects those who must make it work, the sharing of that insight, and the collaborative development of activities that will ease their burden are more accessible to persons in leadership positions than to other practitioners. Sensitive leaders are also better located to identify and ameliorate the anxieties that new tasks and roles often engender. Social rewards, sympathetic understanding of a change's impact, and relieving the anxiety that change engenders are all necessary to maximize pro-change behavior.

Not surprisingly, a primary focus of applied organizational literature has been on the managerial aspects of organizational change. The literature is replete with prescriptions for managers, and since many of these are

---

[6] Workers whose idealism, commitment to clients, or sense of craft impels organizationally "proper" behavior are often burdened with additional assignments without added compensation in money, position, or recognition.

[7] For instance, responsiveness to peers in a work group, unions, professional associations, and the like.

applicable to workers with responsibility for operationalizing an innovation, we need not dwell on them here.[8] We wish only to highlight one further aspect that is especially relevant to change-oriented efforts—the tension of the man in the middle.

Workers who have subordinates as well as superordinates must be responsive to the needs of both. But these needs are frequently in conflict, and a delicate act of balancing is required. A "natural" accommodation—interpreting the interests of each to the other—is sometimes appropriate, but it can also lead to the worst of both worlds. The risk is that each constituency will perceive the worker as primarily loyal to the other. On the other hand, obvious identification with one party is a disincentive for the other party to respond to the worker's wishes.

Implementers have to perceive the practitioner-manager as "on their side" if he is to effectively encourage pro-change behavior. This does not necessarily raise an issue of loyalty, but matters relating to loyalty are likely to arise in the normal course of things and may particularly be an issue when the authority of the worker in charge is temporary. The manager must then take those with whom he works into his confidence while he tries to maintain critical-actor support as well. For example, when he disagrees with a decision, he might share this disagreement instead of rationalizing his acquiescence to authority as agreement with it. Or he might report conversations with decision makers in which he represented the needs of the implementers unsuccessfully, so that his commitment to their interest and his competence in arguing their case can be affirmed even in his defeat. His reportage must, of course, be both truthful and credible—that is, congruent with staff's own observation of how he acts and argues. And his tone must be dispassionate and nonconspiratorial if he hopes to maintain the dual connection.

Paradoxically perhaps, maintaining critical-actor support.is important not only in its own terms but because it develops loyalty to the practitioner-manager as well. An effective means of demonstrating to staff that a manager is "on their side" is by obtaining the resources they need to perform their tasks successfully, along with the rewards they expect for performing them well. Managers are accorded more authority by subordinates when they see the manager as influential with his own boss than when they do not. The dual connection thus has a circular effect. To implement a change, the practitioner-manager must influence the critical actor to provide concrete support, which, in turn, enhances his own "connection" with lesser-ranking staff.

---

[8] For example, discussion about motivation, the delegation of responsibility, leadership development, and other standard managerial tasks may also be relevant for the worker charged with bringing an innovation into being. See John B. Minor, *The Management Process* (New York: Macmillan, 1973).

One Among Many.   Monitoring a change is a relatively simple task when implementers are accountable to the worker who conceived the change. However, when the innovator is a peer working with others, or the responsibility for the change is located elsewhere, indirect means of monitoring the change are necessary. The creation of regular or formal mechanisms to chart and oversee the progress of the change is an important technique for ensuring "indirect" accountability.

Workers need not be in charge of an innovation in order to encourage structural rearrangements. There are two types of structure that particularly facilitate implementation. These are responsibility and coordinating mechanisms. Their use depends, of course, on the specifics of the innovation and the political climate of the organization.

By responsibility mechanisms we mean the formalization of staff responsibility for carrying out aspects of the change. If, as sometimes occurs, no one is assigned specific responsibility for a set of tasks, no one can be held accountable for neglecting to carry them out. Sometimes responsibility is allocated vaguely (e.g., "Why don't a few of you work on that idea?") or informally (e.g., someone simply volunteers at a staff meeting).

Unless there is strong support for the change from others or the worker's own commitment is limited, he will not leave the matter of responsibility for implementing a change to chance. If he suspects that volunteers may be called for, he will try to have volunteers lined up. If his opinion is to be solicited, he will try to have names to suggest. More important, he will try to fix, formalize, and make visible those who are supposed to act in reference to the change. This is accomplished by making sure that assignments are specific, that a date and forum for reporting progress are considered, and that the decision is made public—in writing, if possible. An announcement may be made by memorandum, or if the assignment is decided at a meeting, the minutes should reflect the action. If the innovation has generated controversy, the importance of detailed minutes transcends the fixing of staff responsibility. Since what is included and excluded necessarily entails selectivity, how the language of minutes is shaded often has significant bearing on the ultimate direction and success of a process. Minutes and memoranda constitute an organization's formal memory. What they say occurred is what occurred, regardless of other recollections later on.

Ensuring that the interdependent actions necessary for a change take place and that these actions support rather than subvert the change goal is essential to implementation. A formal coordinate arrangement, either through routinized individual contacts or regular committee meetings, is an effective means by which the worker can stay in touch with the developing change. For example, a child-abuse project within a hospital and the hospital's social services department jointly adopted a procedure for the systematic referral of clients from one to the other unit. The agreement worked only intermittently, however, until such time as a member of the child-abuse staff scheduled regular conferences with a supervisor from the social services department to review each week's experience.

Coordination often entails a variety of units, some more and some less predisposed to the change. The composition and responsibility of any coordinating device stem, of course, from the content of the change and the types of input and information that are necessary. The worker or sympathetic friends should find themselves members of the coordinating device if that is possible. It is only when coordinators share a common purpose that the process can be managed without bargaining or coercion. When goals are mixed and the coordinators are peers, bargaining is essential, and persons whose preferences are compatible with the change goal become important resources for influencing the outcome. The principles noted in Chapter 7 in regard to structural positioning apply here as well. Consideration must be given to who is likely to be included or excluded by using one or another structure. The legitimacy of the coordinating structure and its appearance of representativeness are similarly important.

In addition to staying on top of an innovation by indirect accountability arrangements, the worker must select a consistent strategy and choose his stance from a range of potential roles. While such roles emerge naturally from the context of particular situations, we identify three here.

One is the *change advocate*. As advocate, the worker assumes a strong identification with the change and publicly champions its values. The activity typically involves "hard" persuasion and exerting pressure to gain acceptance of the change idea. By and large, the role is associated with a high worker profile. Three factors are particularly relevant in deciding whether the advocate facilitates support for the change. One has to do with how positively or negatively the worker is perceived by the person(s) who must be won over or neutralized. The second relates to his earlier actions. If he has been strongly identified with the change in the initiation phase of the process, he may wish to maintain a low profile now. Advocacy during implementation can make it appear that his stake overrides the stakes of others and may inhibit them from coming forth as leaders. Finally, engaging in advocacy risks creating the impression that the change is in trouble and can coalesce resistance.

A second role is that of *change interpreter*. The interpreter attempts to influence the perceptions of participants so that the process proceeds smoothly. His approach is not overtly partisan, as is the advocate's, but measured and "objective"; he is interpreting rather than convincing. The role is most effective if the worker was in the background earlier or resistance did not surface during the initiation phase of the change. If resistance then develops during implementation, the worker may now represent the change as a *fait accompli* [9] and hence irreversible. He may try to reassure others that the change does not threaten their interests. Or he may provide early positive data on the benefits of the change.

Troubleshooter is a third possible role. Here, the worker provides assistance to remove the barriers that develop as a change is being implemented. The role is most effective when the worker's activities are associated not with the change per se but with discrete problems that have arisen. The troubleshooter, then, not only helps to overcome snags but enhances his credits with co-workers affected by the problem. These credits can often be exchanged for renewed colleague vigor on behalf of the change. The troubleshooter role is particularly important when organizational participants vested with responsibility for the change lack either the commitment or the ability to engage in creative problem solving as barriers to implementation are encountered.

While there are many other potential roles, these are the most significant, in our judgment. They are important to note because they tend to preclude one another, and the worker must anticipate, as he enters the implementation process, what his general approach will be. So, for example, if the worker begins as a change advocate, a shift to interpreter or troubleshooter will be viewed with suspicion, since his strong pro-change position is already apparent. To a lesser extent, the generalization holds for functions the worker performed during the earlier phases of the change effort as well. Here as elsewhere, the worker who has developed a strategy regarding how to proceed will be able to make day-by-day decisions that are guided by an overall conception of role rather than on an ad hoc and potentially inconsistent basis.

MAINTAINING THE COMMITMENT OF CRITICAL AND FACILITATING ACTORS

The investment of the critical actor and other important participants is a powerful force for staff to "go along" and constitutes a significant resource for implementing a change. It is true that this support can increase restraining forces opposed to the change—for example, triggering a fight with those in a rival but peer relationship with these actors or activating the resistance of lower-ranking staff who have grievances against top management. By and large, however, the willingness of staff to take steps to implement a change is importantly influenced by their perception of its significance to top decision makers.

By definition, the critical actor has endorsed the change before implementation begins. But the attention of critical actors may wander—and

[9] The *fait accompli*, as an approach in intergroup relations, has been described by Gordon Allport, *The Nature of Prejudice* (New York: Doubleday, Anchor Books, 1958), p. 471.

when they are inattentive, covert resistance becomes increasingly difficult to counter. Furthermore, the endorsement of important participants is not necessarily accepted as a binding commitment. The behavior of critical actors during the process is a source of data regarding the intensity of their support. As innovations require more effort, perseverance, or creativity on the part of implementers, it becomes more important for the commitments of decision makers to be concrete and visible.

As in all social processes, however, commitments shift with time. The critical actor's investment in a change can either diminish or intensify, depending on the forces that moved him to embrace it initially, as well as new forces that come into play subsequently. However, a lessening rather than an increase in commitment is the more typical response.

The process of implementation itself encourages the erosion of commitment. There is, first, a honeymoon period. The energy invested in making the change reaches its "high" with the decision to go ahead—for the critical actor, as well as for other organizational participants and the worker himself. As implementation begins, it draws from the energy generated by the acceptance of the change. In this initial period, the attitudes of those who conceived the change and those who accepted it range from enthusiastic support to benign interest. The energy generated by the change may even act as a stimulus to others, and a heightened period of change activity may be triggered within the organization.

Inevitably, however, the "bugs" inherent in any new operation begin to emerge. If there was significant resistance initially, the difficulties will be seized on and exaggerated as they occur. Even without opposition, time may be necessary for "debugging" the change, and as time elapses, agreements tend to get softer, the forces that impelled agreement alter, and negative reactions are likely to occur. The honeymoon over, reconsideration may result, and sometimes the change comes to a standstill.

Knowledge of this process and the timing of worker interventions to coincide with it are central to maintaining the commitment of significant actors. The practitioner must act when the decision maker's support is at its peak, and, except in the particular circumstances that we note below, this is ordinarily at the point of adoption. It is then that elaborating support is most feasible. Decisions are made or resources proffered which might be unavailable once a counterreaction occurs.

When the critical actor is willing, a memorandum or statement is useful to mark the occasion of the change's adoption. Ideally, the statement should include the reasons for the new policy or program and its importance. In some circumstances, it might also cite problems raised by the change, along with why they were set aside in making the decision. In addition, the acts to be taken to begin implementing the innovation might be specified, including an action-enforcing mechanism and provision for future reports of progress. The reader may recognize some of the techniques of persuasion in these suggestions—e.g., a high-status communicator, a message that expresses confidence in its arguments, the contrary position included but effectively countered, the mild suggestion of threat in the request for reports of progress, and the means for dealing with the threat by following the outlined steps.[10]

Workers—whether they are managers or are among many implementers—are not often in a position to exercise discretion over the content of a decision maker's announcement. Sometimes, however, busy decision makers are willing to share influence in terms of a statement's emphasis in exchange for a worker's volunteering to conduct the research and writing tasks necessary to develop and communicate new policy. Sometimes, too, even a critical actor whose support of a change idea is reluctant may share a draft statement with a worker prior to its distribution if the decision maker wants to convince the worker of his support. This is more likely to occur if the worker can find an acceptable rationale for requesting to see it. Indeed, a decision maker's advance knowledge that the statement will be shared may serve to modify its tone—and in any case, the worker's review of a draft offers him a handle to strengthen the positions expressed in the statement.

Workers must also take advantage of any events during the honeymoon period to reinforce commitment to the change. If clients respond favorably to the new policy or staff members react spontaneously and positively to some elements of it, the practitioner will ensure that this feedback reaches those whose support is essential to the maintenance of the change. To the extent possible, the bearer of such glad tidings should be an interpreter rather than an advocate already identified as a partisan of the idea.

There is likely to be some aspect or component of the change that is attractive to critical actors—for example, its cost-reducing potential, its public relations value, or the like. An important element in maintaining early commitment is the facility with which the worker is able to keep attractive aspects of the change central as the organization encounters the bumps or jolts of the implementation period.

If "bugs" are anticipated, they should be publicly identified *before* they occur. In large measure, people evaluate events in light of their expectations. For example, if a supervisor had expected some tension to be generated by the change among staff carrying different responsibilities, he is not likely to perceive the existence of tension as an isssue. However, if he had expected harmonious relations, even mild tension will cause him distress.

Commitment is more difficult to maintain when the nature of the change is such that the practitioner cannot assure early success. Long-

[10] Herbert Abelson, *Persuasion: How Opinions and Attitudes are Changed,* 2nd ed. (New York: Springer, 1970).

range changes that face opposition risk losing critical-actor commitment because the measure of their success cannot be determined at the time that criticism may surface. One technique, then, is to identify a readily achievable interim objective against which to measure the innovation early in its implementation. For example, a new mode of intake may be intended to collect data on which to base improved forms of service. But the payoff is long-range and will not be visible before negative reactions to implementation have occurred. If, however, the new procedure is also likely to save staff time, is so defined by its proponents, and in fact does save time, the innovation may quickly be perceived as a success. In other words, one way of taking advantage of an innovation's credibility early in the implementation stage is to define what might be considered an immediate success, achieve it, and make it visible.

Short of setting interim objectives, the worker may prevent premature judgment by setting a timetable for evaluation of the change. To best protect the integrity of the trial period, the timetable should be incorporated into the proposal before implementation begins. But the worker must, in any case, maintain ongoing contact with critical actors and other influential parties and keep them informed of the process and its progress.

Although we have counseled immediate action by practitioners in moving an adopted change to implementation, some cautionary words are in order. In instances where there has been little organized opposition, the passage of time may work in favor of the change, for by the time the innovation might be questioned, it often seems so familiar as to seem hardly a change at all. One means of blunting challenges to an innovation is to point to earlier agreements—for example, what the group now raising question has already voted on the matter. Although this is perhaps illogical, groups tend to accept that they must live with their mistakes.

A decision that has been reached following controversy, on the other hand, requires a delicate balancing of considerations in regard to timing. If the worker's victory is clear and the risk in delaying operationalization of the change is minor, an excess of zeal is counterproductive. Pressing action does not permit time for consolidation or the thoughtful planning of next steps. It also deprives the opposition of an opportunity to "save face" and thus contravenes a principle of effective negotiation—that is, to assist one's opponent to retreat gracefully, without his seeming to have retreated. When the victory is less certain, however, using the momentum generated by the adoption of the change, as we have advised, is important.

Swift action poses another risk as well. Upper-ranking members may be wary of being pressed too far too fast, with the result that their initial support becomes qualified. Or implementers may feel railroaded into taking actions without time for due consideration and thus resist what they otherwise might accept. In short, as the practitioner explores the benefits of acting quickly during implementation, he must balance them against the costs of appearing to jump the process.

PARTICIPANT PREFERENCES

Some innovations can be realized in the face of hostile reaction by those who must carry them out. Ordinarily, these are one-time changes or those of a largely routine nature. Hostile reactions may also be moderated in the act of experiencing a change, since familiarity reduces threat potential. But gaining or holding the support for workers is nevertheless a significant practice concern in implementing a change. Their preferences for and commitment to the change are central elements in the success of the effort.

Since we have talked much in this volume about participant preferences, it is necessary to highlight only two aspects of the issue here—the first relating to participant decision making and the second having to do with managing resistance and conflict.

There is probably no more pervasive counsel in the literature for developing commitment to a course of action than that one seek the participation of affected staff in decision making. Dalton observes that "participation in goal setting is mentioned most frequently [in the literature] as the key means of promoting [personal ownership in the vital goals and subgoals of the organization]." [11] The prescription, however, is rarely followed, and this raises a question about whether it is possible to follow it. Upper-ranking staff are unlikely to turn over agency direction to a staff group less experienced, less accountable, and less oriented to the overall needs of the organization than themselves, although they may accept informal input or influence by low-ranking members. Usually, when participation in decision making is formally structured, it deals with relatively modest issues or is intended to give the *appearance* of participation more than the fact of it.

Putting aside the value issues inherent in worker participation, empirical studies on the subject are equivocal in their results, though it is clear that participation increases staff morale. [12] A major instrumental argument that has been advanced in favor of participation is that when members feel that they have contributed to goal setting, they are more likely to understand the goal and hence to endorse it. But there is little evidence to support this notion, and one could also argue that participation in making a decision with which a member disagrees or which he perceives as contrary to his interests will not bind him to the decision. It could instead strengthen his resistance, precisely because he understands the meaning of the goal's impact on him or because he carries a reservoir of negative feeling from having lost on the issue.

[11] Gene W. Dalton, "Motivation and Control in Organizations," in Gene W. Dalton and Paul R. Lawrence, eds., *Motivation and Control in Organizations* (Homewood, Ill.: Dorsey, 1971), p. 34.

[12] Warren G. Bennis, *Beyond Bureaucracy* (New York: McGraw-Hill, 1966), pp. 68–69.

This is not to suggest that participation is proscribed, only that it is not a panacea. We believe that it is most useful in the implementation phase of a change process because by then at least the outlines of the change have been officially sanctioned. Although there is still the risk of compromising the character of the change, at this juncture the risk is modest.

Participant decision making is important in implementation under certain circumstances. Often, the differing perspectives that implementers bring to an issue are necessary for effective problem solving; they thus make the change more likely to reach its intended end. Participation also helps in maintaining the preference for change among those who are already predisposed to it. Even those who are neutral, uncertain, or mildly negative can be brought along if the climate within the decision-making unit is affirmative.

Furthermore, staff input is critical in implementation when members *expect* to be involved. Some professionals view participation as a right, and an organization's history or current procedures may encourage such a view. Put differently, *lack* of participation can be a disincentive, creating problems in implementation that participant decision making avoids.

There are two important principles when innovating workers are in a position to influence participant involvement. The first is that the innovator must encourage wide contribution to the decision making of the group. Silence does *not* mean consent, and mere presence at a meeting without actual input will not spur a group member to go along with the decisions made. The second is that the parameters of decision-making responsibility must be set forth in advance. It should be clear before any conclusions are reached which areas are within the purview of the implementers to decide and which areas are reserved for others, although staff opinion regarding the latter may be welcomed. Overriding a group that believes itself to have the authority to decide is a sure formula for inducing resistance.

Paradoxically, a major concern in securing pro-change preferences during implementation is the reduction of stress. Once again, an intervention that is appropriate in one phase of the process is contraindicated in another. Earlier we noted that the worker's task in the beginning phases of change was to influence working forces so as to upset the existent equilibrium and create stress. Once an innovation has been adopted, however, the task is to restore the equilibrium at the newly reached point. The very nature of implementation, however, creates disequilibrium, since old procedures must be discarded, new relationships forged, new roles learned, and the like. Establishing a supportive environment if one is a manager—or expressing respect and approval, proferring help, and sharing concerns if one is a peer—go a long way toward reducing both tension and resistance to the change.

The same may be said for the role of conflict in the respective phases of the process. Early in the process, a worker may precipitate conflict by mobilizing attention to a persistent problem. However, once favorable action has been taken, the desired denouement for the change proponent is that the agency and its decision makers obtain some measure of organizational tranquility.

When resistance is mild, it may be contained by "turning the other cheek." There is a tendency for resistance to be self-generating. Thus, person A responds to person B with antagonism, triggering person B's response in kind, which reinforces person A's initial reaction. Unless the cycle is broken, the resistance builds. For example, a social worker new to a school setting found the school psychologist hostile to the social worker and strongly opposed to his attempt to implement a change. The social worker initially defined the problem as a personality clash and reacted in kind. When he redefined the issue as one of overlapping roles, however, and acted on the basis of his redefinition, consciously attempting to break the cycle, the psychologist's attitude altered. The worker was then able to obtain the psychologist's neutrality with regard to the change he had previously opposed.

Mild forms of resistance can also be dissolved by openness to the objections of opponents, recognizing whatever valid objections may exist. Failing that, the worker may attempt to reduce resistance through bargaining—compromising differences or incorporating elements in the change that are advantageous to the other but that do not violate the integrity of the change.

In the face of profound resistance to change, the techniques suggested above may not be possible, and, as a matter of fact, it is during implementation that the most protracted and highly contentious situations occur.[13] Empirical evidence suggests that when conflict is extended over time, it tends to become increasingly general (i.e., concern about a discrete change is transformed into a philosophic attack), widens in scope (i.e., new issues are precipitated), and moves from disagreement to antagonism (i.e., becomes increasingly personalized and polarized).[14] Thus, workers may be prone to deal with resistance by discrediting their adversaries' competence or motives. They may also attempt to "divide and conquer" by suggesting that their adversaries hold goals antithetical to those of the actors whose support the worker is seeking.

There are compelling practice reasons to restrain this posture. Negative "overkill" can undermine the worker's own credibility and integrity in the eyes of critical actors and other staff. Conversely, the worker who, although provoked, is unwilling to engage in "low blow" tactics will be

[13] This is so for a number of reasons, many of which were indicated in the earlier section of this chapter dealing with barriers to implementation.

[14] James S. Coleman, *Community Conflict* (New York: Free Press, 1957); Morton Deutsch, *The Resolution of Conflict* (New Haven: Yale University Press, 1973).

viewed as statesmanlike. Furthermore, because he has official sanction for the change, it is in the interests of a change proponent to act in a restrained way. Once all this has been said, however, it may be necessary for the worker to deal with resistance by impugning either the credibility or the motivation of the opposition—though this must be done as gracefully as possible.

Sometimes disagreements occur among the supporters of a change as they engage in implementing it. In this case, the worker tries to reduce the tensions among them. He may serve as a conciliator, attempting to mediate differences as they arise. When that is impossible, he will try to reduce contact between contending actors, either physically or through the creation of sharper role boundaries. Or he may try to get the resolution of an agreement postponed by removing it from the group agenda until the change is further established. When circumstances do not allow such interventions, the worker may encourage a confrontation between conflicting implementers in the hope that deepened understanding will result from an open, direct, and honest communication of differences. Confrontation is useful in situations that stem from misunderstandings, misperceptions, and unfounded suspicions. But it ought to be avoided in cases of clashes of interest, when the parties have a greater stake in winning the argument than in ultimate agreement.[15]

COMMUNICATING THE CHANGE

However favorably implementing staff view the change, they must be clear about what is required of them if they are to act as innovators intend. Clarity is essential but is no easy matter to achieve. The reasons have already been noted. One is that generality may have been the only means to garner the support necessary to win the adoption of an idea, whereas specificity is now the major requirement. Another is that the innovators may themselves be unclear about how to translate their intentions into actions. It is through effective communication that these difficulties are overcome.

When the worker is in charge of the process and serves as a manager, the desired clarity is advanced by taking initiative with implementers, increasing his contact with them, providing opportunity for increased inter-worker contacts, and encouraging initiatives back to the manager from the implementers.[16] In other words, a system of increased interaction, the

---

[15] Organizational development theorists especially encourage the use of confrontation as growth-producing for the actors. It exposes them to their own misperceptions and stereotypes and can, as we have suggested, clear the air and deepen mutual understanding. But it can also intensify stress and, in addition, deflect organizational concern from the accomplishment of a task to issues of personality.

[16] These points parallel the description of an implementation process in Leonard R. Sayles, "Accommodating for Change," in Fremont J. Lyden et al., eds., *Policies, Decisions and Organizations* (New York: Meredith, 1969), p. 236.

use of informal channels, and high feedback are useful methods of communication in managing the implementation of a change.

High feedback assures that the meaning of the communication as transmitted is similar to its meaning as received. Feedback reduces the "noise" or distortion that takes place in much communication. To be maximally useful, feedback must be invited that deals with specific and partial reactions to issues rather than general or total ones and focuses on matters that the practitioner-manager can do something about. Feedback that is immediate (i.e., solicited as close as possible in time to the events for which reactions are sought) contributes to increased clarity and also allows the necessary adjustments to be made more quickly than otherwise.[17]

Even when the lack of clarity stems from other factors than communication distortion, feedback is helpful, since it encourages implementers to make their confusion known and opens the possibilities for a shared problem-solving process to take place. Gross and his colleagues note, for example, that a contributing factor in explaining why teachers did not function in the ways hoped for by the open-classroom innovation was that the school's administrators were unclear about what they wanted the teachers to do and the teachers never shared their perception of this lack of clarity with the administrators.[18]

Workers who are not in charge of an innovation must be plugged into the agency's communication network, and the alliances developed during initiation ought be maintained for the purpose. Workers must remain alert to ongoing developments as well. It is not unusual for surprises to occur when implementation appears to be going smoothly, since workers then tend to relax their attention. Attentiveness is particularly important in order that the worker can attempt to influence emergent problems while the problems are discrete and partial and the change can still be effectively "debugged." Problems that are handled before they develop into larger issues are less likely to come to the attention of decision makers or to create undue resistance within the agency.

In addition to eliciting informal feedback from colleagues or supervisors, the change-oriented worker will press for regularized reporting procedures, such as standing progress reports at meetings. This serves the dual function of assuring official attention to the innovation while allowing the worker to stay in touch with and influence its development. He will think twice, however, before attempting to establish regular reporting if the early stages of implementation have been characterized by trouble, unless, of course, the difficulty is related to inadequate information about the change.

[17] For principles of "good" feedback, see Richard A. Schmuck and Philip J. Runkel, *Handbook of Organization Development in Schools* (Palo Alto: National Press Books, 1972), pp. 39–42.

[18] Gross et al., *op. cit.*, pp. 150–59.

It is just such potential trouble that leads practitioner-managers and other innovators to "tune out" communications that are available for the listening. If they do not hear about problems associated with the change, the problems are functionally nonexistent, and proponents do not have to face the possibility that their conception of the change was faulty. Two dubious purposes are thus served. Their commitment to a proposal in which they may have placed much store is not threatened. More importantly, they avoid facing what it might take to solve the difficulties, hoping that the change can be implemented anyway. If the implementation is imperfect, it can be improved on later, for to solve these difficulties often entails organizational costs and can tip the cost-benefit ratio of the innovation against the change.

Although this may constitute a politically correct judgment, it cannot be made rationally by non-listening. For example, the school administrators in the Gross study may have avoided recognizing that open classrooms required further teacher training because the training constituted a too "expensive" investment. But the implementation foundered on this inadequacy, and it would have made more sense to recognize the problem. If training was too expensive to be incorporated into the plan, other accommodations might have been explored. Short of that, the experiment might have been abandoned prior to the considerable input of time and energy and the debilitating effect of the failure. In other words, not listening does not permit an innovator to address the choices that would indicate whether or not the costs of the change exceed its benefits.

In sum, a precondition of effective implementation is that the implementers clearly understand what is expected of them. This prescribes heightened interaction between the worker and other implementers, the solicitation of feedback, and active listening. When the change proponents are themselves unclear or the complexities of the change are such that clarity requires further work, mutual problem solving is the prescribed route to successful implementation of innovative goals.

It should be noted in concluding this discussion of implementation that when a change encounters any serious obstacle, the total change process may have to be undergone again. An example makes the point. Assume that a mental health clinic has followed the change process described in earlier chapters and has adopted a policy of creating a neighborhood advisory committee. As the worker begins to implement this new mandate, he discovers an emergent restraining force in his effort to obtain representation from certain critical neighborhood groups. The leaders of these groups insist that the agency provide technical assistance to the groups in return. The clinic's current focus, however, is the provision of individual and family treatment, and providing technical assistance would entail reallocations of staff time. The worker will thus need to weigh the feasibility of developing the agency's technical-assistance capacity or search for other alternatives. He will then have to shepherd the new idea through the appropriate steps—in other words, repeat the process for a further change in order to implement the adopted one.

Institutionalization

The process does not end when a change is implemented, since its permanence must still be assured. In Lewin's terms, the system has been "unfrozen," and a change has occurred. Now a "refreezing" process must take place.[19] If "refreezing" fails to occur, the change remains vulnerable to countervailing forces and can be rendered inoperative. The final phase, then, is for the change to become an integral part of the organization.

EVALUATING THE CHANGE

Before workers begin the "refreezing" process, they must assess the current status of the change effort. The innovation may now be fully observed in practice and thus evaluated. Two issues are particularly important in this regard. One has to do with whether the change has realized its original purposes; the other, with whether it has caused negative consequences.

Realizing the Goals of the Change.   Determining the extent to which the implemented change achieves its purposes, or has the potential for achieving them, is a central evaluation issue. We distinguish here between short-term goals which are easily observable and long-term outcomes which may require evaluation research. The former asks whether the change achieved its immediate aim. The latter questions whether the result satisfies the underlying rationale or long-term expectation of the goal. In the terms of systems theory, the short-term goal refers to the organization's "through-put," or the service it provides, whereas the long-term objective relates to the organization's output, or the result of its service.

An example will make the point clearer. In a family agency, decisions regarding the treatment modality (i.e., long- or short-term treatment, behaviorist or insight therapy) for a client were made by individual workers, who shared the responsibility for conducting intake interviews through a rotation system. According to one practitioner, the clients were referred to various modalities as a result of each worker's bias in favor of or against the modalities rather than in response to the client's problem or personality. The worker introduced an innovation to move these treatment

[19] Kurt Lewin, *Field Theory in Social Science* (New York: Harper & Row, 1951).

decisions from the private domain of individual staff to case conferences where all clinical staff participated in treatment decision making regarding each client.

The worker's goal—to prevent the individual judgments of the intake workers from forming the sole basis for the assignment of clients to particular interventions—could be validated by simple observation once the change had occurred. The worker assumed that this change would result in an improved treatment outcome, and he may, of course, have been right. But the assumption that enough is known about client problems and personality, as well as about the effects of different modalities, to make appropriate matches between them is questionable. Adequate evaluation of that assumption—and therefore of whether the treatment outcome was in fact improved—requires systematic research regarding the relative efficacy of various modalities under comparable client conditions.

Although we do not underestimate the importance of evaluation research, human service workers, in their need to act, cannot wait for precise answers, and our interest here is the short-term goal. In gross terms at least, the efficacy of short-term goals is observable, and the worker's task is essentially analytic. Three questions must be addressed. Does the change meet the goal that initially moved the practitioner to engage in the effort? Is modification necessary before the change can function as intended? Or does the change so miss the mark that it is not justifiable in terms of its original conception?

An affirmative answer to the first question is likely to reflect thoughtful initial planning by the practitioner. The extent to which the change idea in its initial conception was directly related to the problem to be solved, or was adjusted accordingly as the change process unfolded, is, we believe, the best predictor of successful goal attainment.

A study by Pressman and Wildavsky of the implementation of a federal program in Oakland, for example, concludes that the program's failure to increase minority employment, as intended, was the result of its indirect approach. Instead of taking the direct path of paying the employers a subsidy on wages after they had hired minority personnel, the program subsidized the capital of business enterprises on the promise that the firms would hire minorities. This involved the program operators in a morass of activities such as assessing the viability of marginal enterprises, negotiating loan agreements, and monitoring employment plans—activities that would have been unnecessary if a simple approach had been taken.[20] The point, which is especially relevant in complex undertakings, is worth underscoring as applied to human service workers in regard to simple changes as well. Practitioners frequently choose solutions that only indirectly or tangentially relate to the problems they hope to solve and, more unfortunately still,

[20] Pressman and Wildavsky, *op. cit.*, p. 147.

are frequently unaware they have done so until the change has been implemented.

Sometimes the change as implemented reveals flaws in its design that obviate the initial goal but can be made to work with some modification. Reassessing the problem may then reveal the appropriate remedy. Consider, for example, the change in the family agency we cited above. The case conferences were held informally, and workers controlled the material that each presented. An unrecognized collusion developed between them: none was pressed on the data he or she supplied, and the others deferred to the judgments of the particular worker who presented the case. For these reasons, the change as implemented had little effect on the impact of worker biases on the treatment modalities that were chosen. The situation was salvageable, however. Ultimately, the group was encouraged to devise a format for presenting data in an organized way and to develop a uniform set of criteria for assigning clients to different treatment protocols.

Changes may also entirely miss their mark. Sometimes this reflects a worker's enthusiastic commitment to a particular methodology, leading to its indiscriminate application. An example is the organization-development specialist who suggests "team building" activities to improve staff relations among competing professional groups when, in fact, the solution might actually require restructuring the work to alter patterns of work coordination. Changes also go awry because information is incompletely available, inaccurately interpreted, or because unanticipated events intervene.

In dynamic human processes, outcomes cannot be predicted with precision, and the evaluation of an innovation's effectiveness before it is institutionalized is critical to high standards of professional practice. The point is obvious enough, but there are inherent difficulties in its application. Practitioners are frequently unwilling to give up cherished methodological notions with which they have been identified or identify themselves, and workers who have been associated with a change may feel that its failure will incur a loss of reputation or self-esteem. Professional responsibility requires that flawed innovations be discarded. Furthermore, there is even professional equity to be derived from admitting mistakes (if one has not made *too* many) as well as from being open to a variety of problem-solving approaches. Honesty—in the face of failure as elsewhere—often *is* the best policy, since it can be disarming and fosters respect as well.[21]

Negative Consequences of Change.   In Chapter 1, we referred to the undesirable consequences that often accompany a change and stressed the importance of anticipating them prior to pressing for a problem's solution,

---

[21] Many effective political tacticians use honesty to disarm their audience. It is particularly effective when an audience is suspicious of a speaker or believes that he is trying to convince them of something in his own self-interest.

while we recognized the difficulty for the practitioner of imagining a future state of affairs. Here, the task is simpler since the innovation has been implemented. What must now be emphasized is the worker's responsibility to assess negative consequences before proceeding with the institutionalization of the change.

In the Charter House case discussed earlier, for example, the adoption of a policy outlining specific criteria for discharging youngsters from the group home and moving the jurisdiction for the decision from the child-care staff alone to a team of clinical and other workers is, in itself, a salutory change. But following its implementation, a number of secondary negative consequences are likely to emerge. As discharging youngsters becomes more difficult, the agency's open intake policy (i.e., admitting all runaways who appear at its doors) is endangered since, with less turnover, a waiting list becomes a possibility. Furthermore, as the number of youth with behavior problems increases, the abilities of the child-care staff are taxed, and it is an open question whether Charter House has the mental health resources to deal with its now more difficult population.

Three alternatives exist in response to the discovery of negative consequences accompanying a change. Eliminating the difficulty is the alternative choice, of course, assuming that it is possible. In the Charter House example, this option was unavailable. A second alternative is learning to live with the difficulty. Ordinarily, this requires making a choice between competing values and cannot be addressed apart from specific circumstances and the ideology of the actors. Thus, at Charter House, the decision would have to be based on the weight one gave to the open intake policy and the difficulties incurred for child-care staff, on the one hand, against the weight placed on the rights of youngsters to receive equitable and consistent treatment in relation to discharge, on the other. The third alternative, of course, is to dismantle the change.

We implied earlier that a practitioner who has committed the energy and resources to carry a change through to its implementation tends to resist the notion that the change is not working well, frequently discounting data that reveal problems. The response, more often than not, is a redoubling of efforts to make the change work. So, for example, the organizational-development specialist might step up his team-building activities rather than re-examine his original premises. Although determination and persistence are necessary ingredients in change practice, they are not substitutes, nor should they be, for rigorous evaluation.

Practice Concerns in Institutionalizing a Change

Practitioners reverse their field during institutionalization. In the early stages of a change attempt, their task was to disrupt system stability, creating disequilibrium in forces that impinged on their problem area. In implementation, they began the process of reducing the tension caused by their intervention, an effort that is accelerated in the institutionalization phase. Coming full circle, they seek stability instead of change.

With the task reversed, organizational dynamics, which earlier posed obstacles for workers pressing for change, now promote their purposes. For example, a change sanctioned by a superordinate in a highly centralized organizational structure is more likely to take root than a change implemented in a decentralized setting. Another example is the inertia in organizations that inhibits movement toward change. Once a change has been implemented, this same inertia more easily fixes the permanence of the change.

In the early chapters of this book, we discussed factors in the environment and internal to the organization which, as they impinge on organizational actors, affect organizational stability and change. Our intent was to sensitize practitioners to elements in the setting that predispose it to change so as to help workers assess the feasibility of their change ideas, design their goals in that context, and highlight possible areas of change activity. In institutionalizing a change, the same factors may be considered for the opposite purposes—to enhance the stability of the implemented innovation.

We conclude this chapter by referring to two variables of importance in assuring change permanence. The first—and more critical—has to do with the extent to which the change is linked with other organizational components. The second refers to the need for standardization.

INTERDEPENDENCY

A newly implemented change that has been linked with other organizational elements can more effectively ward off threats from contending ideas than changes that are less ingrained in the organization's fabric. As a change becomes interrelated with other organizational entities, forces for protecting the new state of affairs come into being. Facilitating interdependence, then, is a major task of institutionalization. There are three ways in which it may be accomplished.

The simplest is to identify an organizational or subunit need, as perceived by the relevant participants, and insure that the implemented change makes a contribution to meeting it. Assume, for example, that a practitioner is located in a union and that his change was to effect a contract between the union and a local family agency to provide consultative services to the union's personal services department. The personal services department offers a wide variety of help to its membership but is particularly interested in improving and expanding its program for retirees. From the gamut of possibilities among which the family agency might choose in offering consultation, the worker would urge attention to the retirees program as a clear priority if seeking permanence was the criterion of the decision.

A second means of encouraging interdependence is to promote the visibility of the change and thus reinforce its positive ramifications to others. On an individual level, this may mean no more than providing recognition or praise for those staff members who are involved in the change. The manager of the union's personal services department, for example, may be publicly congratulated for its use of the family-agency team. More broadly, if the change is widely publicized, its value increases. For example, if information on the retirees program and the contribution of the family agency is disseminated throughout the union—or even better, advertised among other unions as well—the personal services department and the union' leadership are likely to feel greater commitment to and payoff for themselves in the change.

To encourage interdependence, practitioners may not only identify and meet a perceived need, or make its accomplishment more visible; they can *generate* needs as well. If, in our example above, the manager of the union's personal services department had been unsure about the need for the family agency's assistance, the worker might have conceived of ways to recruit more or different clients, so as to overwhelm the department and generate the impetus for additional help.

The possibility of developing linkages with other organizational components depends, of course, on the content of the change, where it is located structurally within the agency, and how it impinges on these other components. As practitioners scan the organization for possible areas of connection between their change and other organizational elements, it is useful for them to consider linkages in terms of the three broad requirements that system theorists describe as essential to organizational maintenance and growth: the organization's need for input, the effectiveness of its "through-put" or internal processes, and the impact of its output (or "finished" product) on its environment.

Organizational inputs (i.e., the range of resources that organizations must draw from their environment in order to function) include funds, staff, clients, equipment, and the like. The worker might ask to what extent the innovation can be linked to inputs for which organizational actors feel a need or whether the change can itself generate that need. Client availability offers an example. All human service agencies need "customers," and funding may be contingent on maintaining a steady or rising flow of clients. A mental hygiene clinic whose case load was falling offers a case in point. A group of workers, interested in crisis intervention, developed a hotline for potential suicides. Their focus on attracting hotline clients to use the agency's services, thereby increasing the clinic's client count, contributed to the stabilization of the program within the agency. Even if the clinic's client population had been steady, however, and an increase in case load due to the new program had resulted in the clinic's receipt of third-party payments, the agency would soon have come to depend on the additional funds. In the latter case, the need would have been generated by the innovation.

Subunits within an organization are ordinarily dependent on each other's activities to enhance their own functioning. Here, the practitioner would seek ways of facilitating the positive impact of the change on other organizational subunits. An example may be drawn from the dayroom program that was developed as part of the comprehensive treatment service for alcoholics at Somerville Hospital, noted in Chapter 8. The dayroom absorbed clients who had earlier "hung out" at the facility's counseling clinic, thus permitting counselors to conduct their interviews with less distraction. Further, the dayroom staff developed a procedure to provide information about the group behavior of their clients to the counselors, thus increasing the counselors' dependence on the dayroom program and thereby further stabilizing its place in Somerville's comprehensive service.

Linkages to internal organizational elements is particularly important for innovations that have been defined as demonstrations (whether or not the purpose was legitimately to test a new program or procedure or to make the change more "salable"). As a time-limited experiment, a demonstration constitutes an easily reversible arrangement, often divorced from the organization's mainstream. Until it is legitimized through the establishment of ties to other organizational entities, its stability remains uncertain. At the simplest level, the point may be illustrated by the experience of the second-year social work student, referred to in Chapter 8, who obtained sanction to organize a demonstration group in a mental hospital to prepare patients for re-entry into the community. The group, led by the student, was evaluated positively, but its success alone by no means insured its continuity. The student recruited one of the psychologists to co-lead the group with him, and the latter agreed to carry the assignment when the student left the agency. He also made periodic reports to the staff psychiatrist and other ward team members, thus reinforcing their commitment to the service. The student, in short, created linkages to other actors to assure the permanence of the demonstration.

The third major area where interdependent links can be forged is with components of the organization's environment to which it feels some sense of accountability for its output (i.e., its neighborhood, client organization, special-interest groups, other agencies with which it cooperates or competes, legislative bodies, executive departments, and the like). If the change has the potential of interrelating with any of these in ways that might be perceived by critical actors as advancing the agency's interests, the practitioner attempts to establish a pattern of facilitating relationships. For example, the change may be connected to clients by accompanying it with the organization of a citizen's advisory group; to regional officials of the Department of Health, Education and Welfare through the submission of reports, invitations to meetings, and periodic consultations; and to other agencies by means of referral and coordinating mechanisms. When an innovation can be made to intermesh with these outside elements, it becomes more difficult to wrench from its organizational place.

A word of caution must be noted before we leave the subject of establishing linkages. Interdependence comes at a price. When the visibility of a change is increased through linkages with internal and external organizational components, its vulnerability to outside influence is increased as well. In effect, the change proponent opens the innovation to scrutiny and in so doing trades away some of its autonomy in return for increased stability.

We have argued that this is a price that must be paid. The question still remains regarding the degree of stability that is required against the extent of autonomy to be forfeited in relation to a particular change at a particular moment in time. We suggest two guidelines in seeking an answer.

One relates to the goal of the change and its fit with the ongoing purposes and activities of the organization. When the change goal marks a radical departure from the "normal" protocol of the organization, it is likely to constitute a threat to other components and may need the protection of isolation in order to maintain its integrity from challenges by these competing organizational interests. In this instance, only after the innovation has been firmly established would it seek ties with other elements.

The second criterion for weighing autonomy against interdependence is a related one. The issue is not only how markedly the goal of the innovation differs from traditional agency practices but also the extent to which the innovation is supported by powerful organizational interests. The point has a paradoxical element. The more powerful the sources of support available to a change, the less risk there is to its autonomy in making linkages to other components—but the less need it has for developing links to a variety of other organizational elements. Conversely, the softer the support for an innovation, the greater its need for linkages, which, at the same time, pose a greater risk to its autonomy. By and large, when support for a change is tenuous and its direction might be threatened by involvement with other components, it is well to seek these connections cautiously. In effect, the integration of an innovation into an organizational system must follow its establishment of its own integrity, if that is at all possible.

STANDARDIZATION

In our discussion of organizational structure in Chapter 3, we pointed out that routinization is change-inhibiting. Once again, what works against a worker in initiating a change works in his favor in institutionalizing it. An important means of fixing an innovation as an integral part of an organizational system is to standardize its operations within the agency as soon as possible.

There is probably a chicken-egg quality to the process. Does standardization follow the acceptance and integration of a change into an organization, or is its integration promoted by its development of standardized procedures? We believe that both occur, and to the extent that this is the case, our advice to the worker to standardize operations holds.

The form taken by a change represents a factor in its stability; in other words, as a change appears, so it tends to be perceived. Thus, if it functions erratically, it may be viewed as unstable. If it is seen as orderly, it is more likely to be accepted as an integral part of the agency.

Standardizing a change to encourage its institutionalization is not so simple a matter as it might appear. Since some amount of trial and error is necessary to maximize the potential of an innovation, the question of when one moves to cloture is a difficult one. If premature standardization takes place, the full benefit of the change may be vitiated; if standardization takes too long, however, the entire innovation could be put at risk.

At the least, however, consistent and predictable patterns of interaction with other organizational components can be facilitated. First, staff engaged in the change attempt must internalize—and make their own— the new behaviors demanded by the change. Secondly, those who are identified with the change in the agency must be especially consistent in their dealings with other organizational participants. The appearance and reality of responsible performance accrue credit to the stability of the change itself. Finally, as aspects of the new operations become fixed— rules and regulations spelled out, job requirements specified—these need to be highlighted and diffused.

It is perhaps fitting that we close this discussion about assuring the permanence of change—and conclude this book as well—by noting that nothing within a formal organization is immune to the possibility of evolution and obsolescence; "permanence" is never more than relative and a matter of probabilities.

The change process, as described in this book, begins with identifying a problem that impinges on the needs and rights of clients. It moves to designing a solution, assessing its feasibility, preparing for the introduction of the change, seeking and winning its adoption, and, finally, implementing and assuring the stability of the solution in the agency. But the process does not end there. Forces within the environment and the organization continue to generate tensions for organizational actors—and as old problems are solved, new problems emerge. Thus does the process begin again.

Index

Printed in the United States
By Bookmasters